Shakespeare's Storytelling

Nate Eastman

Shakespeare's Storytelling

An Introduction to Genre, Character, and Technique

Nate Eastman
Earlham College
Richmond, IN, USA

ISBN 978-3-030-62992-2   ISBN 978-3-030-62993-9 (eBook)
https://doi.org/10.1007/978-3-030-62993-9

© The Editor(s) (if applicable) and The Author(s), under exclusive license to Springer Nature Switzerland AG 2021
This work is subject to copyright. All rights are solely and exclusively licensed by the Publisher, whether the whole or part of the material is concerned, specifically the rights of translation, reprinting, reuse of illustrations, recitation, broadcasting, reproduction on microfilms or in any other physical way, and transmission or information storage and retrieval, electronic adaptation, computer software, or by similar or dissimilar methodology now known or hereafter developed. The use of general descriptive names, registered names, trademarks, service marks, etc. in this publication does not imply, even in the absence of a specific statement, that such names are exempt from the relevant protective laws and regulations and therefore free for general use.
The publisher, the authors and the editors are safe to assume that the advice and information in this book are believed to be true and accurate at the date of publication. Neither the publisher nor the authors or the editors give a warranty, expressed or implied, with respect to the material contained herein or for any errors or omissions that may have been made. The publisher remains neutral with regard to jurisdictional claims in published maps and institutional affiliations.

Cover design by Isaac

This Palgrave Macmillan imprint is published by the registered company Springer Nature Switzerland AG
The registered company address is: Gewerbestrasse 11, 6330 Cham, Switzerland

Preface

Aspiring professional Shakespeareans need to learn all kinds of things before they go to graduate school: the differences between fair and foul copies, between quartos and folios, and between the typesetting habits of A and B compositors. They need to read North's translations of Plutarch's *Lives*, and Holinshed's *Chronicles*, and histories from Conrad Russell and Christopher Hill. They need to know what influential Shakespeare critics—from Samuel Taylor Coleridge and Samuel Johnson to Jean Howard and Margarita de Grazia—have had to say about *Hamlet*. And so most undergraduate Shakespeare courses focus on these topics.

This is wonderful for aspiring professional Shakespeareans, who see clear connections between what they learn in Shakespeare, what they think is important, and what they'll do in the future. But in my sections of Shakespeare, every aspiring Shakespeare professor enrolls in the company of about fifty aspiring software developers. That one Shakespearean is also in the company of about fifty aspiring doctors, accountants, and engineers. The world might need Shakespeare professors, but it doesn't need that many of them.

I wrote this book because every student—not just the aspiring Shakespeare professor—deserves a Shakespeare course that speaks to their interests, that helps them make sense of Shakespeare's plays, and that helps them discover why Shakespeare is worthwhile. And so this book is about Shakespeare's storytelling.

A *story* is any relation of events in which a character tries to get something they want. As a genre, it includes most novels, movies, comic books, and television shows. Unless you have a shriveled-up turd for a heart, you know and love at least one story. Maybe you read *Harry Potter and the Sorcerer's Stone* (1999) as a child (or still read it as an adult) or keep up with Hugo winners like N. K. Jemisin's *The Fifth Season* (2015). Maybe you watch Disney movies. Maybe you dig on sprawling, multiple-narrative pieces of storytelling like George R. R. Martin's *A Game of Thrones* (1996), or Stephen King's

IT (1986), or multi-generational pieces of storytelling like Amy Tan's *The Joy Luck Club* (1989) or Gabriel Garcia Marquez's *One Hundred Years of Solitude* (1967).

Stories bring us joy. They prompt us to reflect on the hows and whys of life, and to develop the kind of emotional intelligence that used to be called *wisdom*. Unless you are seriously unlucky, you will read, or see, at least one more story before the universe packs you up for recycling. This book will help you understand how that story does what it does, and why that story has Shakespeare's fingerprints all over it.

Shakespeare defined the modern story and invented what are now indispensable storytelling techniques. We talk about Shakespeare in the same ways that programmers talk about Grace Hopper (who invented the compiler), the way that science fiction writers talk about N. K. Jemisin (who won three Best Novel Hugo Awards *in a row*), or the way that directors talk about Steven Spielberg (who invented the Summer blockbuster). These are players who, like Shakespeare, gamed so well that they changed the rules.

This book will help you better understand storytelling: what storytellers do, and which techniques they use to do it. This is important because you might have already learned other concepts that allegedly help you understand how stories are put together— concepts like "rising action," "climax," or "protagonist"—and, well, you might as well try to understand a story by throwing rocks at it. Who is the protagonist in *A Midsummer Night's Dream*? Which scene is the climax? What does applying these labels to the play, or to its characters, teach you about how they work? Luckily, this book will help you learn to use a better set of tools.

This book will also help you better understand Shakespeare's stories. If you understand why Shakespeare has both Laertes and Hamlet ask Claudius's permission to leave Denmark, or understand why the ghost of Old Hamlet complains about how gross his poisoning was, you'll also understand how the pieces of a play fit together, and why these pieces look the way they do. That's useful if you're interested in Shakespeare, or in reading other pieces of storytelling, or in writing pieces of your own.

This book will also help you understand why Shakespeare is such a big deal. It's hard to overstate just how often writers use Shakespeare's storytelling tools. Once you know how to spot those tools, you'll see them everywhere.

If you're teaching Shakespeare, this book should help you design a course that's challenging, accessible, and relevant. A course that focuses on Shakespeare's storytelling tools—on concepts, rather than on content—lets students focus on making connections between Shakespeare and the hundreds of other pieces of storytelling they see and read. This isn't about re-treading Shakespeare by talking about how *The Lion King* (1994) and *Hamlet* are basically the same story. It's about helping students see how Shakespeare's symbols work in *Hamlet* so that they can discover how other pieces of *Hamlet*-style storytelling, like *Fences* (1986), *Star Wars* (1977), *Beloved* (1987), or *The Mist* (1980), use symbols the same way.

I wrote this book because its concept-driven approach has a lot of advantages. One is that it promotes close reading. Too often, close reading of Shakespeare means discussing the rhyme, meter, and imagery of a short passage—say, Hamlet's first soliloquy—to no clear purpose. Too often, it means throwing around a few terms like "enjambment" or "feminine rhyme" before using a line like "'tis an unweeded garden" to segue into a more sustainable discussion of, say, Shakespeare's ecophobia, or of Early Modern horticulture.

Close reading should do more. Good close readers ought to be able to explain why *King Lear* has a subplot. They ought to be able to explain how Shakespeare's presentation of a subplot character like Gloucester affects our perception of a main plot character like Lear. If these close readers are career students of literature, they also ought to be able to explain how other subplots—in, say, N. K. Jemisin's *The Fifth Season* (2015), J. R. R. Tolkien's *The Lord of the Rings* (1955), or the movie *The Silence of the Lambs* (1991)—work in ways that are like or unlike *King Lear*'s.

A second advantage to this book's approach is inclusiveness. A course on a subject as historically and culturally vexed as Shakespeare needs to welcome students. It needs to recognize that who they are, and what they love, is legitimate. A typical Shakespeare course—meaning one that focuses on Shakespeare's poems and plays and their historical and cultural context—tells students that they are welcome to enjoy Shakespeare as long as they also appreciate Jonathan Goldberg and Terry Eagleton.

But a concept-driven course on Shakespeare—one that, like this book, focuses on making connections between Shakespeare's plays and other pieces of storytelling—lets you welcome students gracefully. You can start by including readings from writers who reflect different student identities and interests, and continue by having students discover how Shakespeare's storytelling tools are used in their own favorite shows, books, and films.

This point is important enough to make twice: some students believe that people like them don't belong in your Shakespeare class. Some of these students are from traditionally marginalized groups. Others are English language learners, or student athletes, or neurodiverse students, or engineers, or rural students, or students who love science fiction, fantasy, detective stories, or romance novels, and who don't think that a course on Shakespeare will tolerate—let alone welcome—their identities and interests. This book can help you show students that their stories, and the stories that they love, have a place in your classroom.

Richmond, USA   Nate Eastman

Acknowledgments This book wouldn't exist without the help of a very patient editor, Allie Troyanos, or without the Shakespeare classes who suffered through early drafts of it. Together, they talked me out of a lot of bad ideas. Only they know how much work that takes.

References

Allers, Roger, and Rob Minkoff. 1994. *The Lion King*. Directed by Roger Allers and Rob Minkoff. Burbank: Walt Disney Studios, 2014. Blu-Ray.
Garcia Marquez, Gabriel. (1967) 2006. *One Hundred Years of Solitude*, trans. Gregory Rabassa. New York: HarperCollins.
Jemisin, N. K. 2015. *The Fifth Season*. London: Orbit Books.
King, Stephen. (1980) 2018. *The Mist*. New York: Scribner.
King, Stephen. 1986. *IT*. New York: Signet.
Lucas, George. 1977. *Star Wars Episode IV: A New Hope*. Directed by George Lucas. 1977. Los Angeles: Twentieth Century Fox, 2013. Blu-Ray.
Martin, George R. R. 1996. *A Game of Thrones*. New York: Bantam Books.
Morrison, Toni. (1987) 2004. *Beloved*. Vancouver: Vintage.
Rowling, J. K. 1999. *Harry Potter and the Sorcerer's Stone*. New York: Scholastic Books.
Tally, Ted. 1991. *The Silence of the Lambs*. Directed by Jonathan Demme. Beverly Hills: MGM Studios, 2007. DVD.
Tan, Amy. (1989) 2006. *The Joy Luck Club*. New York: Penguin.
Tolkien, J. R. R. (1955) 1987. *The Lord of the Rings*. New York: Houghton Mifflin Harcourt.
Wilson, August. 1986. *Fences*. New York: Plume.

Contents

1 Introduction — 1
  1.1 What Is This Book? — 1
  1.2 Exclusions and Limitations — 5
  1.3 Further Reading — 7
  References — 8

2 Shakespeare the Storyteller — 11
  2.1 What Is a Story? — 11
  2.2 Why Read Shakespeare? — 14
  2.3 Shakespeare and Storytelling — 16
  2.4 Further Reading — 18
  References — 19

3 Characters and Their Stories — 21
  3.1 Motivations — 24
  3.2 Goals (and Plans) — 27
  3.3 Flaws — 34
  3.4 Revelations — 39
  3.5 Further Reading — 48
  References — 49

4	**Relationships Between Characters**	51
	4.1 Conflicts	56
	4.2 Opponents and Opposition	64
	4.3 Character Webs	73
	4.4 Further Reading	92
	References	93
5	**Structure**	95
	5.1 Scene Weave	98
	5.2 Symbols	115
	5.3 Moral Vision	125
	5.4 Further Reading	132
	References	133
6	**Shakespeare's Genres**	135
	6.1 What is Genre?	135
	6.2 Character Histories	138
	6.3 Coming of Age Stories	140
	6.4 Romantic Comedies	142
	6.5 Revenge Tragedies	144
	6.6 Runaway Villains	145
	6.7 One-Trick Ponies	147
	6.8 Contest Stories	149
	6.9 Further Reading	151
	References	153
7	**Applications and Exercises**	155
	7.1 Application: Introduction and Starter Questions	155
	7.2 Application: King Lear	159
	7.3 Application: Hamlet and Star Wars: Episode IV	161
	7.4 Application: From Story to Shakespeare	169
	7.4.1 Step One: Motivations, Goals, and Flaws	170
	7.4.2 Step Two: Conflict and Opponents	171
	7.4.3 Step Three: Plans	173
	7.4.4 Step Four: Battles and Revelations	174
	7.4.5 Step Five: New Equilibrium	177
	References	178
8	**Conclusion**	181
	References	184
Index		187

CHAPTER 1

Introduction

1.1 WHAT IS THIS BOOK?

Most courses about Shakespeare are actually about the past. As a typical *Hamlet*-reading student in a typical twenty-first-century section of Shakespeare, you might read Stephen Greenblatt's *Hamlet in Purgatory* (2001) to learn what, exactly, Shakespeare's audience would have thought about ghosts. You might also read Nabil Matar's *Turks, Moors, and Englishmen* (1999) to learn how Shakespeare and his fellow Londoners thought about a Muslim like Othello,[1] or James Shapiro's *Shakespeare and the Jews* (1996) to learn how they might have thought about Shylock,[2] or Natasha Korda's *Shakespeare's Domestic Economies* (2002) to learn how they thought about difficult women like Kate.[3] Shakespeare courses are rich in history.

Modern editions of Shakespeare's plays are, too. Whether you're reading a Norton Shakespeare or a humble Signet, your introduction to *The Comedy of Errors* will inevitably mention that *Comedy* is based on Plautus's *Menaechmi* ("The Menaechmus Brothers"), was entered into the Stationers' Register in 1594, and was first printed in Shakespeare's First Folio (1623).

Along with this, you'll get notes on Shakespeare's life. There, you'll learn that Shakespeare was the son of a one-time Stratford glove-maker, and was educated at the King's New School, and that he married Anne Hathaway (who was eight years his senior), fathered some children with her, and then disappeared for a few years before Robert Greene—a fellow playwright—sniped at

---

[1] From *Othello*.
[2] From *The Merchant of Venice*.
[3] From *The Taming of the Shrew*.

© The Author(s), under exclusive license to Springer Nature Switzerland AG 2021
N. Eastman, *Shakespeare's Storytelling*,
https://doi.org/10.1007/978-3-030-62993-9_1

him in a 1592 pamphlet titled "Groats-Worth of Wit."[4] It will go on from there.

I like history. But that so much study of Shakespeare is actually a closeted study of history seems misguided. My Shakespeare classes are full of aspiring doctors, accountants, chemists, biologists, and engineers. Their futures will not be improved by knowing how Early Modern Europeans understood Muslims, or that Shakespeare's England hosted thriving home-based textile businesses. My students will never, ever read Plautus. That's not a lament for how, Once Upon A Time and In Better Days, every student knew the name of Alexander the Great's horse.[5] I have excellent students. They deserve a course that speaks to them. They deserve a course that understands the difference between Shakespeare and history.

History is about how we understand the dead. It makes sense to talk about Chaucer, Wyatt, Amelia Lanier, and so many other writers as history. They are no longer active. The train of their influence has arrived at its final destination, never to depart again.

But Shakespeare is alive. Whenever you read a book like *Beloved* (1987), or watch a movie like *The Wrestler* (2008), read a comic like *Watchmen* (1987), binge a show like *Breaking Bad* (2008), or see plays like *Angels in America* (1991),[6] you're seeing Shakespeare come to life. I don't mean that these books and plays and movies are all just thinly veiled adaptations of Shakespeare, like how *The Lion King* is just *Hamlet* in a cat mask.[7] I mean that all of these books, movies, plays, and shows, along with thousands of others, use storytelling concepts that were developed by Shakespeare in roughly the same way that every piece of lighting in your home, whether it's LED, CFL, or incandescent bulb, uses a technological concept—electric light—developed by Thomas Edison.[8]

If you're wondering why Shakespeare is important, or why Shakespeare matters, it's because he was an *inventor*. The first thing he invented was a type of story, in which a character changes in order to get what they want. The second thing he invented was a set of tools that allow this type of story

---

[4] History gave Robert Greene one chance to send William Shakespeare to the burn unit, and Greene came up with this: "here is an upstart Crow, beautified with our feathers, that with his *Tiger's heart wrapped in a Player's hide*, supposes he is as well able to bombast out a blank verse as the best of you: and being an absolute *Johannes factotum*, is in his own conceit the only Shake-scene in a country."

This quote is well known, but I've sourced it from Stephen Greenblatt's *Will in the World: How Shakespeare Became Shakespeare* (2004).

[5] Bucephalus.

[6] The work commonly referred to as *Angels in America* actually consists of two plays (*Millennium Approaches* and *Perestroika*) published in 1991 and 1993.

[7] This is true of both the 1994 and 2019 version of *The Lion King*.

[8] And his hundreds of anonymous employees at Menlo Park, and a half-dozen predecessors like Humphry Davy, Warren de la Rue, Joseph Swan, and Henry Woodward, whose light bulbs were impractically short-lived. See Robert Friedel and Paul Israel's *Edison's Electric Light: The Art of Invention*.

to be told effectively. While much—but not all—modern-day storytelling is Shakespearean, almost all modern storytelling uses Shakespeare's tools.

Just for instance: the last movie that I saw in a theater was *Moana* (2016).[9] If you've never seen *Moana*, it's about a young girl (Moana) who leaves her native island to find a demigod, Maui, so that they (Moana and Maui) can complete an ocean journey to save the world. That's not Shakespeare. In fact, *Moana*'s "return the magic doodad to its rightful place" mission, its cast of gods and demigods, and its periodic musical numbers mean that *Moana* looks more like *The Lord of the Rings* (1955) than *Hamlet*.[10]

But there are traces of *Hamlet* in *Moana*: Moana's father, Chief Tui, wants Moana to spend the rest of her life on her home island. That way, she'll be safe. In contrast, an assembly of other characters—especially her grandmother, Tala—want something different for Moana. They believe in exploration, or in finding yourself by leaving the place where you grew up. In their own ways, they each want Moana to leave her island for parts unknown.

This is very like *Hamlet*. *Hamlet* is a story about a prince with two father figures. There's Hamlet's dead father, Old Hamlet: a warrior who solved problems with his sword. And there's Hamlet's stepfather, Claudius: a scheming manipulator who solves problems with a combination of plotting and treachery. Hamlet's story is about him choosing which kind of adult he'll become: a warrior or a schemer.

In both *Moana* and *Hamlet*, in other words, we see a young character who chooses between two different systems of values, each of which is represented by a parental figure. Both Moana and Hamlet ask similar questions about themselves as they stand on the cusp of adulthood: Do I choose a life of safety or adventure? Do I become a warrior or a politician? Am I a Chief Tui, or a Maui? Am I an Old Hamlet, or a Claudius?

That's Shakespearean, or at least one of Shakespeare's storytelling tools. And once you start looking for it, you'll see it all over the place. It's in the first *Star Wars* trilogy (1977–1983),[11] where Luke Skywalker chooses loyalties between Obi Wan Kenobi and Darth Vader.[12] It's also in the film *Coraline* (2009), where Coraline chooses between her Mother (a typically exasperated, under-attentive parent) and her Other Mother (the Beldam, who steals the souls of runaway children).[13] This tool is widespread because, on the one hand, it's interesting to see young characters struggle with the values they'll

---

[9] This means that I have not been to a movie theater in some time.

[10] Except that *Moana*'s songs are good.

[11] For the sake of clarity, I mean *Episode IV: A New Hope*, along with bits of Episodes V and VI (that is, *The Empire Strikes Back* and *Return of the Jedi*).

[12] In 1977's *Episode IV*, Luke chooses between Uncle Owen and Obi-Wan. In 1983's *Return of the Jedi*, he chooses between Vader and the Emperor.

[13] It's in a lot of other books and movies, too. Think movies like *Interstellar* (2014) and *Get Rich or Die Tryin'* (2005), and books like *The Golden Compass* (1995), *True Grit* (1968), *Dune* (1965) or any other story in which a young person chooses loyalties between two parental figures who represent different sets of values.

live by as adults. On the other, hearing characters describe their values is tedious.

But attaching values to *symbols*—in this case, to father (or parent) figures—lets characters accept or reject ideas about how to live without a lot of tedious philosophizing. When Moana argues with her father, she's arguing against the idea of staying on her island, and for the idea that becoming who her people need her to be requires that she take a dangerous journey into the unknown. When Luke rejects Darth Vader, he's rejecting brutality and intimidation, and accepting that the use of might for right, according to an elegant and civilized mysticism, is the Right Way to Live. When Coraline chooses her Mother over her Other Mother, she's accepting that real people are imperfect, and rejecting the well-manicured order of illusions over which her Other Mother magically presides. The acceptance or rejection of a parent figure, in other words, represents a profound, value-driven act of self-discovery and change.

As an audience, we understand this intuitively. That's good. If Moana, Luke, or Coraline had to explain their changing inner states in the same ways that characters in pre-Shakespearean plays like *Gorboduc* (1561) and *Mankind* (1470) did, *Moana*, *Star Wars*, and *Coraline* would be five hours long. Shakespeare's storytelling tools make these kinds of stories—Shakespearean stories—possible. That's what this book is about. In the following chapters, we'll look at the patterns that Shakespearean stories follow, and at how stories are told using Shakespeare's tools.

Other books about stories, storytelling, characters, and plays often refer to Shakespeare's storytelling tools in different ways, and by using different names. If you read Stanislavski's *An Actor Prepares* (1936), for instance, you'll notice that what Stanislavski calls *super-objectives* look a lot like what this book calls *motivation*. Truby's *Anatomy of Story* (2007) uses the term *need*. In her chapter of the Gotham Writers' Workshop's *Writing Fiction* (2003), Brandi Reissenweber calls the same concept—or something like it—*desire*.

There's no single, standardized vocabulary that academics, actors, playwrights, or storytellers use to name the parts of storytelling. That can be frustrating. Why not call the force that drives a character from the beginning to the end of a story "motivation" (or "super-objective") and be done with it? One answer is that, while each of these concepts is broadly similar, there are significant differences between them. For Stanislavski, Truby, and Reissenweber, for instance, a character's motivation (or super-objective, need, or desire) can be nearly anything. It can be a glass of water. That has to be true in the sense that Stanislavski, Truby, and Reissenweber talk about an incredible diversity of stories and at least one of them, somewhere, is about someone getting a glass of water.

But for us, motivation is very, very specific. We're mainly concerned with Shakespeare's storytelling, and Shakespeare's characters are motivated by *how they want to be seen*.[14]

This doesn't mean that Stanislavski, Truby, Reissenweber, or dozens of other writers are wrong. All of them have perceptive things to say about Shakespeare's characters and, if you're interested in learning more about storytelling techniques—many of which were invented by Shakespeare—you ought to read their books and others. This book is only a beginning.

So let's recap.

There are three things I want you to understand about this book. The first is that Shakespeare's plays aren't about history. Even the Histories aren't about history. Shakespeare's plays are stories, and understanding them means understanding how stories are told.

This means understanding Shakespeare's storytelling tools. If you want to write your own novels, plays, or movies, or if you're just interested in how storytelling works, you'll have to understand how storytelling uses Shakespearean tools like motivations, character webs, and symbols. This is true no matter what you think each of those tools ought to be called.

Finally: Storytelling is a craft. It is technically complex and demanding. It is detailed, meticulous, and complicated. When stories are told well, they look and feel natural. But don't be fooled. Over the next five chapters, we'll learn just how involved a piece of storytelling can be.

1.2 Exclusions and Limitations

This book doesn't deal in history. This means that this book, while illustrating some of its key concepts, will make statements that other Shakespeareans would find insufficiently complicated. Sometimes it will completely ignore what they consider a major part of this field. I'm fine with that. They can write their own books.

But it's important to talk about what this book won't talk about. You should know what you're missing.

Later on, in our chapter on characters, I'm going to write something like this:

> It's important to Egeon that other people see him as a good father.

You don't need to know who Egeon is right now, except that he's a character in *The Comedy of Errors*. But you should know where I'm generalizing: what it means to be a good father is really very complicated. As of this writing, my daughter is three. Her favorite movie is *Aliens* (1986), and we watch it nearly

---

[14] That said, I've used John Truby's terms throughout much of this book. *The Anatomy of Story* talks about relationships between characters (like conflicts and character webs) and the structural elements of stories (like scene weave, symbols, and moral vision) in ways that are especially well-suited to Shakespearian stories.

every weekend. You and your classmates might disagree over whether this is good (or bad) parenting.

History makes this kind of disagreement even more complicated. For instance: Thomas Wyatt, a poet who lived a generation before Shakespeare, wrote a series of letters to his son. In one of them, he explains that his (that is, Thomas Wyatt's) marriage has been strained and distant. Wyatt partly blames his wife for this, writing "the fault is both in your mother and me, but chiefly in her."[15] If you were in a restaurant and overheard that line in a father/son conversation at a neighboring table, it might be hard to know whether Wyatt was telling the truth, or passing his son a self-serving fiction. It might be hard to know whether Wyatt understood his own behavior, or the dynamics of his marriage, well enough to pass judgment on either. For those and dozens of other reasons, it would be hard to know whether we were hearing good or bad parenting.

But Wyatt wasn't taking his son to a weekend-dad dinner at the local spaghetti grotto. He was writing in a culture where people thought about marriage, parenthood, and manners differently than we do. Maybe the manners of Wyatt's day dictated that he was supposed to pretend that his marriage was happy. Maybe those manners led Wyatt's son to expect a notarized list of his mother's infidelities. We don't know.

But if we were enterprising researchers, we might try to find out. Maybe we'd read a conduct manual like Castiglione's 1528 *The Book of the Courtier* (a Shakespeare-era version of an advice column) to see how well-mannered Elizabethans were supposed to talk about their unhappy marriages.

Here's the thing: Even if *Courtier* gave us a top-ten list of things that you should never tell your son about your estranged spouse, our job still wouldn't be finished. A single book can't speak for everyone. We'd need to read more to get a sense of how different people thought. Maybe they'd all agree, but probably not.

After that, we could open up some sixteenth-century letter collections to find out how often unhappy parents confessed each other's sins to their children. Even if Wyatt's behavior were technically impolite, it might also have been perfectly normal, like farting on the subway or texting in a movie theater.

There would be no end to it. No matter how much research we did, we'd be left with the same questions: What does it mean to be a good father? What did it mean to be a good father? Can we find out, based on what Thomas Wyatt wrote to his son? You could write a book about any of these questions. I'm not about to. That book might help you better understand the world that Shakespeare lived in, but probably won't help you understand the wholly imaginary world of *The Comedy of Errors*.

This book won't discuss the differences between our world and Shakespeare's. It won't deal in history. Other books do a fine job of that already, just as they also do a fine job of discussing the most complex and interesting

---

[15] See Wyatt's letter to his son on April 15, 1537.

dimensions of Shakespeare's culture and life. I've included several such books in the list of Further Reading that appears at the end of each chapter.

For our purposes, each of Shakespeare's plays operates in its own world that may (or may not) have anything in common with either our own world or the world of Shakespeare's England. In those worlds, as diverse as they are, characters operate according to the same basic rules: they want things, try to get them and, in the process, learn how to stop hurting themselves and other people. While each of Shakespeare's characters is different, each of them operates according to this same basic pattern: their *story*.

1.3 FURTHER READING

Shakespeare and History

These books—both monographs and anthologies—are great starting points if you want to understand more about Shakespeare's life, times, and culture.

Gajowski, Evelyn. *The Arden Research Handbook of Contemporary Shakespeare Criticism*. **Arden Shakespeare, 2020.**

The *Handbook of Contemporary Shakespeare Criticism* is a wide-ranging guide to the critical approaches most often used to interpret Shakespeare. It catalogs about twenty of these, ranging from the traditional (like character studies and genre studies) to the contemporary (like queer studies and critical race studies), and features chapters dedicated to significant late-twentieth-century approaches (like cultural materialism and New Historicism). Helpfully, each critical approach is grounded in a reading of one of Shakespeare's plays.

Greenblatt, Stephen. *Will in the World: How Shakespeare Became Shakespeare*. **Norton, 2004.**

The documentary evidence of Shakespeare's life is sparse and so, like most Shakespeare biographies, *Will in the World* is highly speculative. That said, this book does an excellent job of separating direct evidence from theories and conjecture, and of providing readers with useful historical, dramatic, and critical context.

McDonald, Russ. *The Bedford Companion to Shakespeare*. **Bedford/St. Martins, 2001.**

This is the best of the many Shakespeare companions that attempt an overview of Shakespeare's life, times, and culture. It also approaches matters such as Shakespeare's language, playwriting and playgoing conventions, and the editorial practices that shape modern-day editions of Shakespearean plays. Each of these subjects is treated in a single, brief chapter, each of which features a discerning list of suggested reading and well-chosen excerpts from period texts.

Pritchard, R.E. *Shakespeare's England: Life in Elizabethan and Jacobean Times*. **Sutton Publishing Ltd, 2000.**

Shakespeare's England is an anthology of writings by Shakespeare's contemporaries, sorted by topic. While this approach is similar to the one taken by McDonald's *Companion to Shakespeare*, *Shakespeare's England* focuses on the details of everyday life: how doctors treated patients, how Londoners gardened, and what to expect during an afternoon at the theater. It also includes a wider range of voices and, as a consequence, more persuasively represents the vitality, variety, and harsh reality of life in Shakespeare's England. All that aside, *Shakespeare's England* is a classic for a reason: it's equal parts informative and fun.

REFERENCES

Allers, Roger, and Rob Minkoff. *The Lion King*. Directed by Roger Allers and Rob Minkoff. 1994; Burbank: Walt Disney Studios, 2014. Blu-Ray.

Anonymous. "Mankind." In *Three Late Medieval Morality Plays: Mankind, Everyman, Mundus et Infans*, ed. G.A Lester, 66–104. London: Methuen, 2008.

Cameron, James. *Aliens*. Directed by James Cameron. 1986; Los Angeles: Twentieth Century Fox, 2016. Blu-Ray.

Castiglione, Baldesar. (1528) 1978. *The Book of the Courtier*. Trans. George Bull. New York: Penguin.

Clements, Ron, and John Musker. *Moana*. Directed by John Musker and Ron Clements. 2016; Burbank: Walt Disney Studios, 2017. Blu-Ray.

Friedel, Robert, and Paul Israel. 2010. *Edison's Electric Light: The Art of Invention*. Baltimore: Johns Hopkins University Press.

Gilligan, Vince. *Breaking Bad*. Aired January 20, 2008, to September 29, 2013, on AMC.

Greenblatt, Stephen. 2001. *Hamlet in Purgatory*. Princeton: Princeton University Press.

Greenblatt, Stephen. 2004. *Will in the World*. New York: W. W. Norton & Co.

Herbert, Frank. 1965. *Dune*. New York: Chilton.

Korda, Natasha. 2002. *Shakespeare's Domestic Economies*. Philadelphia: University of Pennsylvania Press.

Kushner, Tony. 1991. *Angels in America, Part One: Millennium Approaches*. New York: Theater Communications Group.

Kushner, Tony. 1993. *Angels in America, Part Two: Perestroika*. New York: Theater Communications Group.

Lee, Gary. 1982. *Family Structure and Interaction: A Comparative Analysis*. Minneapolis: University of Minnesota Press.

Lucas, George, and Lawrence Kasdan. *Star Wars Episode VI: Return of the Jedi*. Directed by Richard Marquand. 1983; Los Angeles: Twentieth Century Fox, 2013. Blu-Ray.

Lucas, George, Leigh Brackett, and Lawrence Kasden. *Star Wars Episode V: The Empire Strikes Back*. Directed by Irvin Kershner. 1980; Los Angeles: Twentieth Century Fox, 2013. Blu-Ray.

Lucas, George. *Star Wars Episode IV: A New Hope*. Directed by George Lucas. 1977; Los Angeles: Twentieth Century Fox, 2013. Blu-Ray.

Matar, Nabil. (1999) 2007. *Turks, Moors and Englishmen in the Age of Discovery*. New York: Columbia University Press.

Moore, Alan. 1987. *Watchmen*. New York: D.C. Comics.

Morrison, Toni. 1987. *Beloved*. New York: Alfred A. Knopf, Inc.

Nolan, Christopher. *Interstellar*. Directed by Christopher Nolan. 2014; Burbank: Warner Brothers, 2015. Blu-Ray.
Norton, Thomas. "Gorboduc." In *Two Tudor Tragedies*, ed. William Tyndeman, 44–105. New York: Penguin Classics, 1992.
Portis, Charles. (1968) 2012. *True Grit: A Novel*. New York: Harry N. Abrams.
Pullman, Philip. (1995) 2001. *The Golden Compass*. New York: Knopf Books for Young Readers.
Reissenweber, Brandi. 2003. "Character: Casting Shadows." In *Writing Fiction*, ed. Alexander Steele, 29–51. New York: Bloomsbury.
Selick, Henry. *Coraline*. Directed by Henry Selick. 2009; Los Angeles: Focus Features, 2011. Blu-Ray.
Shakespeare, William, and Stephen Greenblatt (ed.). 2015. *The Norton Shakespeare (Third Edition)*. London: W. W. Norton & Co.
Shakespeare, William, Sylvan Barnet, and Harry Levin (ed.). 2002. *The Comedy of Errors*. New York: Signet.
Shapiro, James. (1996) 2016. *Shakespeare and the Jews*. New York: Columbia University Press.
Siegel, Robert. *The Wrestler*. Directed by Darren Aronofsky. 2008; Los Angeles: Fox Searchlight, 2009. Blu-Ray.
Stanislavski, Konstantin. (1936) 1989. *An Actor Prepares*. London: Routledge.
Tolkien, J.R.R. (1955) 1987. *The Lord of the Rings*. New York: Houghton Mifflin Harcourt.
Truby, John. 2007. *The Anatomy of Story: 22 Steps to Becoming a Master Storyteller*. New York: Farrar, Strauss, & Giroux.
Winter, Terence. *Get Rich or Die Tryin'*. Directed by Jim Sheridan. 2005; Hollywood: Paramount Pictures, 2006. DVD.
Wyatt, Thomas. "A Letter to His Son." In *The Broadview Anthology of British Literature, Volume 2*, ed. Joseph Black, 113. Ontario: Broadview Press, 2010.

CHAPTER 2

Shakespeare the Storyteller

2.1 What Is a Story?

This is a book about stories or, more specifically, about Shakespeare's stories, how Shakespeare tells them, and how writers use Shakespeare's tools to tell stories today. So what is a *story*?

A story is an experience—something an audience reads, sees, witnesses, or creates—which tells its audience what a character wants and how they try to get it. A *character* is usually a person, but doesn't have to be. *Watership Down* (1972), *The Caves of Steel* (1954), *Wild Seed* (1980), and *The Fifth Season* (2015) focus on characters who are rabbits, robots, gods, and (animate) rocks. Likewise, *The Curious Incident of the Dog in the Night-Time* (2003), *Forrest Gump* (1986), and *The Bride Test* (2019) focus on characters whose ways of thinking and feeling are profoundly atypical. A character does not need to be a human being, or need to demonstrate a normative range of thoughts and feelings. The only thing that a character needs to do is want something and try to get it.

According to that definition of a story, two things are true: the first is that any movie, play, or novel contains as many stories as it has major characters. The second is that a character can want anything. A short story could be about a young woman trying to climb a chain-link fence so she can help a sick kitten. "I'm going to rescue that kitten," she might say to herself, "no matter what it takes."

And so our fence climber—let's call her Mary Sue—could fall down nine times but actually get over the fence on the tenth, and the story could end with her telling her sick kitten a neat little aphorism about the importance of persistence: "I had to keep trying," Mary Sue might say, "no matter what it took."

Mary Sue, in other words, could start her story believing something ("I can climb that fence to help that kitten") and end the story believing the same thing ("I *knew* I could climb that fence to help that kitten!"). She could begin and end her story as essentially the same person.

But if you read a novel, or watch a play or movie, you'll often see something different. A character will begin their story wanting something—love, or a vacation, or a Mickey Mantle rookie card. As they pursue what they want, they will learn and grow. By the end of the story, they will have become (or failed to become) a different person: the person their desire requires them to be.

This is a specific kind of story: the *Shakespearean* story. Shakespeare didn't invent the idea that people want things, or that they change, but he gave the relationship between (a) wanting something and (b) changing in order to get it, a clarity and focus that earlier storytellers never managed. There were smartphones before the iPhone, and some of them were interesting. But none of them were good in the ways the iPhone was good, or as influential as the iPhone has been. Shakespeare's formula for storytelling is much the same kind of invention. It's hard to imagine what life (or storytelling) was like before it.

But there is more. In his storytelling, Shakespeare weaves stories together so that each story defines and highlights elements of the others. For instance: We learn who Hamlet is by seeing how he is different from Laertes. Where Laertes is direct and confrontational, Hamlet is secretive and broody. This tells us that, in the world of *Hamlet*, people have different ways of dealing with grief. Some—like Laertes—draw swords over it. Others—like Hamlet—dress in black and gripe about their stepfathers.

Each of Shakespeare's plays, in other words, tells several characters' stories in ways that highlight similarities and differences between them. We'll call this practice of arranging multiple stories *storytelling*. A story helps us learn who a character is, and how they change, by showing us what they do. A piece of storytelling helps us learn who each character is by comparing and contrasting characters with one another.

Not every piece of storytelling you read is Shakespearean. Greek tragedies allow their heroes enough space to learn just one piece of information—usually something so repellant that they declare they would be better off never to have been born. But the characters do not grow. Like Mary Sue, patron saint of fence climbing and abandoned kittens, they end each of their stories much the same person as they began.

The same is true of Everyman, of Mak in the *Second Shepherd's Play* (c. 1500), and of Chaucer's Pilgrims. However colorful she is, and however varied her experience, the Wife of Bath is incapable of introspection. Despite being on pilgrimage to Canterbury, there's no evidence that she learns anything about herself. Neither does Marlowe's Faustus. The great joke of Faustus, and of his deal with the devil, is that despite being a man of learning he is unable to learn from his mistakes.

The same is also true of modern characters. There are plenty of perfectly serviceable horror movies in which people never change, and in which the audience would not expect them to. Joe Parkman—the Brave Young Warrior in American International's movie *The Deadly Mantis* (1957)[1]—begins his story with every emotional and psychological tool he needs in order to Defeat the Monster, Save the World, and Get the Girl. All he needs is for the Brilliant Scientist with Just a Touch of Gray in his Hair to build him the right kind of bomb.

If Ancient Greece, Chaucer, and 1957's worst giant insect movie are too far away for you to see clearly, the things that are true of Joe Parkman's character are also true of Harry Potter. Harry learns things as he ages—he's a student, so he ought to—but Harry never struggles with how he needs to change. This doesn't make the Harry Potter books or *The Deadly Mantis* bad pieces of storytelling (although *The Deadly Mantis* probably is). It just makes them not Shakespearean.

While Harry Potter and Joe Parkman begin their stories by thinking and acting The Right Way, Shakespeare's characters begin their stories with at least one *flaw*: a way of thinking or acting that causes them to hurt themselves and other people. Characters struggle with that flaw until they either overcome it or are forced to stop trying.

This means that Shakespearean characters make bad choices. They don't need perverse gods, giant insects, or Voldemorts to cause them problems. (Villains sometimes show up in Shakespeare, but when it comes to causing problems they're rarely any match for what the characters do to themselves.) Characters' flaws are sometimes complex but never subtle. Early in each play— usually in the first act—it will be clear how each character needs to think and act differently.

Sometimes, Shakespeare's characters learn to become different and better people. Other times, the audience watches in terrified fascination as a character spends scene after scene tripping over the same mistakes, chasing the same bad idea, in the face of ever-escalating consequences.

In a few cases—as with Brutus in *Julius Caesar*—this makes characters difficult to like. Other characters—like Richard of Gloucester, Aaron the Moor, Iago, Cleopatra, Malvolio, and *All's Well that Ends Well*'s Helena and Bertram—are likable precisely because they are deeply and completely horrible.

---

[1] *The Deadly Mantis* is one of many films dating from the late 1950s in which a giant insect ravages a city until it is stopped by a Brave Young Warrior.

2.2 Why Read Shakespeare?

So why read Shakespeare if it's full of characters who are (mostly) bad people? One answer is that it's entertaining.

Later on, we'll discuss *moral vision*, which is a play's baseline statement about how people (or characters) ought to behave toward one another. Shakespeare's plays often have pronounced, sensible moral visions—the kind that would impress your grandparents. In the Romantic Comedies, the moral vision is usually that people who want to be loved ought to also be authentic, honest, and vulnerable. That's what makes Romantic Comedies *romantic*. But what makes them *comedies* is that characters aren't authentic, honest, and vulnerable. The problems that they create by lying to themselves and manipulating one another are—for the audience—a lot of fun.

It's also fun to know where stories come from. When I watch Disney movies with my daughter, I'm watching mostly Shakespearean stories. In Disney's Princess movies, the princess's first song is always an "I want" song (in which—brace yourself—the princess tells us what she wants). Usually what she wants is to escape. This is a specific type of Shakespearean story—the Coming of Age story—in which a young person is inaugurated into adulthood by confronting their weaknesses for the first time. They do this by looking at the world around them, seeing how people in that world do things, and deciding to do them differently.

This may seem like part of growing up. You might think, "every teenager looks at the world around them and says, 'I'm going to be different.' That's not Shakespeare. That's life."

Maybe it is. But stories aren't life. They are life distilled to its salient, meaningful experiences. During the Middle Ages, and for the Morality Plays that preceded Shakespeare, those salient, meaningful experiences involved every person's relationship with God. For Chaucer, the Miller's fart jokes and the Nun's pretentiousness, and the eccentricities of all the other pilgrims, fit together like the gears of an old watch. Life wasn't about understanding your experiences, but understanding how your experiences fit the intricacies of a divine plan.

In contrast: For Shakespeare, and for us, life is about plasticity, change, and self-discovery. Questions like "are you who you want to be?" point to qualities of our collective thinking that would have made little sense either to Chaucer or to the Romans who proceeded him. The Wakefield Master—author of the *Second Shepherd's Play*—would be quick to correct us. "Life is about being who God wants you to be," the Master might have said. "You have a choice about that, and there are right and wrong answers." Sophocles—author of *Oedipus the King* (429 BCE)—might say, "Life is about playing the role that fate has assigned you. The less you fight against that fate the less unhappy you'll be."

This is not the stuff of Disney movies. Cinderella does not marry Prince Charming only to find out that he's actually her father. We are more interested in her (and Moana, and Pocahontas, and the rest) overcoming their childhood deference to authority. We are interested in the process by which these characters become who they need to be in order to get what they want.

In other words: Stories, whether Classic, Medieval, or Modern, are about the hows and whys of human life. For writers before Shakespeare, these hows and whys mostly involved characters discovering how to fit into a story that was already written by God or by fate. For Shakespeare, and for us, the hows and whys involve *discovering who we need to become in order to get what we want*. This often means learning something about how we ought to relate toward other people. I like to say that stories, like life, are about becoming the person the world needs us to be.

Shakespeare's plays are not the greatest storytelling of all time. Some of them (like *The Two Noble Kinsmen*, *Henry VIII*, and *The Two Gentlemen of Verona*) are memorable for a single character, or a single line, or not at all. And they are sometimes sloppy.

But Shakespeare's storytelling is often very, very good. As an innovator, or as one who changed the kinds of stories that we tell, and the tools we use to tell them, Shakespeare is unparalleled. The artistic and technical differences between a pre-Shakespearean play like *Gorboduc* (1562) and Shakespeare's *King Lear* is baffling when compared to the differences between *King Lear* and *Fences* (1986). *Lear* and *Fences* are different but recognizable versions of the same story. They focus on relationships between fathers and children, and see those relationships become complicated as characters exercise their senses of self-importance and entitlement.[2]

Gorboduc is not this story. While it is technically similar to *Lear* in the sense that it involves the division of a kingdom between two squabbling heirs (Ferrex and Porrex), it reads like a set of IKEA furniture instructions. There are characters, but only in the strict sense that representations of human beings are required in order to illustrate a process.

Another matter: Shakespeare's human insight. A good performance of *Hamlet* will get laughs on Hamlet's opening line (I.ii.66: "a little more than kin and less than kind")—mostly from stepparents who are too familiar with their stepchildren's resentment. The relationship between the Nurse and Juliet, too, is instantly recognizable. Who hasn't met an adult who's just a bit too willing to enable a child's bad decisions—not out of malice, but out of the vicarious thrill that comes with reliving their own?

Shakespeare didn't invent these types of people. They have always been around. But Shakespeare was the first to think about them as characters on their way to finding what they want, and becoming different people—better and wiser people—as they search for it. Someday, some new understanding of our own experience may fully replace the one that Shakespeare pioneered. But

---

[2] *Death of a Salesman* (1949) is another version of the same story.

until then, his plays are the earliest version of our modern answer to a much older question: What does life mean, and how do we discover and create that meaning?

2.3 Shakespeare and Storytelling

While Shakespeare's plays each focus on how characters discover who they are and try to live into that vision, they do this in several different ways. As a piece of storytelling, each play includes several different stories. The number of stories that each play includes, how closely the play explores each, and how each play constructs relationships between these stories, differ.

Sometimes, a play mainly follows the development of a single character, with minimal time given to the stories of others. *Hamlet* and *Othello* are both plays of this type, although there are perhaps a dozen more.

At other times, the play follows the development of several characters whose stories are given roughly equal weight. *Romeo and Juliet*, *A Midsummer Night's Dream*, and *King Lear* are plays of this type.

Regardless of whether a play follows one or several characters, each character's story—that is, their journey of self-discovery and change—follows the same basic pattern. It has five steps:

1. *Motivations, Goals and Flaws*: We are introduced to the character(s), and learn:

   - How they need to be seen in order to feel validated (their *motivation*)
   - What specific things they think they need in order to be seen that way (their *goals*), and
   - How elements of their personality hurt them and other people (their *flaws*).

2. *Conflicts and Opponents*: We are introduced to a conflict, in which other characters want the same thing as our story's character does. Sometimes, this is something tangible (like to marry Juliet). At other times, it is intangible (like to decide who Juliet will marry). Sometimes this conflict features an *opponent*, who not only wants the same thing as another character, but also attacks their weaknesses.

3. *Plans*: The character develops a plan to negotiate their conflicts and achieve their goals. Sometimes this plan fails, and the character develops a new plan. In *Hamlet*, for instance, both Claudius and Hamlet need to revise their plans several times.

4. *Battles and Revelations*: A character discovers how they ought to change in order to stop hurting themselves, to stop hurting others, or to get

what they want. I call this a *revelation*. In some cases, the audience learns how characters ought to change, but the characters themselves do not.

The battle (or battles) in this step are often literal military conflicts or duels; if the play has an opponent, it may be fought directly against them.

More often, a battle is indirect. A good Shakespearean opponent will use innuendo and trickery to get what they want, and resort to direct confrontation (like a battle or duel) only when there are no other options.

5. *New Equilibrium*: A new equilibrium is established. Sometimes this means that the character, having grown and changed, will have become king or will have married the man or woman of their dreams. Sometimes it means that the character hasn't changed, or hasn't gotten what they wanted and will be forced to stop trying. Either way, the story ends. The character has gotten what they wanted, or they never will.

This five-step structure might seem formulaic, but no two Shakespearean plays present it in exactly the same way. Major characters—Hamlets, Othellos, and Cleopatras—will see their stories treated in great detail. Less central characters will have their stories sketched only in outline; as we'll see later on, Laertes's story (in *Hamlet*) is told with remarkable economy.

Regardless of the level of detail in which a character's story is presented, every character in a play will usually progress through their story at roughly the same pace. Their motivations and flaws will be established in their first moments on stage, which (for major characters) is usually in Act I. Likewise, characters' revelations will also occur in clusters—late in Act IV and sometimes in Act V.

This simultaneity is no coincidence. Shakespeare writes his characters so that each step in each of their stories defines and highlights the qualities of other stories. One character's flaw (that he is too arrogant) will be established at the same time as another's (that she is too self-effacing), so that the audience can (a) see the spectrum of confidence available to characters in the world of the play and (b) understand that each of these two characters is at an opposite end of it. If, in *King Lear*, Gloucester didn't have a good son, Edgar, the audience might assume that Gloucester's evil son, Edmund, was ordinary. For that matter, the fact that *King Lear* has two fathers (Lear and Gloucester) help us understand the range of ways that they misparent.

This technique, the *character web*, is one that we'll discuss in greater detail later on. It, along with *symbols*, *scene weave*, and *moral vision*, is part of the toolkit that Shakespeare uses to build the relationships between stories that ultimately define a play.

> **Points of Review**
>
> We've learned a lot about stories and storytelling in this chapter. For now, it's important to remember three things:
> 1. Each of Shakespeare's plays is composed of several stories. Each story describes a single character's desire-fueled journey of self-discovery and change.
> 2. Each of Shakespeare's plays is also a piece of storytelling. This means that characters' stories mutually define and highlight one another. Storytelling shows us who characters are by differentiating them from one another.
> 3. However different each of Shakespeare's characters and their individual stories seem, they all follow the same five steps. Each story begins by establishing a character's motivations, goals, and flaws (usually) in Act I, and ends by establishing a new equilibrium (usually) in Act V.
>
> Let's look at the five steps more closely.

2.4 Further Reading

Stories and Storytelling

These books are about the art and craft of storytelling. They are not about Shakespeare, although some may mention *Hamlet* incidentally (in a discussion of, say, scene construction).

These books are also mainly written for aspiring novelists, actors, directors, and playwrights, rather than for students of literature. Still, their discussions of character, plot, and storytelling are perceptive, accessible, and illuminating.

Stanislavski, Constantin. The Acting Trilogy (*An Actor Prepares*, *Building a Character*, and *Creating a Role*).

Since their first publication in the early twentieth century, Stanislavski's books on acting have been consistently reissued, most recently by Routledge (2012) and Bloomsbury (2013). While they are intended for theater students and aspiring actors, they also include illuminating discussions of characters' motivations, and some fantastic reads of *Richard III* and *Othello*.

Steele, Alexander (ed.). *Writing Fiction*. Bloomsbury, 2003.

Writing Fiction is a collection of essays and exercises written by the faculty of the Gotham Writers' Workshop. Each chapter of *Writing Fiction* discusses a single topic like character, point of view, pacing, or dialogue using a combination of short, concept-based introductions and sometimes-lengthy writing exercises.

I recommend *Writing Fiction* over perhaps a dozen similar books because each chapter is written by a frankly excellent teacher of creative writing (like Allison Amend, Chris Lombardi, Brandi Reissenweber, or David Ebenbach).

This means that you don't need to be a veteran of creative writing workshops to get something out of it.

Truby, John. *The Anatomy of Story.* Farrar, Strauss, and Giroux, 2007.
The Anatomy of Story is a comprehensive, integrated guide to storytelling. *Anatomy* also informs many of the concepts in this book—especially character webs and moral vision—which makes it the book to read if you're looking to learn more about them.

Truby's work as a screenwriter means that many of the concepts and examples in *Anatomy* involve film, although the occasional examples from Shakespeare, and from novels like *The Adventures of Huckleberry Finn* or *Great Expectations*, provide both depth and variety.

REFERENCES

Adams, Richard. (1972) 1975. *Watership Down*. London: Avon Books.
Anonymous. "The Second Shepherd's Play." In Everyman *and Other Miracle and Morality Plays*, ed. Candace Ward, 24–56. Dover: Dover Publications, 1995.
Asimov, Isaac. (1954) 1991. *The Caves of Steel*. New York: Spectra.
Berkeley, Martin. *The Deadly Mantis*. Directed by Nathan Juran. 1957; Los Angeles: Shout Factory, 2019. Blu-Ray.
Butler, Octavia. (1980) 2020. *Wild Seed*. New York: Grand Central Publishing.
Chaucer, Geoffrey. (c. 1380) 2005. *The Canterbury Tales*. New York: Penguin Classics.
Groom, Winston. (1986) 2012. *Forrest Gump*. Vancouver: Vintage Books.
Haddon, Mark. (2003) 2004. *The Curious Incident of the Dog in the Night-Time*. Vancouver: Vintage Contemporaries.
Hoang, Helen. 2019. *The Bride Test*. New York: Penguin Publishing Group.
Jemisin, N.K. 2015. *The Fifth Season*. London: Orbit Books.
Marlowe, Christopher. (1589) 1994. *Doctor* Faustus. Dover: Dover Publications.
Miller, Arthur. (1949) 1976. *Death of a Salesman*. New York: Penguin Books.
Norton, Thomas. "Gorboduc." In *Two Tudor Tragedies*, ed. William Tyndeman, 44–105. New York: Penguin Classics, 1992.
Rowling, J.K. 1999. *Harry Potter and the Sorcerer's Stone*. New York: Scholastic Books.
Sophocles. (429 BCE) 1991. *Oedipus Rex*. Trans. George Young. Dover: Dover Publications.
Wilson, August. 1986. *Fences*. New York: Plume.

CHAPTER 3

Characters and Their Stories

There is a profound difference between a person and a character. For instance: When a person is interviewed for a documentary, we intuitively understand that they have wants, needs, and anxieties, regrets about their past, hopes for their future, and a thousand other human concerns that go unrepresented in their interview. It's a common mistake to think of characters the same way. Characters are created word by word. They do not have wants, needs, anxieties, regrets, or hopes that exist independent of their stories.

This difference between people and characters can be confusing, especially when Shakespeare's characters are modeled on historical figures. In *Macbeth* I.vii, Lady Macbeth mentions that she has had a child. No other character or circumstance in the play tells us whether she has had more than one child, whether her children are boys or girls, alive or dead, or have children of their own. Lady Macbeth's children, unlike real human beings, exist in a sort of supposed, indefinite state, like Schrödinger's cat. We'll call this state *unwritten*.[1]

Everything that a story tells us about a character involves either what that character wants or how they need to change in order to get it. This is true whether the character is a merciless grasper like Gordon Gekko in *Wall Street* (1987), an outright villain like Aaron in *Titus Andronicus*, or a well-intentioned rabbit like Hazel in *Watership Down* (1972).

[1] For the last century, "how many children had Lady Macbeth?" has been a kind of contemptuous shorthand for the practice of asking questions about matters that might be relevant to understanding a person but not to understanding a character (such as their astrological sign or favorite Burgerville shake). For a history of the phrase, including its misunderstandings and misattributions, see Britton (1961).

It might seem impossible that a character who's limited to wanting something and trying to get it could be the center of a complex, interesting, meaningful story. But it turns out that while wanting and getting—what we'll call *desire*—can be simple, Shakespeare rarely presents it that way. For Shakespeare, desire drives a process of self-discovery that touches the center of human experience. Shakespeare's storytelling techniques present this process to us with unnatural clarity, but in a way that looks and feels natural. Over the next three chapters, we'll learn how.

You'll remember that Shakespeare's stories follow five steps:

1. Motivations, Goals, and Flaws
2. Conflict and Opponents
3. Plans
4. Battles and Revelations
5. New Equilibrium.

Some of these steps involve individual characters and their desires. Others involve relationships between characters—their conflicts, oppositions, and battles. In this chapter, we'll focus on the first kind of step—that is, on characters' individual stories. Shakespeare tells these stories by describing characters' *motivations*, *goals*, *flaws*, and *revelations*.

Characters' motivations are long-term needs. In non-Shakespearean stories, these needs might be anything from food to freedom. But in Shakespeare's stories, characters' motivations are psychological, emotional, and social. These characters are after a specific kind of public validation: They need other people to see them in the way they want to be seen.

One common form of this motivation involves a character wanting to be seen as significant. That is, they simply want other characters to consider, and care about, their thoughts and feelings. At other times, however, characters will want to be seen as honest, clever, loyal, or capable, as good fathers and sons, or as good mothers and daughters.

Once established, a character's motivation will remain constant throughout their story and throughout the play. A character who wants to be seen as a good father in Act I will still want to be seen that way in Act V. A single motivation, in other words, propels a character through their entire story.

Act by act, and scene by scene, characters are driven by goals: the concrete, specific achievements that characters believe will help them attain their motivation. A character whose motivation is to be seen as the cleverest man in the kingdom might have several goals: out-argue the lawyers, outwit the conmen, and outclass the court poets. As a story progresses, a character's goals will change.

For instance: Hamlet wants to be seen as loyal to his father. That's his motivation. Before the play begins, Hamlet has been moping around Elsinore dressed in black—an act of mourning his father's death that both Gertrude

(Hamlet's mother) and Claudius (his uncle/stepfather) think is excessive. Hamlet making the depth of his grief public is his first goal. It's not an ambitious goal, but Hamlet thinks that by achieving it he can show the rest of Elsinore that he's a loyal son to his dead father.

But Hamlet actually has several other goals, too. He snipes at his stepfather, Claudius, because he thinks that showing everyone that he resents his stepfather is a way of being loyal to his father. Hamlet also wants to go back to college, fleeing the scene of his mother's second marriage so that he can show the rest of Elsinore he wants no part of her new family.

None of those goals excludes the others. Hamlet would happily fire a couple snide parting shots at Claudius and then abandon Denmark for Wittenberg if the world of his play would let him. But as Hamlet learns more about his father's death, and becomes compelled to avenge his father's murder, what it means to be seen as a loyal son changes. Hamlet's goals become progressively more challenging, dynamic, and violent.

Hamlet, like all of Shakespeare's characters, also begins his story with flaws: habits of thinking and acting that hurt himself and others. Most of the time, there's at least one flaw at work in the way a character connects their motivations to their goals.

Consider Hamlet: His goals at the beginning of the play don't actually demonstrate loyalty to his father. Old Hamlet was a warrior king—everybody who recognizes Old Hamlet's ghost remembers how Old Hamlet led a battle, or killed someone in single combat. Old Hamlet solved problems with his sword, not with snide remarks. So (young) Hamlet's flaw—at least the first flaw we discover—is that he thinks he can solve problems by being broody and theatrical, when what he actually needs to do is shed some blood.

Other characters, especially in the comedies, exhibit flaws that amount to being insufficiently authentic, honest, or vulnerable. Shakespearean characters often begin their plays not understanding (or not taking responsibility) for what they want. They lie to other people, or concoct outrageous plans to avoid being held accountable for their desires. Often, they do these things because they are afraid that being who they really are, and saying what they really feel, will lead to them getting hurt.

Either way, the result is the same: Characters who act on their flaws will hurt themselves and other people, and will do so until they learn to act differently. That moment of learning is their revelation. *Hamlet* ends with Prince Hamlet acting differently than he began: storming a pirate ship, leaping into Ophelia's grave, dueling Laertes, and—finally—avenging both his father's and mother's deaths by murdering Claudius.

But while every character of Shakespeare's, no matter how minor, has motivations, goals, and flaws, not every character has a revelation. Some characters, like some people, never learn.

But you will. In this chapter, we'll explore Shakespeare's characters' motivations, goals, flaws, and revelations in greater detail, using examples from *The Comedy of Errors, Richard III, Hamlet, The Merchant of Venice, The*

Taming of the Shrew and *Much Ado About Nothing*. By the end, you should be able to discover any of Shakespeare's characters' motivations, goals, and flaws by closely reading the first thing they say or do. You should also be able to discover these characters' revelations—if they have them—by tracking how their thoughts and actions change throughout the play.

Finally, you'll be able to identify how modern-day writers use these tools of Shakespeare's in their own work. Here, as elsewhere, these tools define the craft of modern storytelling.

3.1 Motivations

Motivations are characters' general and ongoing needs. Outside of Shakespeare's world, in the universe of stories, motivations touch every level of Maslow's hierarchy, from food, water, and shelter to the peculiar form of fulfilled happiness that Maslow called "self-actualization."

For example: When I was in school, Jack London's stories were required reading. In each of them (like 1902's "To Build a Fire" and 1909's "A Piece of Steak") a character needed exactly what each story's title would suggest. London's characters were Arctic explorers or middle-aged boxers who tried (and failed) to do, or to obtain, a seemingly simple and tangible thing.

Other stories involve characters whose motivations are things like money or freedom. These are also tangible motivations, and fodder for all kinds of familiar stories—heists and escapes, for instance. Heist stories focus on a theft, and in the most basic and forgettable ones the motive for the theft is money. Escape stories focus on escape, and in the most basic and forgettable versions of these the motive for escape is literally to set foot outside prison walls.

If these don't sound Shakespearean, there's a good reason: Shakespeare never wrote a play where characters are motivated by survival, money, or freedom. These are tangible motives, and Shakespeare's characters' motives are intangible.

In most good heists and escapes, characters' motives are also intangible. You could say that Butch Cassidy and the Sundance Kid[2] were both motivated by money, or that Luke Jackson (in 1967's *Cool Hand Luke*) or Andy Dufresne (in 1994's *Shawshank Redemption*) were motivated to get out of prison. That's not totally wrong, but it's criminally incomplete.

A later generation of Disney princesses—Belle, Moana, Rapunzel—have motivations that are similar to Butch and Sundance, Luke and Andy. In their stories, they need to explore the world in order to discover who they are. This discovery is central to decisions about how they ought to live. Those princesses, and characters like them, are playing for different stakes: They need to learn, and become, the people that their worlds need them to be.

In that sense, Shakespeare's characters look more like Disney princesses than they look like Jack London's Toms. Shakespearean characters always have one

---

[2] In *Butch Cassidy and the Sundance Kid* (1969).

motive: validation. They are consistently concerned that other people see them in the way they want to be seen.[3] This doesn't mean that Shakespeare's characters don't care about things like money or freedom; just that those things are tools that characters use in order to serve what they see as a higher purpose.

If there's one rule of character motivation, it's this: A character's motivation explains every decision they make. This includes why they say what they say and do what they do, and who they say or do it to, and when. I like to test this by looking at the actions a character chooses not to take. Motivation needs to account for why a character chooses one course of action over another.

Consider *The Comedy of Errors*, which opens with Egeon (a trader) facing execution because he's caught trespassing in Ephesus. The Ephesian policy on executing trespassers, as related by the Duke in I.i.18–25, goes like this:

> if any Syracusian born
> Come to the bay of Ephesus, he dies,
> His goods confiscate to the duke's dispose
> Unless a thousand marks be levied
> To quit the penalty and to ransom him.
> Thy substance, valued at the highest rate,
> Cannot amount unto a hundred marks.
> Therefore, by law, thou art condemned to die.

This is a complicated situation. Egeon, being caught in it, could want a lot of things: money (like the thousand marks that he can pay in order to avoid the death penalty), or a lawyer, or a key to his handcuffs.

Egeon doesn't angle for anything like that.[4] Instead, when the Duke asks him how he came to Ephesus, he tells a story. In summary: The story begins with a shipwreck in which Egeon and his family (a wife and twin sons) were separated—Egeon with one son and his wife with the other. About eighteen years later, Egeon's son (Antipholus) left in search of his lost brother (also named Antipholus), and Egeon has spent the last five years searching for them both. He concludes his story (in I.i.137–39) like so:

> But here must end the story of my life
> And happy were I in my timely death
> Could all my travels warrant me they live.

These words are deceptively complicated. A first read would make you think that Egeon wants to find his sons. That's not wrong, but it's not his motivation. It doesn't explain why Egeon chooses this course of action over another.

---

[3]This is Shakespeare's presentation of a more complex and socially pervasive Early Modern concern about one's public persona. For more on this, see Greenblatt (2005) and Maus (1995).

[4]Egeon's plan is to convince the Duke that he's a good father (and a good person) in order to elicit the Duke's sympathy.

For instance: Why doesn't Egeon lie to the Duke during this opening scene? The death-penalty-for-trespassing bit of Ephesian law is reserved for people who hail from Syracuse. A reasonable Syracusian might say he's from Messina, Verona, or Venice for the same reasons that American tourists sometimes pretend to be from Canada.

The answer is that Egeon wants to be seen as a dedicated father. Egeon's suffering and self-sacrifice, risking his life to search for his lost son, help him be seen that way. That's exactly the point he hammers home in his last lines of this opening scene: "happy were I in my timely death / Could all my travels warrant me they live." *I'm such a good father that I would die to know that my children were alive.*

Being seen as a good father is more important to Egeon than life or money. Egeon hasn't taken step one to find his missing wife, so there's a chance it's more important to him than sex, too. Egeon's motivation is, in fact, more important to him than anything else.

Hamlet works the same way. Prince Hamlet begins the play as the presumed heir to Denmark's throne (after his uncle Claudius), and having found love with Ophelia. At the beginning of the play—before he suspects that there's anything rotten in the state of Denmark—he should be happy.

But he's not. Love, financial security, and all the perks that come with being well-educated royalty don't touch Hamlet because his motivation is to be seen as a loyal son. We learn that during Hamlet's first moments on stage (I.ii.71–87).

> QUEEN
> Do not for ever with thy vailed lids
> Seek for thy noble father in the dust.
> Thou knowest it is common: all that lives must die,
> Passing through nature to eternity.
> HAMLET
> Ay, madam, it is common.
> QUEEN
> If it be, why seems it so particular with thee?
> HAMLET
> Seems, madam! Nay it is! I know not "seems."
> It is not alone my inky cloak, good mother,
> Nor customary suits of solemn black,
> […]
> Together with all forms, moods, shapes of grief,
> That can denote me truly. These indeed "seem,"
> For they are actions that a man might play.
> But I have that within which passeth show,
> These but the trappings and the suits of woe.

"I have that within which passeth show," Hamlet assures us. *I feel*. He's sensitive to the Queen (his mother's) accidental implication that he only "seems" to be grieving his dead father. Given the choice to say or do anything, including leave the room, stay silent, or ask for money, Hamlet uses his first speech to tell the Danish court that his grief over his father's death is genuine.

So Hamlet begins his play wanting to be seen as a loyal son. At the beginning of the play, this means protesting to the Danish court that his grief over his dead father is more than a performance. But when Hamlet's father's ghost reveals that he was murdered, and that the murderer was none other than the current king—Hamlet's uncle Claudius—loyalty suddenly means something different. In order to be seen as a loyal son, Hamlet will have to avenge his father's death. That leads him down a darker path. Hamlet's motivation ends up costing him everything.

In summary: While characters' motivations remain constant during the course of Shakespeare's plays, and characters serve their motivations to the exclusion of other things, the ways that they pursue those motivations change. We can track how characters pursue their motivations by talking about the specific things that each character wants to achieve from moment to moment, from scene to scene, and from act to act. In other words, their goals.

3.2 Goals (and Plans)

Goals are the specific things a character believes they need to have, or do, in order to fulfill their motivation. If I want other people to think I'm smart, I might start by finding the right pair of glasses. I might talk openly about going to the library, or even read in public.

All of those specific things—the glasses, the rare Dostoyevsky edition I page through at the local coffee shop—those are goals. I think that once I get, do, or achieve them, people will see me as the smart person that I want to be seen as.

Goals may be simple ("wear glasses that make me look smart"), or steps in a well-developed plan for achieving larger goals ("sell my collection of 1980s Chicago Bears memorabilia so I can afford designer frames"). They might be straightforward ("look smart") or mated to a complex set of tactics and expectations ("look smart and sophisticated while Amy the Barista is working so that she'll yearn for me—truly, madly, and deeply. That way, I can get free coffee.")

Over the course of their story, every character will have dozens of goals that each—at least in the character's own mind—serves their motivation of being seen in the way that they want to be seen. If there's one rule for goals, it's this: Goals account precisely for what a character does at every specific moment, and connect the character's every specific word and action to their motivation.

Let's look at Shakespeare's famous hunchback, Richard of Gloucester. Richard wants to be valued. In his opening monologue (I.i. in *Richard III*) he tells us how he'll go about this in lines 24–31:

> Why I, in this weak piping time of peace,

> Have no delight to pass away the time —
> Unless to spy my shadow in the sun
> And descant on mine own deformity.
> And therefore, since I cannot prove a lover,
> To entertain these fair well-spoken days,
> I am determined to prove a villain
> And hate the idle pleasures of these days.

Richard thinks that, because he can't find love, the only way that he can be valued is by becoming a villain. That's one of his goals. Later, we also find out that he intends to be king. That's the endpoint of his plan, his proof to himself that he's played the villain well. That's another goal, and one that he pursues for the first half of the play.

This pursuit requires a plan. Everybody who's ahead of Richard in line for the throne needs to be removed. So Richard's step-by-step (or goal-by-goal) plan for becoming king looks like this:

1. Kill my brother George (Duke of Clarence), so that when our oldest brother Edward (now the king) dies of natural causes, George won't be in line for the throne.
2. Kill or disinherit Edward's sons, so that when Edward dies neither of them will be in line for the throne either.

But it's not that simple. Each of these goals has another plan, with another series of steps (or goals) attached to it. Let's take killing George:

1. Hire a fake wizard to convince my brother (King Edward) that there is a prophecy suggesting that my other brother (George) will murder Edward's children, and that the only way they can be safe is if George is imprisoned and executed.
2. Because King Edward's mind is easily changed by things like fake wizards, and he might later decide to release George, I'll hire murderers to kill George while he's in prison, and make it look like they were actually executioners sent by the king.
3. Intercept George as he is being led to prison, and act puzzled by his arrest. That way, George will never suspect that I'm behind the whole fake wizard/false prophecy/murder situation.
4. While I'm talking to George, I'll also insinuate that the prophecy is one of many seeds of political turbulence planted by King Edward's wife, who is opportunistically using her marriage to Edward to elevate members of her own family. This conversation, overheard by the guard escorting George, will deflect suspicion of George's eventual murder to the Queen's family.
5. Because (again) King Edward's mind is easily changed by things like fake wizards, I'll contact the murderers I've hired as soon as George is safely

in prison, and delay any messenger that Edward sends to countermand his original order for George's execution.

Each of these steps (goals) has sub-steps (sub-goals) too. Take the murderers:

1. Give the murderers a warrant so that they can be admitted to the prison where George is being held.
2. Make a plan for the murderers' escape (so that they don't end up getting caught and confessing the details of my plan).
3. Make sure that George can't talk his way out of being murdered.

And each of these has sub-steps. Take the last point (making sure that George can't talk his way out of the murder):

1. Advise the murderers to kill George quickly, before he gets time to say anything.
2. Warn the murderers that George is persuasive and articulate, and might try to talk them out of the murder.
3. Since murder is a morale-driven enterprise: be more, and differently, likable than George. That way, if George does say anything, the murderers have more reason to be loyal to me than to him.

Once we've granulated Richard's goals to that degree, we can account for every word of his exchange with the murderers in I.iii.343–58:

> RICHARD
> *Gives the warrant*
> When you have done, repair to Crosby Place.
> But sirs, be sudden in the execution,
> Withal obdurate. Do not hear him plead,
> For Clarence is well-spoken, and perhaps
> May move your hearts to pity if you mark him.
> FIRST MURDERER
> Tush!
> Fear not, my lord, we will not stand to prate.
> Talkers are no good doers. Be assured
> We come to use our hands and not our tongues.
> RICHARD
> Your eyes drop millstones when fools' eyes drop tears.
> I like you lads. About your business straight.
> Go, go, dispatch!

Note the praise at the end: "Your eyes drop millstones when fools' eyes drop tears. / I like you lads." *You're good at your job, just like I'm good at mine. Only fools get sentimental about things like this.* These lines, like every other line of Richard's, are part of a coordinated plan which relies on achieving hundreds of goals, large and small, one after another after another.

You'll usually discover a character's first goal, along with their motivation, when the character is introduced. Consider Baptista Minola's first lines in *The Taming of the Shrew* I.i.48–55:

> BAPTISTA
> Gentlemen, importune me no farther,
> For how I firmly am resolved you know:
> That is, not bestow my youngest daughter
> Before I have a husband for the elder.
> If either of you both love Katharina,
> Because I know you well and love you well,
> Leave shall you have to court her at your pleasure.
> GREMIO
> [*Aside*] To cart her, rather. She's too rough for me.

Baptista has two daughters (Kate and Bianca) and one problem: nobody wants to marry Kate. So he's set up a condition to solve that problem. Bianca (Baptista's younger, easier-to-handle daughter) won't be able to marry until her older sister, Kate, does.

Baptista wants to be seen as a competent, responsible parent. That's his motivation. In the world of *Shrew*, this means arranging marriages for both his daughters—it's his way of securing their futures. But because Bianca has no shortage of suitors, his goal is more specific: find a husband for Kate. If he can do that, he thinks, everyone will see him as the competent father that he wants to be.

In this first speech, we can also see Baptista's larger goal granulated into several smaller goals: to convince Bianca's suitors that he's being reasonable, to convince them that he likes them, and to convince at least one of them to court Kate. Those are all prerequisites to marrying her off.

Baptista's goals evolve as *The Taming of the Shrew* progresses. In order to achieve his larger plan of marrying off both his daughters, he needs to protect Bianca from her sister Kate (who, at the opening of Act II, has tied Bianca up and started beating her). And then he needs to protect Bianca's suitors from one another. Each moment in the play brings him a different goal, each one in service of seeing his daughters married so that the rest of Padua will see him as a responsible father.

Another example: In *Hamlet*, Claudius (Hamlet's uncle, stepfather, and part-time king killer) wants to be seen as judicious, patient, and pious. The first sentence of his first speech (in I.ii.1–7) looks like this:

> KING CLAUDIUS
> Though yet of Hamlet our dear brother's death
> The memory be green, and that it us befitted
> To bear our hearts in grief, and our whole kingdom

> To be contracted in one brow of woe,
> Yet so far hath discretion fought with nature
> That we with wisest sorrow think on him,
> Together with remembrance of ourselves.

The tone of this speech is calm, formal, and measured, and it describes Claudius himself in the way he wants to be seen—his thinking tempered with the "wisest sorrow" over his "dear brother's death."

This may be important to Claudius because he's so quickly married his brother's widow and (as *Hamlet* tells us in I.iv.8–12) has a habit of staying up too late, drinking too much, and firing off cannons. He knows that he has not yet demonstrated his capacity for balanced judgment.

So his goal in this first speech is specific. After naming the virtues that he wants his audience to believe he has, Claudius proposes a solution to a problem the play has related to us in I.i: A rival king, Fortinbras, means to invade Denmark. Here is how Claudius intends to deal with Fortinbras's invasion (I.ii.27–38):

> [...] we have here writ
> To Norway, uncle of young Fortinbras, [...]
> to suppress
> His further gait herein, in that the levies,
> The lists, and full proportions are all made
> Out of his subject; And we here dispatch
> You, good Cornelius, and you, Voltimand,
> For bearers of this greeting to old Norway,
> Giving to you no further personal power
> To business with the king, more than the scope
> Of these delated articles allow.

That is: Claudius declares to the court that his plan is to send ambassadors to Fortinbras's uncle, the King of Norway, and get Norway to stop Fortinbras's invasion. Claudius's goal isn't simply to stop Fortinbras's invasion—although that's probably necessary. It's to impress the court that his solution to the problem of Fortinbras's invasion is judicious and patient. That goal accomplished, he takes on the next order of business in lines 42–50:

> And now, Laertes, what's the news with you?
> You told us of some suit. What is it, Laertes?
> You cannot speak of reason to the Dane
> And lose your voice. What wouldst thou beg, Laertes,
> That shall not be my offer, not thy asking?
> The head is not more native to the heart,
> The hand more instrumental to the mouth,
> Than is the throne of Denmark to thy father.
> What wouldst thou have, Laertes?

Again, Claudius paints himself as judicious. "You cannot speak of reason to the Dane," says Claudius (referring to himself), "and lose your voice." *If you're reasonable here*, Claudius means, *I'll hear you.*

In that scene, Claudius's goals change—although only slightly. His motivation is to be seen as a judicious king, and his first goal is to demonstrate that he's judicious by handling Fortinbras's invasion diplomatically (rather than by marching Denmark into war). That accomplished, his second goal is to demonstrate his judiciousness by treating Laertes's request in a way that is transparently and publicly fair.

Shakespeare lays out both Baptista's and Claudius's goals immediately—a careful reading of their first few lines will tell you most of what you need to know. But it doesn't always work this way. Sometimes, understanding a character's first significant goal will require some exposition: you'll need to learn who the character is, and how their society operates, before you can understand why they want whatever it is they want. Consider the opening conversation in *The Merchant of Venice* I.i.1–7:

> ANTONIO
> In sooth, I know not why I am so sad.
> It wearies me. You say it wearies you.
> But how I caught it, found it, or came by it,
> What stuff it is made of, whereof it is born,
> I am to learn.
> And such a want-wit sadness makes of me,
> That I have much ado to know myself.

This sounds like Antonio tells us exactly what he wants: not to be sad. But if you know people, you know how this situation is more complicated. People don't complain about their problems because they want solutions.

So Antonio's friends, Salerino and Salanio, know better than to take a statement like Antonio's at face value. It's less a declaration of feeling than a plea for attention: someone who tells you that they're sad for no good reason probably knows the reason perfectly well, and wants you to invest some time and effort in sympathetic conversation.

Being good friends, this is exactly what Salerino and Salanio do and, in a handy bit of exposition, we find out that Antonio is, in fact, the merchant in the play's title:

> SALARINO
> Your mind is tossing on the ocean.
> [...]
> SALANIO
> Believe me, sir, had I such venture forth,
> The better part of my affections would
> Be with my hopes abroad. [...]
> SALARINO

My wind cooling my broth
Would blow me to an ague, when I thought
What harm a wind too great at sea might do.
[...] Should I go to church
And see the holy edifice of stone,
And not bethink me straight of dangerous rocks
Which, touching but my gentle vessel's side,
Would scatter all her spices on the stream,
Enrobe the roaring waters with my silks,
And, in a word, but even now worth this,
And now worth nothing? Shall I have the thought
To think on this, and shall I lack the thought
That such a thing bechanced would make me sad?
But tell not me. I know Antonio
Is sad to think upon his merchandise. (I.i.8–40)

But even though Antonio says he doesn't know why he's sad, he knows why he's not sad:

ANTONIO
Believe me, no. I thank my fortune for it:
My ventures are not in one bottom trusted,
Nor to one place, nor is my whole estate
Upon the fortune of this present year.
Therefore my merchandise makes me not sad. (41–45)

And that gets us to the heart of the matter. In case we couldn't diagnose Antonio's moodiness for ourselves, Salarino hands it to us:

SALARINO
Why, then you are in love! (46)

And Antonio—who has been listless and wordy when his friends offer other explanations of what's wrong—responds like this:

ANTONIO
Fie, fie! (47)

You don't have to be a World Series of Poker finalist to see Antonio's tell. We don't need to be an advanced student of drama, either. It's always a safe bet that a character who insists they're not in love is actually in love.

By now, we've traveled dozens of lines into the play. Lots of things have happened—at least conversationally. We've found out that Antonio is a merchant, and has several ships abroad, and that merchants (in the world of the play) risk losing everything if they lose their ships. There's no maritime insurance in the world of Shakespeare's play, although there was in Shakespeare's London (and, for that matter, in Venice).

But nothing important has happened. No messenger has arrived with any news. No king has been murdered. We have not, as of yet, met what some writers call the first beat of the story.

And then Bassanio walks in. Again, Salarino and Salanio tell us everything we need to know:

> SALANIO
> Here comes Bassanio [...]. Fare ye well.
> We leave you now with better company.
> SALARINO
> I would have stayed till I had made you merry,
> If worthier friends had not prevented me. (57–61)

Antonio, whether he admits it to his friends, is in love with Bassanio. They see this as clearly as we do, and take their cue to leave Antonio in Bassanio's "better company."

It's worth noting what we've learned about Antonio. It should be plain that he wants attention, and thinks that he can get it by acting hopelessly sad: he tells his friends that this is how he feels, and resists their efforts to cheer him up. Antonio's complementary goal of pursuing a relationship with Bassanio—whatever form that relationship takes—is probably ill-conceived. Congenitally unhappy people don't build happy relationships, romantic or otherwise. Most people understand this after a few innings on love's softball field.

But not Antonio. In pursuing a relationship with Bassanio, Antonio is likely to hurt people—especially if he insists on playing the role of the moody and perpetually dissatisfied partner. There is, in other words, a significant gap between Antonio's motivation (to be seen as emotionally significant) and his goal (a relationship with Bassanio) that arises from the way that Antonio treats other people (making them feel responsible for his misery).

That problem with Antonio's perspective—which, if he exercises it, will hurt both himself and others—is a flaw.

3.3 Flaws

Interesting characters are more often defined by what they do wrong than by what they do right. The qualities that make a person a good friend—say, the ability to have an argument without escalating it—make them a poor vehicle for interesting drama.

So each of Shakespeare's characters begins their story with flaws—that is, with misconceptions about the world, or about their place in it, or about how they ought to treat themselves and others. Generally speaking, a character's flaws will be apparent in the ways that they connect their motivation to their first goal. We'll explore this connection in detail in a moment.

First: Central characters in Shakespeare's stories will usually have both *psychological* and *moral* flaws:

- Psychological flaws hurt only the character, and usually involve a character's inability to understand themselves. This might mean that, like Richard of Gloucester, they don't understand the likely long-term consequences of pursuing their motivation. Richard completely understands that being seen as a villain means hurting other people—he's fine with that. He doesn't understand that playing the villain also means that he'll inevitably hurt himself.
- Moral flaws cause a character to hurt others in ways that run counter to the *moral vision* of the play. We'll examine moral vision in detail later on, but for our purposes a moral vision is the play's baseline statement about how people ought to behave toward one another. Characters are flawed to the degree they deviate from that statement, regardless of how good or bad their actions might seem from a vantage point outside the text.

Morality is always complicated, so moral flaws and moral visions probably warrant some examples from outside the world of Shakespeare.

Let's start with the Harry Potter books. As a boy wizard whose birth predestines him to confront the unrelenting evildoing of Lord Voldemort and his followers, Harry makes plenty of mistakes that end up hurting other people. Most of those involve not killing evil people soon enough. Imagine that Harry had toilet-drowned Draco Malfoy[5] the night before their first Quidditch match. Lives would have been saved.

But the moral vision of the Harry Potter books—meaning their baseline assumptions about how people ought to behave toward one another—isn't "kill people who are clearly evil." It's more like "only harm other people when (a) they are directly and immediately threatening, and (b) you're out of better options." Harry might have saved lives by killing Draco on day one, but J.K. Rowling never takes him to court for it.

You don't get that kind of moral vision from the film *Silence of the Lambs* (1991). There, characters are effectively good or evil based on how much they respect Clarice Starling's personhood. There's nothing wrong with respecting a person as a person, but in *Silence* this vision delivers a set of bizarre (but, in the world of the movie, perfectly sensible) moral verdicts. For instance: Dr. Hannibal Lecter, cannibal and erstwhile serial killer, is one of the film's good guys because he's one of the few who treats Clarice as a person rather than a sex object.

And what about *Charlie and the Chocolate Factory* (1964)? If you've never read it, *Charlie and the Chocolate Factory* involves a group of children who tour a whimsical candy factory that horribly disfigures them whenever they do anything wrong. For instance: They might eat a piece of candy when Willy Wonka tells them not to and turn into a Volkswagen-sized blueberry. Those are the wages of sin in Charlie Bucket's world, and his story is perfectly at peace with them. According to *Charlie and the Chocolate Factory*'s moral vision, it is

---

[5] One of the Harry Potter series's villains.

perfectly reasonable for an adult to disfigure a child in the process of teaching them how to behave.

Both inside and outside of Shakespeare's world, a character's flaws also often depend on context. A way of thinking and acting that serves characters well in one situation may hurt them, or others, when they press it into service somewhere else.

Shakespeare's military men are especially prone to this: *Othello*, *Coriolanus*, and *Titus Andronicus* focus especially on their title characters' inability to negotiate the political and social uncertainties of civilian society. These characters hurt themselves, and others, by inadvertently turning open-ended social and political questions into intense, factional conflicts.

The clearest example of this may be in *Othello*, in which:

1. Othello and Desdemona fall in love.
2. Under the presumption that Desdemona's father and Othello's friend, Brabantio, might object to Desdemona and Othello's marriage, they marry in secret, without leaving a message to inform Brabantio of their intentions.
3. Brabantio, assuming that his daughter has been kidnapped, rouses armed guards to search Venice for Othello and Desdemona.

Othello's reasoning may not be flawed when he assumes that Brabantio will object to Desdemona's marriage—he might, since Othello is a Muslim and there's a significant age difference between him and Desdemona. But Othello's reasoning probably is flawed if he thinks that the best possible way to deal with that objection is through a secret marriage.

This gets Othello and Desdemona what they want, but also leads Brabantio to think that his daughter has been kidnapped. Sowing confusion among enemies is great on the battlefield, but Othello's choice to see Brabantio as an enemy to be defeated—rather than as a friend whose feelings and perspectives about his daughter's marriage ought to be considered—ends with Othello losing a friend and Desdemona losing a father.

This isn't the only time that Othello escalates an open-ended social complication into a bitter factional conflict. It's just the first time, and he spends the rest of the play turning every moment of doubt or uncertainty into a winner-take-all conflict played for the highest possible stakes.

If there's one rule for flaws, it's this: A character's flaws will lead them to make the same kinds of mistakes several times. If you don't see a character's flaws when Shakespeare first introduces them, just wait. You'll see their flaws at work again, and again, and again.

With that in mind, let's return to Antonio's first few lines in *The Merchant of Venice* I.i.1–7, and look for the ways his flaws become apparent in how he connects his motivation to his first goal:

ANTONIO
In sooth, I know not why I am so sad.
It wearies me. You say it wearies you.
But how I caught it, found it, or came by it,
What stuff it is made of, whereof it is born,
I am to learn.
And such a want-wit sadness makes of me,
That I have much ado to know myself.

"I don't know why I'm so sad," Antonio says. Except, of course, that he does. So do Salarino and Salanio, which is why they leave the moment Bassanio shows up. They know better company when they see it.

But Antonio doesn't open the play by saying "I'm in love with Bassanio and I don't know what to do." He opens it by making an attention-getting spectacle out of his own misery. Regardless of Antonio's intentions, this behavior is also manipulative—playing on Salarino and Salanio's feelings of guilt and obligation. It should also go without saying that Antonio's inability (or unwillingness) to take responsibility for his own emotions is unlikely to impress Bassanio and reasonably sure to isolate Antonio from his friends. Advertising your own misery won't get you love, and doing it too often will run out all your friends' reserves of sympathy.

That's complicated, but it breaks down neatly into motivations, goals, and flaws.

- *Antonio's motivation*: he wants to be seen as central to his friends' (and Bassanio's) lives. There are other ways to say this that amount to much the same thing—for instance, that Antonio wants to be seen as deserving of his friends' attention.
- *Antonio's goal*: In this opening scene, Antonio thinks that he can become, or remain, central to Salanio and Salarino's lives by using an ongoing emotional crisis to demand their attention.
- *Antonio's flaw*: Antonio looks for attention (or love) from people by manufacturing crises and acting powerless to solve them. Although this is a fine way to become the momentary center of attention, it's a bad strategy for sustaining a friendship.

But Antonio doesn't know this. Two acts later (in III.ii.317-24)—after Bassanio has run off after Portia and Antonio fails to repay his "pound of flesh" loan to Shylock—Antonio sends Bassanio this letter:

SWEET BASSANIO
My ships have all miscarried, my creditors grow cruel,
my estate is very low, my bond to the Jew is forfeit.
And since, in paying it, it is impossible I should
live, all debts are cleared between you and I if I
might but see you at my death. Notwithstanding, use

> your pleasure. If your love do not persuade you to
> come, let not my letter.

This last sentence is another version of "in sooth, I know not why I am so sad"—the one-two punch of a manufactured crisis and the Sufferer's Threat, or "do what I want, or it's your fault that I'll feel bad." And it works. To be fair, there is something at stake other than Antonio's feelings. Antonio wasn't lying when he said he couldn't outlive repaying Shylock.

But from Bassanio's wife Portia's perspective, Bassanio ought to have recognized Antonio's flaws (that is, the way that Antonio demands attention by creating an emotional crisis) the moment he opened Antonio's "Sweet Bassanio" letter. For that matter, Antonio ought to know better than to manipulate her husband.

So Portia decides to test Antonio and Bassanio. When she hears Antonio's "Sweet Bassanio" letter, she disguises herself as a lawyer, delivers a (fraudulent) legal opinion that saves Antonio's life and—as payment—asks for a ring that she had earlier given Bassanio, and which Bassanio had promised on his life to keep.

Antonio, ever ready to play on his friend's feelings of guilt and obligation, springs into action again. This time it's in IV.i.449–51:

> ANTONIO
> My Lord Bassanio, let him [the disguised Portia] have the ring.
> Let his deservings and my love withal
> Be valued against your wife's commandment.

This strategy of Antonio's looks subtle—it turns on pointing out how much (or how little) Bassanio values Antonio's love—but it's the same game he's played before: "if you don't do what I want, it's your fault that I'll feel bad." More specifically, it's "choose my feelings over your wife's, or I'll feel bad, and you should feel bad about that because my feelings are your responsibility." Instead of "look at what you made me do," it's "look at how you made me feel."

You get the point, but Bassanio doesn't. Much to Antonio's satisfaction, Bassanio gives his ring to the lawyer (who is really his wife, Portia, in disguise), and the two of them return to Belmont—Portia's home and now Bassanio's—with what they think is good news: Antonio is alive and well, and hasn't had to face the consequences of his manipulative behavior because its only public victim happened to be Jewish.

But Portia is ready for him. When she feigns an argument over her ring with Bassanio (in V.i.252), Antonio tries to insinuate himself into it. "I am the unhappy subject of these quarrels," he says—once again using his suffering to claim the center of attention—but Portia outwits him. "Sir, grieve not you," she says, "you are welcome notwithstanding." And then she cuts Antonio's suffering out from under him. The scene continues:

PORTIA
[…] Antonio, you are welcome,
And I have better news in store for you
Than you expect: unseal this letter soon.
There you shall find three of your argosies
Are richly come to harbor suddenly.
You shall not know by what strange accident
I chanced on this letter.
ANTONIO
I am dumb […]
Sweet lady, you have given me life and living,
For here I read for certain that my ships
Are safely come to road. (289–305)

This moment neatly mirrors the play's opening, in which Antonio used his misery to get his friends' attention. Here, for the first time, Antonio may be genuinely happy—not because he's finally found a foolproof way to suffer himself into his friends' lives, but because he realizes for the first time that he doesn't have to. Portia has shown him attention before he requested it—gone out of her way to consider his needs—even though she knows that he's one reason that Bassanio broke his promise to her, and she has every reason to shun him for all the inconvenience his melodramas cost her.

Antonio has every reason to suffer at the end of this play—he's spent most of it being a terrible person. But Portia's welcome to Belmont, her gift of good news about Antonio's ships, teaches Antonio that he doesn't have to play the martyr in order for people to respect his feelings.

At the end of the play, in other words, Antonio has learned something about how to act in the world, and how to behave toward other people, that helps him overcome his flaws. That kind of learning is a *revelation*.

3.4 Revelations

So far, we've seen that characters are representations of people, and the scope of their representation is limited to what they want and how they try to get it. The most important thing a Shakespearean character wants is validation: characters do what they do, and say what they say, because they need to be seen in a certain way.

We've also seen that characters have goals: specific accomplishments that they believe will cause them to be seen in the way that they want to be seen.

Finally, characters have flaws: ways of thinking about how the world works, and how people ought to relate to one another, that lead them to hurt themselves and others.

One thing that unites motivations, goals, and flaws in Shakespeare is that you'll usually discover all three during a character's first moments on stage. Consider Laertes's first appearance in *Hamlet* (I.ii.42–57). Claudius opens for him:

CLAUDIUS
And now, Laertes, what's the news with you?
You told us of some suit. What is it, Laertes?
You cannot speak of reason to the Dane
And lose your voice. What wouldst thou beg, Laertes,
That shall not be my offer, not thy asking?
The head is not more native to the heart,
The hand more instrumental to the mouth,
Than is the throne of Denmark to thy father.
What wouldst thou have, Laertes?
LAERTES
My dread lord,
Your leave and favor to return to France
From whence, though willingly I came to Denmark
To show my duty in your coronation,
Yet now, I must confess, that duty done,
My thoughts and wishes bend again toward France
And bow them to your gracious leave and pardon.

Laertes's motivation is clear, at least in outline: he wants to be seen as loyal and honorable. We know that because he tells everyone in attendance that he returned to Denmark because he felt duty-bound to attend Claudius's coronation.

Laertes's first goal is also clear. He wants Claudius's permission to return to France. That's what he's after at this specific moment, and he thinks he can get it by reminding Claudius that he's a loyal subject.

Laertes's flaw is revealed next, with Claudius's reply:

KING CLAUDIUS
Have you your father's leave? What says Polonius? (58)

That question shows us the misperception that lives between Laertes's motivation and his goal. Laertes thought that he could get Claudius's permission to return to France by emphasizing how loyal he was in attending the king's coronation. But it turns out that Claudius doesn't think that way. In fact, his permission seems to depend on what Polonius has to say—not on Laertes's loyalty at all. The scene continues:

LORD POLONIUS
He hath, my lord, wrung from me my slow leave
By laborsome petition, and at last
Upon his will I sealed my hard consent.
I do beseech you, give him leave to go.
KING CLAUDIUS
Take thy fair hour, Laertes, time be thine,
And thy best graces spend it at thy will! (59–64)

And so Claudius takes Polonius's advice, and Laertes leaves for France.

This is only the outline of Laertes's flaw, which Shakespeare sketches in further detail as *Hamlet* progresses. But Shakespeare also takes care to introduce it at the first moment we meet Laertes. One way to describe that flaw, knowing no more than what we see in this first conversation, is that Laertes thinks too highly of himself, and is too morally certain, to be perceptive.

Let's start with Laertes's obtuseness. Claudius takes great pains to tell Laertes that he respects Laertes's father, Polonius. One-third of his first speech to Laertes (three of the first nine lines) gets spent on that point. Another character, one who's a better listener, might reply with something like "Can I go back to France? My father, who you respect, has given me permission."

But Laertes doesn't. Instead, he focuses on two points: what he wants (to return to France) and that he's done his duty (by returning to Denmark when he didn't want to). That adds up to a peculiar view about how he thinks Claudius ought to act. *I followed the rules*, Laertes seems to think, *and I did my duty; in turn, Claudius ought to recognize the legitimacy of what I want and give it to me.*

There's nothing objectively wrong with that way of thinking—at first, it looks like treating other people the way you'd like to be treated. But it is self-centered for Laertes to assume that what he wants ought to be important to the king. That's only true for important people like Polonius.

It's also clear that Laertes expects other people to play by his rules. His request to Claudius is, implicitly, an exchange: *I gave you something* (my presence at the coronation) *and so you should give me something in return* (your permission to leave). It's one thing to ask for something, and another to tell somebody why they ought to give it to you. Laertes might begin his speech to Claudius with honorifics like "dread lord," but that doesn't make him humble. Behind his language of deference, he treats Claudius as his equal rather than his superior.

Laertes discovers that this isn't how he ought to think and act, eventually. He is one of many characters in *Hamlet* who have a revelation. And if there's one rule for revelations, it's this: Revelations change a character in ways that specifically address their flaws. Let's look at how this works for Laertes.

Once Claudius suspects that Hamlet means to murder him, he plays on Laertes's arrogance and moral certainty in order to convince Laertes to murder Hamlet. The plan is for this to happen during a fencing match in which Laertes will wield a poisoned sword. During the match (in V.ii), Laertes wounds Hamlet—poisoning him—but then Hamlet disarms Laertes and, in the scramble that follows, wounds and poisons him. Hamlet doesn't know it yet, but neither he nor Laertes has long to live.

Claudius, meantime, has also poisoned a cup of wine that he plans to offer Hamlet, but Gertrude (Claudius's wife, Hamlet's mother, and the queen) drinks it and dies instead. Here's what follows:

> HAMLET
> O villany! Ho! Let the door be locked!
> Treachery! Seek it out.
> LAERTES
> It is here, Hamlet. Hamlet, thou art slain.
> No medicine in the world can do thee good.
> In thee there is not half an hour of life.
> The treacherous instrument is in thy hand,
> Unbated and envenomed. The foul practice
> Hath turned itself on me. Lo, here I lie,
> Never to rise again. Thy mother's poisoned.
> I can no more. The king! The king's to blame! (296–305)

This is quite a pivot for Laertes who, at the beginning of the play, seemed only to care about himself. He hardly mentions that he's dying—instead, his last concern is to explain what happened and how, and to see that Claudius is brought to justice by his confession.

But Laertes isn't finished changing. Hamlet kills Claudius, and Laertes has one last thing to say:

> LAERTES
> He is justly served.
> It is a poison tempered by himself.
> Exchange forgiveness with me, noble Hamlet —
> Mine and my father's death come not upon thee,
> Nor thine on me. (313–17)

Here, we see a reflection of Laertes's first lines. He expects an exchange with Hamlet here in the same way that he expected an exchange with Claudius at the beginning of the play.

But here, that exchange is tempered by humility. Laertes asks for forgiveness from Hamlet, rather than implicitly insisting that he deserves it. For the first time in the play, Laertes recognizes—and regrets—that he was wrong about something, that he's not the most important person in the world. What matters most to him in this dying moment isn't paying lip-service to Denmark's customs. It is the integrity of the place he once called home.

That's revelation. The way that Laertes sees the world and his place in it, the way he thinks about how he ought to behave toward other people, has changed. Those changes are intelligible against the flaws that Shakespeare introduced to us in Laertes's first conversation.

Hamlet is full of stories, and the focal one (Hamlet's) takes time to develop. This means that Laertes's story, like Ophelia's, is told quickly. For a character so central to the structure of *Hamlet*, Laertes spends remarkably little time on stage. His revelation, a handful of lines sandwiched between a swordfight and a murder, might seem easy to miss.

But most revelations aren't. Most of the time, characters need to change in order for the conflicts in their story to resolve. In order for that to happen in a way that is clear to the audience, characters' revelations are highly focused—addressing a single, well-defined character flaw—and afforded conspicuous amounts of stage time. The simplest, and most common, examples of these kinds of revelations are in Shakespeare's Romantic Comedies.

In Shakespeare's Romantic Comedy formula, the romantically eligible characters look like this:

> *Motivations*: Characters in Romantic Comedies need other people's emotional attention. They want to be seen as central to other characters' emotional lives.
> *Goals*: These characters will command other people's emotional attention by using different variations of the same dysfunctional strategy (usually, being manipulative or controlling).
> *Flaws*: In the world of Romantic Comedy, characters ought to seek emotional attention (a.k.a. love) by being authentic, honest, and vulnerable. They ought to know themselves and their desires, and speak and act directly from that knowledge, even when this risks social or romantic rejection. Characters' flaws are defined by how, and how far, they deviate from that universal path.
> *Revelations*: Characters who have revelations discover that they should seek love by being (or becoming) authentic, honest, and vulnerable. They do this, and (usually) end up married as a result.

In what is arguably Shakespeare's most well-crafted and best-loved Romantic Comedy, *Much Ado About Nothing*, two lovers (Beatrice and Benedick) begin their stories at "a kind of merry war" with one another.

While their bickering is entertaining, it's also a familiar cover: both Beatrice and Benedick are afraid of taking emotional risks, and use casual contempt for the opposite sex to make this fear seem like a clever matter of sexual principle. But neither of them keeps this private—they use it to make jokes and draw attention to themselves. Consider Beatrice:

> BEATRICE
> [...] Lord, I could not endure a husband with a
> beard on his face. I had rather lie in the woollen.
> LEONATO
> You may light on a husband that hath no beard.
> BEATRICE
> What should I do with him? Dress him in my apparel
> and make him my waiting-gentlewoman? He that hath a
> beard is more than a youth, and he that hath no
> beard is less than a man. And he that is more than
> a youth is not for me, and he that is less than a
> man, I am not for him [...] (II.i.26–34)

Men, in other words, are either too manly for Beatrice to be comfortable with, or not manly enough to be comfortable with Beatrice. In the eternal manner of lonelyhearts, she frames this as a problem with the world (rather than as a problem with her expectations) and tries to bond with other people by complaining about it.

But that's not the only strategy she uses to get attention. Beatrice is also flirtatious. In II.i.295–96 she tells Don Pedro that "your father got excellent husbands, if a maid could come by them"—that is, "your father's sons were such great husbands that we've nearly run out of them." In this play, that's as direct an invitation as anybody gets, and Don Pedro instantly proposes a marriage:

> DON PEDRO
> Will you have me, lady?
> BEATRICE
> No, my lord, unless I might have another for
> working-days. Your grace is too costly to wear
> every day. But, I beseech your grace, pardon me: I
> was born to speak all mirth and no matter. (297–301)

This is a flaw in action: Don Pedro is clearly hurt. To her credit, Beatrice apologizes.

Benedick presents in roughly the same way. Like Beatrice, he defends himself from the threat of intimacy by having impossible standards. Here's an example from II.iii:

> One woman is fair, yet I am well. Another is wise, yet I am well. Another virtuous, yet I am well. But till all graces be in one woman, one woman shall not come in my grace. Rich she shall be, that's certain. Wise, or I'll none. Virtuous, or I'll never cheapen her. Fair, or I'll never look on her. Mild, or come not near me. Noble, or not I for an angel. Of good discourse, an excellent musician, and her hair shall be of what color it please God. (24–33)

The further joke on Benedick is that he does not possess any of these qualities himself. *Much Ado* goes out of its way to show us that Benedick "cannot woo in festival terms" like poetry and music. In V.ii he declares:

> I cannot show it in rhyme. I have tried. I can find out no rhyme to "lady" but "baby,"—an innocent rhyme. For "scorn," "horn,"—a hard rhyme. For "school," "fool,"—a babbling rhyme. Very ominous endings. No, I was not born under a rhyming planet[...] (31–35)

Benedick's behavior also threatens other people's happiness. Like Beatrice with Don Pedro, Benedick also tries to get (or keep) other people's attention by being romantically misleading. Here he is in I.i, trying to talk his friend Claudio out of being attracted to Hero:

> CLAUDIO
> In mine eye she is the sweetest lady that ever I

looked on.
BENEDICK
I can see yet without spectacles and I see no such
matter. (174–75)

But the stage is set for change. After Shakespeare introduces us to Beatrice and Benedick, he has their friends plot to convince Beatrice that Benedick loves her, and to convince Benedick that Beatrice loves him.

Meanwhile, another plotter (Don John) works to derail Claudio's impending marriage to Hero by convincing him of Hero's infidelity. At the wedding, Claudio publicly accuses Hero of cheating on him. She hasn't, but Don John's plan is executed well enough that there are eyewitnesses to the supposed act.

And so there is argument and spectacle and the marriage is called off. Hero's family (which includes Beatrice) and Claudio's friends (which include Benedick) each exit the wedding, differently mortified by what they believe is appalling behavior by the other party.

Afterward, Benedick finds Beatrice crying. This leads each of them to their moment of revelation in IV.i.251–67:

BENEDICK
Lady Beatrice, have you wept all this while?
BEATRICE
Yea, and I will weep a while longer
BENEDICK
I will not desire that.
[…]
I do love nothing in the world so well as you. Is
not that strange?
BEATRICE
As strange as the thing I know not. It were as
possible for me to say I loved nothing so well as
you. But believe me not, and yet I lie not. I
confess nothing, nor I deny nothing. I am sorry for my cousin.

This exchange catches both Beatrice and Benedick halfway into the process of learning something about themselves. For Benedick, suddenly, love isn't about poetry and songwriting. It's about authenticity, about taking the emotional risks that come with plain speaking. Benedick has spent the better half of the play using a kind of calculated insincerity to protect himself from feeling, and his forays into poetry and songwriting are very much a different expression of the same strategy. Here, however, he falls back on the time-tested method of simply naming his feelings. This is a change for him.

Beatrice changes, too. She has spent most of the play using her wit to keep her feelings at arm's length. But this exchange with Benedick is all matter and no mirth. Beatrice acknowledges her actual feelings to another person for the first time in the play.

In other words, both Beatrice and Benedick have learned (or are learning) that the best way to deal with the complexities of romance in post-war Messina is to be authentic, honest, and vulnerable, rather than by making attention-getting jokes.

Not every character has a revelation. Some characters, especially in the comedies, are interesting specifically because they fail to change even when confronted with the overwhelming, obvious need to do so. Other characters—like Bardolph in *Henry V*—see their worlds change out from under them. Bardolph is a longtime associate of Prince Harry, who begins in Shakespeare's *Henry IV Part 1* (the second play in the four-play sequence that ends with *Henry V*) as part of the raucous, charming, petty criminal entourage surrounding Falstaff, whose creative shamelessness and opportunism have made him one of Shakespeare's most endearing characters.

But as Harry discovers his responsibilities, first as prince and then as king, the antics of Falstaff and his crew become increasingly out of place—a therapist might use words like "maladaptive." Falstaff drinks himself to death. Bardolph, who has joined the army for a bit of opportunistic looting, is hanged for it; Henry, when he learns that his one-time friend has been hanged for robbing a church, says that he "would have all such offenders so cut off." If Falstaff and Bardolph's impending deaths brought them anything like Laertes's moment of moral clarity, we never hear of it. Instead, their inability to understand that the rules of life have changed highlights just how different those rules have become.

Among major characters, Shakespeare's villains are also (mostly) exempt from revelation. A few, like Edmund in *King Lear*, have what may be last-minute changes of heart. But Richard of Gloucester, Claudius, Iago, and even the comic Malvolio exit the play carrying the same flaws with which they entered.

Points of Review

In this chapter, we've learned that Shakespeare's characters are defined by, and essentially limited to, their desires. The story attached to each character's desire is in turn defined by four things: motivations, goals, flaws, and revelations.

Motivations and goals involve the what and how of a character's needs. In Shakespeare, what characters need (their motivation) is to be seen in a specific way—as a loyal son, for instance. How they will be seen that way is a matter of their goals: the decisions they make, and the steps they take, in order to present themselves convincingly.

Motivations are single and constant. A character's motives at the beginning and at the end of their story will be the same, even though everything else in the play may have changed.

Goals, on the other hand, change from moment to moment. Sometimes this is because a character needs to do one thing before they can do the next one (Laertes needs to get Claudius's permission to return to France, for instance, and Richard needs to murder his brother and nephews in order to become king). At other times the terrain of a play changes—a ghost-king reveals that he's been murdered by his brother—and the how of being seen as a good son changes with it.

Shakespeare introduces us to each character's motivations and goals with the first thing that character says or does. At that moment of introduction, Shakespeare also shows us a character's flaws—that is, a character's ways of thinking and acting that hurt themselves and other people.

Unlike motivations (which never change) and goals (which change all the time), characters' flaws change only once—at the point of revelation. Characters begin their stories hurting themselves and others. As their stories progress, we get a more detailed understanding of how they act, and what's wrong with it, until the character either discovers these things for themselves or conspicuously fails to change.

Finally, we've learned four rules that can help you discover and clarify your readings of characters' motivations, goals, flaws, and revelations:

1. Motivation ultimately explains every decision a character makes. This includes why they say what they say (and why they do what they do), and who they say (or do) it to, and when. Test this by asking yourself why a character chooses one course of action over another.
2. Goals account precisely for what a character does at every specific moment, and connect the character's every specific word and action to their motivation.
3. Flaws will lead a character to make the same kinds of mistakes several times, usually in contravention of a play's moral vision.
4. Revelations change a character in ways that specifically address their flaws, and that align with their play's moral vision. Often, this means that a character becomes more authentic, honest, or vulnerable.

You can check your understanding of these concepts by answering the questions in Chapter 7. If you do, you'll also see how other, modern-day writers have used these concepts in their own work.

If you understand them, we can comfortably move on to our next chapter. There, we'll see how Shakespeare combines several stories to create a piece of storytelling—like a play.

3.5 Further Reading

Approaches to Character

These monographs and anthologies present a range of recent approaches to defining and interpreting Shakespearean character. I've omitted criticism written earlier than about 1980, since its approaches largely fall outside what students might expect to find in most ordinary Shakespeare classrooms. For an excellent overview of works by earlier critics, see Arthur Eastman's *Short History of Shakespearean Criticism* (1974).

Desmet, Christy. *Reading Shakespeare's Characters: Rhetoric, Ethics, and Identity.* **University of Massachusetts Press, 1992.**

Reading Shakespeare's Characters examines the ways that character (as presented in Shakespeare's plays) is shaped by, and is principally an effect of, rhetoric. This involves a nuanced engagement with specific rhetorical techniques and theories associated with Aristotle, Kenneth Burke, and Paul de Man.

Hutson, Lorna. *Circumstantial Shakespeare.* **Oxford University Press, 2015.**

Circumstantial Shakespeare outlines a theory of character in which the rhetorical, dialectical, and poetic elements of language ("circumstances," in the sense of rhetorical topics) describe complex relationships between character and other dramatic elements (such as the world of the play).

Ko, Yu Gin and Michael W. Shurgot (eds.). *Shakespeare's Sense of Character: On the Page and From the Stage.* **Routledge, 2012.**

Shakespeare's Sense of Character is an anthology that surveys several different approaches to Shakespearean character as described by both literary scholars and theater practitioners. It treats topics such as character motivation both from the perspective of critics concerned with matters of Early Modern subjectivity, and from the perspective of actors and directors who mean to communicate a character's motivation to modern-day audiences using specific performance techniques.

Yachnin, Paul and Jessica Slights (eds.). *Shakespeare and Character: Theory, History, Performance, and Theatrical Persons.* **Palgrave, 2009.**

Shakespeare and Character is an anthology in two sections. The first, and longest, presents the ways that different modern-day critical theories treat character as an analytic category (that is, the different ways that different types of theories answer the question "what is a character?"). A second section of three chapters (on *Timon of Athens*, *King John*, and *King Lear*) produces readings of Shakespeare's characters using combinations of these theoretical approaches.

Character Motivation

These two monographs elaborate on how characters' wanting to be seen in a specific way was a complicated social concern at Shakespeare's specific historical moment.

Greenblatt, Stephen. *Renaissance Self-Fashioning: From More to Shakespeare.* **University of Chicago Press, 1980.**

Renaissance Self-Fashioning is an extraordinarily influential exploration of the ways that Early Moderns considered the fashioning of one's own identity as an intentional and subtle process, and of the ways that they both enacted and represented this process of identity fashioning in art. This book's publication in 1980, followed by the founding of the journal *Representations* in 1983, established an approach, now known as New Historicism, that has defined the last four decades of Shakespearean criticism.

Maus, Katherine Eisaman. *Inwardness and Theater in the English Renaissance.* **University of Chicago Press, 1995.**

Inwardness and Theater in the English Renaissance explores the ways in which Early Modern anxieties concerning differences between avowed and actual feeling, or between one's inward state and outward appearance, were represented both in writing and in dramatic performance.

Literary and Dramatic Traditions

These three books focus on the conventions that Shakespearean drama inherited from Medieval and Early Tudor England, from specific Classical texts, and from Renaissance Italy. Students especially interested in Shakespeare's source material might consult Stuart Gillespie's *Dictionary of Shakespeare's Sources* (2016).

Happé, Peter. *English Drama Before Shakespeare.* **Longman, 1999.**

English Drama Before Shakespeare discusses the range of dramatic and theatrical forms presented in England before 1590, including mystery cycles, interludes, liturgical drama, royal entries, and local (parish) entertainments, with an emphasis on the evolution of these forms and their relationships to plays presented on the professional stage.

Martindale, Michelle. *Shakespeare and the Uses of Antiquity.* **Routledge, 1994.**

Shakespeare and the Uses of Antiquity discusses the ways that Shakespeare used his reading of Ovid, Seneca, Homer, and Plutarch to develop the characters and worlds of his Roman plays.

Marrapodi, Michele (ed.). *Shakespeare and Renaissance Literary Theories.* **Ashgate, 2011.**

Shakespeare and Renaissance Literary Theories places Shakespeare's plays in the context of Italian cultural, dramatic, and literary traditions, and considers Italian novellas, theater, and other texts (such as travel and courtesy books) as direct or indirect sources for Shakespeare.

References

Adams, Richard. (1972) 1975. *Watership Down.* London: Avon Books.
Britton, John. 1961. "A. C. Bradley and Those Children of Lady Macbeth." *Shakespeare Quarterly* 12: 349–51.

Dahl, Roald. (1964) 2007. *Charlie and the Chocolate Factory*. New York: Puffin Books.
Darabont, Frank. *The Shawshank Redemption*. Directed by Frank Darabont. 1994. Burbank: Warner Brothers, 2018. Blu-Ray.
Eastman, Arthur. 1974. *A Short History of Shakespearean Criticism*. New York: W. W. Norton & Co.
Gillespie, Stuart. 2016. *Shakespeare's Books: A Dictionary of Shakespeare's Sources*. London: Arden.
Goldman, William. *Butch Cassidy and the Sundance Kid*. Directed by George Roy Hill. 1969; Los Angeles: Twentieth Century Fox, 2008. Blu-Ray.
Greenblatt, Stephen. 2005. *Renaissance Self-Fashioning: From More to Shakespeare*. Chicago: University of Chicago Press.
London, Jack. (1909) 1986. "A Piece of Steak." In *"To Build a Fire" and Other Stories*, 56–64. New York: Bantam Books.
London, Jack. (1902) 1986. "To Build a Fire." In *"To Build a Fire" and Other Stories*, 17–28. New York: Bantam Books.
Maus, Katherine Eisaman. 1995. *Inwardness and Theater in the English Renaissance*. Chicago: University of Chicago Press.
Pierce, Don, and Frank Pierson. *Cool Hand Luke*. Directed by Stuart Rosenberg. 1967; Burbank: Warner Brothers, 2018. DVD.
Rowling, J.K. 1999. *Harry Potter and the Sorcerer's Stone*. New York: Scholastic Books.
Stone, Oliver. *Wall Street*. Directed by Oliver Stone. 1987; Los Angeles: Twentieth Century Fox, 2014. Blu-Ray.
Tally, Ted. *Silence of the Lambs*. Directed by Jonathan Demme. 1991; Beverly Hills: MGM Studios, 2007. DVD.

CHAPTER 4

Relationships Between Characters

Let's review.

So far, we've learned that Shakespeare invented a type of story that focuses on what a character wants, how they try to get it, and how they change in the process. Each of Shakespeare's characters follows this basic story, regardless of whether they are brooding adolescents (like Romeo and Hamlet), middle-aged lovers (like Gertrude and Cleopatra), or military commanders (like Titus and Othello). Although these characters are of different ages and genders, from different times and different nations, and although the details of each of their stories differ, each of their stories follows the same five steps:

1. Motivations, Goals, and Flaws
2. Conflict and Opponents
3. Plans
4. Battles and Revelations
5. New Equilibrium.

In the last chapter, we learned how five elements of these steps—motivations, goals, flaws, plans, and revelations—work.

First: Shakespearean characters crave validation. This is what motivates them, and we can usually frame this in terms of how a character wants to be seen. A character's motivation—or how they want to be seen—never changes. If a character begins their story wanting to be seen as a good father, son, or daughter, they will end it the same way.

Second: What characters do in a play—every word they say, and every action they take—is in service of a goal. Goals are immediate achievements that characters believe will help them be seen in the way they want to be seen. Characters string these goals together in coordinated sequences, or plans, in order to achieve their motivation.

Third: Characters begin their stories by thinking and behaving in ways that hurt both themselves and other people. These hurtful ways of thinking and behaving are flaws. Eventually, most Shakespearean characters discover that, in order to achieve their motivation, they will need to think and behave differently. This discovery is a revelation.

These are the elements of each character's story. But part of the art of Shakespeare's plays is the art of composition, or of arranging stories so that elements of each story highlight and define elements of the others. The similarities and differences between characters' stories provide us with a clearer understanding of who the characters are—that is, of their motivations, flaws, and revelations.

In this chapter, we'll focus on three storytelling techniques that Shakespeare uses to structure characters' relationships with one another: *conflict*, *character webs*, and *opposition*.

Conflict and character webs are so alike that you'll often see them at work simultaneously. The simplest, most common version of both conflicts and character webs places different characters in similar situations. Their different responses to those situations tell us who they are.

In a conflict, characters both want the same thing and only one of them can have it. How each character tries to get that thing, whatever it is, tells us how they're different.

For instance: Imagine a group of roommates who all share one TV. One night, one of them—let's call her Harmony—calls the roommates together to negotiate who will use the TV when. As the roommates gradually agree to watch *The Notebook* (2004) one of them—call her Melody—turns on the TV and then stomps on the remote.

"Sorry, nerds," she says. "It's *Cop Rock* or nothing."

At first, it might look like Melody and Harmony want something different: Harmony (and the other roommates) want to watch *The Notebook*. Melody wants to watch *Cop Rock*. They couldn't be less alike.

But actually, Melody, Harmony, and all the other roommates want the same thing: to decide what will be on TV. How they decide—by building consensus or by stomping on the remote—tells us how they're different. This kind of conflict, a who-gets-to-decide type of conflict, is frequent in Shakespeare.

For instance: In *Hamlet*, the opening conflict between Hamlet, Claudius, and Gertrude sees each character offer a different explanation for Hamlet's mopey, irritating behavior. This is a conflict because each character wants their explanation for Hamlet's behavior to be the one that everybody else accepts. Here's how this plays out in I.ii.66–72:

> KING CLAUDIUS
> But now, my cousin Hamlet, and my son —
> HAMLET
> A little more than kin and less than kind.
> KING CLAUDIUS
> How is it that the clouds still hang on you?
> HAMLET
> Not so, my lord. I am too much in the sun.
> QUEEN GERTRUDE
> Good Hamlet, cast thy nighted color off
> And let thine eye look like a friend on Denmark.
> Do not forever with thy vailed lids
> Seek for thy noble father in the dust [...]

The first, and most obvious, point of disagreement is between Queen Gertrude and Claudius. Gertrude wants everybody to believe that Hamlet's behavior is driven solely by grief. "Do not forever with thy vailed lids / Seek for thy noble father in the dust," she says to Hamlet. *Don't keep meditating on your father's death.* She thinks that Hamlet's obsession over his dead father is The Problem.

Claudius, on the other hand, thinks that his own stepfather/stepson relationship has something to do with it. Claudius presents himself as a friendly, open stepfather. He calls Hamlet "son." After Hamlet interrupts him, Claudius's next line is clear enough: "How is it that the clouds still hang on you?" he asks. *I've been open, accepted you as my son. How is it that you keep returning my kindness with snide remarks?* He sees Hamlet's resentment of him as The Problem.

Hamlet, for his part, posits that his feelings, rather than his behavior, are what everybody ought to be paying attention to. As he does throughout the play, Hamlet presents his own behavior as a natural, immutable extension of his inward state:

> HAMLET
> [...]
> It is not alone my inky cloak, good mother,
> Nor customary suits of solemn black,
> Nor windy suspiration of forced breath,
> No, nor the fruitful river in the eye,
> Nor the dejected behavior of the visage,
> Together with all forms, moods, shapes of grief,
> That can denote me truly. These indeed "seem,"
> For they are actions that a man might play.
> But I have that within which passeth show;
> These but the trappings and the suits of woe. (79–86)

In short, Claudius, Hamlet, and Gertrude all have a different explanation for Hamlet's behavior. Only one of these explanations can become the truth that everybody else accepts. But the way these characters see Hamlet also tells us something about them.

To Claudius, Hamlet is a reluctant stepson whose petulant behavior is exasperating. Because (as we've seen earlier) Claudius wants to be seen as patient and evenhanded, his response to Hamlet's bad behavior takes the form of a polite, concerned question.

To Gertrude, Hamlet is a vulnerable near-child who doesn't want his father to be forgotten. Because she wants to be seen as a good mother—where "good" means "having only the best intentions in her hasty marriage to her dead husband's brother"—she attributes Hamlet's troublesome behavior to grief over Old Hamlet's death. This is the one factor that isn't accountable to any bad decision making on her part.

Hamlet, finally, presents himself as entirely authentic. It's not his behavior that's at issue so much as how his behavior ought to be interpreted. While both Claudius and Gertrude see Hamlet's behavior as theatrical and (maybe) manipulative, Hamlet insists that it is genuine. Part of being seen as a good son is not feigning grief over your father's death.

In other words: Gertrude, Claudius, and Hamlet all start in the same place. Each of them is prompted to explain Hamlet's behavior. That each of them offers a different explanation leads to conflict, but also tells us how Gertrude, Claudius, and Hamlet see Hamlet's behavior differently. This helps us understand how each character is different from the others.

Character webs work the same way, except that they don't always involve characters directly interacting with one another. Instead, character webs place different characters in similar situations to show us how each character is different from the others. On an ordinary Friday night, we might find Harmony and her roommates playing *Settlers of Catan* in the living room, while Melody one-hands a game of *Cards Against Humanity* on her bed. How Melody and Harmony choose to spend the evening tells us something about each of them—even when they're not in conflict with one another.

Shakespeare does this a lot, too. For instance: All of the children we meet in *Hamlet* (Fortinbras, Hamlet, Laertes, and Ophelia) have to figure out what to do when somebody kills their dad.

Three of these children—the sons—pursue vengeance against their father's murderer. Two of them—Laertes and Fortinbras—do it by immediately invading Denmark and storming Elsinore. In the world of *Hamlet*, in other words, it is standard operating procedure for sons to avenge their murdered fathers by storming a castle.

This matters. Without Laertes and Fortinbras to show us how the sons in *Hamlet*'s world prosecute revenge, we wouldn't see how Hamlet himself is unusual. Hamlet waits to take revenge, and thinks about what revenge would mean. That combination of hesitation and thoughtfulness is one of Hamlet's defining characteristics.

If you ever read *Titus Andronicus*, you'll see the same thing—except instead of dead fathers, *Titus* deals in dead children. As the play progresses, Titus himself, as well as the Emperor Saturninus, the villains Tamora and Aaron, and Titus's son Lucius are all faced with the same question: When is it OK to kill someone else's child?

The answers are telling. Titus kills one of Tamora's sons (and one of his own) out of a sense of duty. Just after this, Lavinia, Titus's daughter, is raped and murdered on the converging orders of Saturninus, Tamora, and Aaron. Their orders come for reasons of political expediency (Saturninus), revenge (Tamora), and simple, malicious joy (Aaron). When is it OK to kill somebody else's kid? The play gives us four answers: when duty demands it (Titus), when it's to your political advantage (Saturninus), when it's payback (Tamora), and when it makes things exciting (Aaron).

The depredations continue. Titus bakes Tamora's sons into a pie and tricks Tamora into eating them. It's hard to say that he does this out of a sense of duty, but that's hardly the point: so far, each murder has been more spectacular and vicious than the last.

But then the issue comes to Titus's son, Lucius. At the end of the play, Lucius becomes emperor, and is asked to dispense some kind of justice. While he chooses to have Aaron—one of the play's many villains—executed, he allows Aaron's infant son to live. The cycle of violence is broken. When is it OK to kill somebody else's kid? For Lucius, if the kid isn't guilty of a crime, the answer is never.

That's a totally different answer than any of the play's other characters have given.

This matters, too. Without Lucius being posed the same question as Titus, Aaron, Saturninus, and Tamora, and without his providing a fundamentally different answer, we might (mistakenly) see Lucius as nothing more than a second edition of his father, Titus, whose misguided decisions in Act I have driven Rome to civil war. Shakespeare's character web helps us understand how Lucius is different from the other characters, and how the events of *Titus Andronicus* have ultimately changed its fictional Rome for the better.

Finally, many of Shakespeare's characters—especially the tricksters and villains—engage in an ascendant form of conflict called opposition. While all conflict involves characters who all want the same thing, opponents try to get that thing by using a unique strategy: attacking the weaknesses of other characters.

Suppose we're back with our house full of roommates, and they're figuring out who's going to do what with the TV. Suppose Harmony gathers all the roommates around her computer so they can hash out a schedule. Just as Harmony fires up her spreadsheet, Melody speaks up.

"Watch out," she says. "This spreadsheet-and-schedule business is how Harmony ended up with the biggest room." Then, as the roommates fall to bickering, Melody sneaks downstairs to watch *Cop Rock*. This isn't a piece of brute force, like breaking the remote. It's manipulative. It relies on Melody understanding who Harmony is.

Shakespeare's villains do the same thing. We've already seen how one of Shakespeare's most notorious villains, Richard of Gloucester, makes plans. You might have noticed that key pieces of Richard's plan—like hiring a fake wizard to deliver a prophecy to Edward—only work because Edward is, specifically, Edward. He takes prophecy seriously. Had Richard's other brother, George, been king, Richard's plan would have been different.

In *Othello*, much the same goes for Iago. He gives us a window into his thinking in his first soliloquy (I.iii.395–401):

> IAGO
> Cassio's a proper man. Let me see now…
> To get his place, and to plume up my will
> In double knavery… How, how? Let's see.
> After some time, to abuse Othello's ear
> That he [Cassio] is too familiar with his [Othello's] wife.
> He [Cassio] hath a person and a smooth dispose
> To be suspected, framed to make women false.

Iago spells out how his plan relies on Cassio's attractiveness. Were Cassio a paunchy, middle-aged nose-picker, Iago's plan would have to look different.

That's opposition. In other plays, villains like Iachimo, Don John, and Edmund the Bastard manipulate nominally innocent characters into wrongdoing by attacking their flaws. That said, opposition isn't always malicious. In some of Shakespeare's plays—like *As You Like It* and *Much Ado About Nothing*—characters trick each other into becoming better people.

When it occurs, opposition is often at the center of a play. Along with conflict and character webs, opposition makes connections between different characters' stories. In this chapter, we'll learn how by looking at examples of conflict, character webs, and opposition from *Richard III*, *Hamlet*, and *A Midsummer Night's Dream*, as well as a handful of modern-day novels, movies, and plays.

By the end of this chapter, you should be able to discover the conflict that animates any interaction between characters—whether that interaction is snappy patter dialogue, a duel, or a battle between armies. You should also be able to discover the conflicts, and the relationships of opposition, that shape an entire play. Finally, you should be able to describe the character webs that highlight and define any individual character's motivations, goals, and flaws. As an added bonus, you should also be able to read, or watch, any modern-day piece of storytelling—a novel, a movie, a comic book, or a play—and see Shakespearean conflicts, oppositions, and character webs at work.

4.1 Conflicts

Any book about drama will tell you that drama is conflict. It's a truth of the trade, like dentists recommending that you brush your teeth after every meal. Again: Drama is conflict. So what's conflict?

Stories of all kinds—Shakespearean and non-Shakespearean—are about what characters do in order to get what they want. In non-Shakespearean stories, conflict is what happens when anything—literally anything—gets in a character's way.

Imagine that I want to buy a Tropical Island card for my *Magic: The Gathering* deck. If I have the money, I can walk down to the corner coffee shop and buy one. There's no conflict there, and no story. There's only conflict if I can't afford to buy the card, or if somebody else is also trying to buy it, or if my family has some principled objection to my spending money on *Magic* cards instead of on, say, baby formula. The moment that one of those things happens, I have the beginning of a story.

Books about drama will tell you that conflict can involve a character set against huge, impersonal forces such as nature or fate. Movies like *All Is Lost* (2013) and *Never Cry Wolf* (1983), along with stories like "To Build a Fire" (1902), exemplify conflict of this type. In them, a single character tries to survive a case of bad weather.

Books about drama will also tell you that conflict can involve a character set against their entire society—either because their society exploits them, or because it condemns them for who they are or what they believe. Novels like *The Fifth Season* (2015), *The Handmaid's Tale* (1985), and *The Stranger* (1942) exemplify conflict of this type. Characters in those stories look very much like characters in Coming of Age stories. "Everybody around me does things this way," they say, "but I'm going to do something different."

Those books about drama are right. Conflict can involve a character set against nature, fate, or society, but in Shakespearean storytelling it rarely does. The most famous representation of nature in Shakespeare is storms, most notably in *The Tempest* and *King Lear*. But storms mostly maneuver characters into position. They separate Egeus's family in *The Comedy of Errors*, wash Stephano, Gonzalo, Antonio, and company onto Prospero's island in *The Tempest*, and drive characters to shelter in *King Lear*. In each case, they produce conflict by introducing new characters to one another. None of Shakespeare's plays is five acts of surviving a thunderstorm.

The same thing goes for characters' conflicts with society. These conflicts do happen in Shakespeare but, like conflicts with nature, they mostly position characters against each other. Consider Richard of Gloucester's opening monologue in *Richard III*, I.i.9–13:

> GLOUCESTER
> [...] Grim-visaged war hath smoothed his wrinkled front
> And now, instead of mounting barbed steeds
> To fright the souls of fearful adversaries,
> He capers nimbly in a lady's chamber
> To the lascivious pleasing of a lute.

In short: the wars are over, and England has settled down to repopulating. That's society, and Richard is at odds with it. He continues:

> But I, that am not shaped for sportive tricks,
> Nor made to court an amorous looking-glass;
> I, that am rudely stamped and want love's majesty,
> [...]
> I, that am curtailed of this fair proportion,
> Cheated of feature by dissembling nature,
> Deformed, unfinished, sent before my time
> Into this breathing world scarce half made up,
> And that so lamely and unfashionable
> That dogs bark at me as I halt by them —
> Why, I, in this weak piping time of peace
> Have no delight to pass away the time,
> Unless to spy my shadow in the sun
> And descant on mine own deformity.
> And therefore, since I cannot prove a lover
> To entertain these fair well-spoken days,
> I am determined to prove a villain,
> And hate the idle pleasures of these days. (14–31)

Everybody's playing love games, but Richard of Gloucester thinks that he's too ugly to get on the field. While this difference between Richard and his society would be enough conflict to drive a play, *Richard III* is not that play. Shakespeare pivots. Richard's next words are:

> Plots have I laid, inductions dangerous,
> By drunken prophecies, libels, and dreams,
> To set my brother Clarence and the king
> In deadly hate the one against the other. (32–35)

The conflict between Richard and his society, it turns out, was just background for his plot against his brothers. Richard kicks that plot into action the moment his monologue ends.

In short: Shakespeare's major conflicts occur between individual characters. Shakespeare's major conflicts all also take a specific form: several characters all want the same thing, and only one of them can have it.

If there's one rule about conflict, it's this: Every interaction between characters involves conflict. A character who isn't in conflict will say and do nothing.

Sometimes, characters will be in conflict over something tangible. In *A Midsummer Night's Dream* I.i, Demetrius and Lysander both want to marry Hermia, but only one of them can. They have different plans to accomplish that goal, too: Demetrius aims to get the approval of Hermia's father, Egeus, knowing that Hermia is legally obligated to marry whichever person her father chooses for her. Lysander, in contrast, wins Hermia's love. This initial difference between their plans tells us something about each character. If Hermia has a choice, we want her to choose Lysander.

But much Shakespearean conflict involves the intangible. Here's an example from *Hamlet* I.i.21–29:

MARCELLUS
What, has this thing appeared again to-night?
BERNARDO
I have seen nothing.
MARCELLUS
Horatio says it is but our fantasy,
And will not let belief take hold of him
Touching this dreaded sight, twice seen of us.
Therefore I have entreated him along
With us to watch the minutes of this night
That, if again this apparition come,
He may approve our eyes and speak to it.
HORATIO
Tush, tush. It will not appear.

The "thing" that Marcellus mentions—the "dreaded sight, twice seen of us"—is the ghost of the dead king, Old Hamlet. Horatio doesn't believe that Bernardo and Marcellus have actually seen Old Hamlet's ghost. Bernardo and Marcellus, of course, think they have.

There are different ways to describe this conflict. We could say that Marcellus and Horatio are in conflict over which version of a story becomes the truth. Marcellus wants people to believe that he and Bernardo have seen the dead king's ghost. Horatio wants people to believe that Marcellus and Bernardo *imagined* seeing a ghost.

There's also another conflict in this scene: it's about the nature of the world, and it plays out as characters set each other's expectations about what will happen next. Marcellus thinks that the ghost will show up again. Horatio thinks it won't.

But what about Bernardo? When Marcellus asks him if the ghost has appeared again, Bernardo says "I have seen nothing." That's a long way from the other answers that he could have given. (A true believer might have said "not yet.") Bernardo has a different view of the world from Horatio's and Marcellus's. Maybe he's not certain that the ghost was real. Maybe he's not certain of the rules this ghost will play by. Just because it's shown up two nights in a row doesn't mean that it will show up for a third.

However we read this scene, one thing is clear: In their conflicts over the nature of the past, and over what's likely to happen in the future, Bernardo, Horatio, and Marcellus each want to tell the story about the ghost that will become official. All three of them know that their stories are different, and that only one story can become the truth.

This is *overt* conflict. To all the characters in this scene, the conflict looks like exactly what it is: three people jockeying over who gets to be right. In most stories, overt conflict brings characters closer together. The moment that the ghost arrives, Horatio, Marcellus, and Bernardo show remarkable unity of purpose. While they disagree about how to handle the ghost, they still work as a team to make it speak.

Shakespeare is full of overt conflict. The bickering between Antipholus and Dromio, or Beatrice and Benedick, ends with each pair uniting in service of a common cause. Sometimes that resolution comes at the end of the play, but it doesn't have to. Consider Sampson and Gregory (servants of the Capulets) in *Romeo and Juliet* I.i.5–6:

> SAMPSON
> I strike quickly, being moved.
> GREGORY
> But thou art not quickly moved to strike.

Sampson and Gregory are in conflict. The issue? How willing Sampson is to fight with servants from the rival house of Montague. They carry the issue for several lines, using typically Shakespearean wordplay in their bickering over whether Sampson is a coward, and how much of one, and what ought to be made of Sampson's disturbing aspirations toward the Montague women. Their conflict is over who Sampson is.

When a Montague shows up ready for a fight, Sampson and Gregory's bickering continues up until the moment the fight begins:

> SAMPSON
> My naked weapon is out. Quarrel! I will back thee.
> GREGORY
> How? Turn thy back and run? (27–28)

There's another exchange after this—Sampson and Gregory engineer an insult (thumb biting) that's aggressive enough to bait the Montagues into a fight, but just meek enough that they can claim the Montagues started it. But the moment the actual fighting begins, Sampson and Gregory stop arguing and take on the Montague servants as an inept—but united—team.

Conflict can also be *covert*: concealed from, or misrepresented to, one of the characters involved in the conflict. Covert conflict involves deception, and usually drives characters apart.

Consider this conflict from *Richard III*, in which Richard (the Duke of Gloucester, and therefore also known as *Gloucester*) and his brother George (Duke of Clarence, and therefore also known as *Clarence*) are in conflict. Like Marcellus and Horatio in *Hamlet*, Richard and George are in conflict over a story: why their brother, King Edward, has ordered that George be imprisoned in the Tower.

To set up this conflict, Shakespeare has Richard tell us about his plan. That way, when we see Richard talk to George, we know what he's lying about and why. I.i.32–42 has Richard begin:

> Plots have I laid, inductions dangerous,
> By drunken prophecies, libels, and dreams,
> To set my brother Clarence and the king
> In deadly hate the one against the other.
> And if King Edward be as true and just
> As I am subtle, false, and treacherous,
> This day should Clarence closely be mewed up
> About a prophecy, which says that "G"
> Of Edward's heirs the murderer shall be.
> Dive thoughts, down to my soul. Here
> Clarence comes.

We learn two things here. One is Richard's goal: he plans to set his brothers, George and Edward (the king) against each other. The second is something that Richard has already done: hired a fake wizard to convince Edward of a prophecy which says that George will murder Edward's children.[1]

When George (Clarence) and Richard (Gloucester) speak a moment later (in lines 44–51), we see the conflict between them begin to play out:

> CLARENCE
> His majesty,
> Tendering my person's safety, hath appointed
> This conduct to convey me to the Tower.
> GLOUCESTER
> Upon what cause?
> CLARENCE
> Because my name is George.
> GLOUCESTER
> Alack, my lord. That fault is none of yours.
> He should for that commit your godfathers.
> Or belike his majesty hath some intent
> That you shall be new-christened in the Tower.
> But what's the matter, Clarence? May I know?

This is covert conflict. Richard knows that in this conflict, both he and George will each try to establish the reason that George believes he's been arrested. George, however, doesn't know this. Instead, his goal is to discover why he's been imprisoned. Richard knows that he and George are in conflict, while George thinks that he and Richard are working together.

He says as much in answering Richard's question:

> GLOUCESTER
> But what's the matter, Clarence? May I know?
> CLARENCE

---

[1] In this speech, Richard tells us that the prophecy is what's led to George's arrest and imprisonment, but not that there was a fake wizard involved. That bit comes later.

> Yea, Richard, when I know—for I protest
> As yet I do not. But, as I can learn,
> He hearkens after prophecies and dreams,
> And from the cross-row plucks the letter G,
> And says a wizard told him that by G
> His issue disinherited should be.
> And, for my name of George begins with G,
> It follows in his thought that I am he.
> These, as I learn, and such like toys as these,
> Have moved his highness to commit me now.
> GLOUCESTER
> Why, this it is when men are ruled by women.
> It is not the king that sends you to the Tower.
> My Lady Grey—his wife, Clarence—it is she
> That tempers him to this extremity.
> [...]
> We are not safe, Clarence! We are not safe! (51–70)

This is Richard's plan in action. George was first inclined to believe that his imprisonment was due to an eccentricity of his brother, King Edward. As we saw in our last chapter, Edward is fickle. He's inclined to be convinced by things like fake wizards, and then un-convinced by a few hours' reflection.

Because George knows this, he first thinks of his imprisonment as a problem that could be solved by convincing King Edward to base his decisions on something other than superstition. But Richard wants George to believe something else: that Edward's wife, Lady Grey, is up to no good, and that she—and not Edward's superstition—is the motive for his imprisonment.

The plan is subtle, but makes perfect sense: In order to set his brothers (George and Edward) against one another, Richard wants George to accuse Edward's wife of a conspiracy. If George tries to talk Edward out of his superstitions, he might succeed and be set free. But if he accuses Lady Grey of a conspiracy, he's aiming at the wrong target, and one likely to worsen his relationship with Edward.

Just in case that's not enough, Richard takes it one step further, changing the conflict over why George has been imprisoned to a conflict over what George ought to do next.

> CLARENCE
> By heaven, I think there's no man is secure
> But the queen's kindred and night-walking heralds
> That trudge betwixt the king and Mistress Shore.
> Heard ye not what a humble suppliant
> Lord Hastings was to her for his delivery?
> GLOUCESTER
> Humbly complaining to her deity
> Got my lord chamberlain his liberty.
> I'll tell you what: I think it is our way,

If we will keep in favor with the king,
To be her men and wear her livery. (71–80)

If accusing Edward's wife of conspiracy wasn't a bad enough idea, Richard also wants George to invite Edward's mistress, Jane Shore, into it. This won't end well for anybody.

It's tempting to think of this exchange as two people chasing two different desires: Richard wants Edward and George to fight, and George wants to get out of prison. But—again—the conflict is actually over two characters wanting the same thing: Richard and George both want to decide what George ought to do next.

So: Conflict happens when characters want the same thing. Open, or overt, conflict eventually brings characters closer together. Concealed, or covert, conflict leads to intrigue and plotting that drives characters apart.

But there's one more type of conflict: *structural* conflict. So far, we've looked at the ways that conflict plays out between characters in a single scene, or at a single, specific moment in a play. But conflict doesn't only work this way. Characters are often involved in conflicts that shape their goals and plans for their entire story.

Consider *Hamlet*. At first glance, a revenge tragedy like *Hamlet* might look like it's built around two characters—a revenger (Hamlet) and a criminal (Claudius)—who want two different things: the revenger wants to do justice, and the criminal wants to escape it. A close reading will reveal that the revenger and criminal actually want the same thing: to determine which version of a story becomes the truth. This conflict drives a revenge tragedy from its first moments to its last.

In *Hamlet*, the competing stories concern how Old Hamlet, one-time king of Denmark, died. Claudius's story—a cover-up—is that Old Hamlet was bitten by a snake while napping in his garden. Hamlet's story is that Old Hamlet was murdered by his brother, Claudius, who is now the king. *Hamlet* tells us how that second story, Hamlet's story, becomes the truth: Old Hamlet's ghost reveals the story to Hamlet, Hamlet has a version of the story publicly performed, and Horatio passes the story to Denmark's new king, Fortinbras, as an official record of what's happened.

In *Romeo and Juliet* the structural conflict—between Romeo, Juliet, the Nurse, Paris, Lord Capulet, and Friar Lawrence—is not over who Juliet will marry but over who gets to decide. If *Romeo and Juliet* were a simple love triangle whose points were Paris, Romeo, and Juliet, it would be a shorter play with significantly fewer characters. One death—either Romeo's, Paris's, or Juliet's—would solve everybody's problems.

But because Friar Lawrence sees Juliet's marriage as a chance to end the feud between the Capulets and the Montagues, he wants to decide that she should marry Romeo. Because Lord Capulet sees Juliet's marriage as a way to smooth over his relationship with the prince, he wants her to marry Paris. Because the Nurse sees Juliet's marriage as a chance for somebody to press her (Juliet's) baby button, she's happy for Juliet to marry anyone—even if the marriage happens secretly. Thanks to all those outside interests, we get a more interesting play. Juliet's marriage gets embedded in Verona's duel-happy, three-family politics, and so the audience gets treated to more swordfighting, dirty jokes, and surprise deaths.

Not every Shakespeare play has a clearly defined structural conflict, but many of them do. In *A Midsummer Night's Dream*, we get fairies, kings, two young men, and an upset father embroiled in a structural conflict that looks very much like the one in *Romeo and Juliet*: everybody wants to decide who Hermia will marry. In others of Shakespeare's plays—*King Lear*, *Macbeth*, and *Richard III*—the conflict isn't over who will be king, but over who gets to decide. Very often, these abstract structural conflicts place characters in a special form of adversarial conflict: opposition.

4.2 Opponents and Opposition

Opposition is a specific kind of conflict. Unlike most other concepts in this book, opposition is about things that happen over the course of a play rather than in a single moment or even in a single scene. You can't look at a single speech from a single character and decide that they're in opposition. You've got to look at everything they do, in the same way you'd discover how a character's revelation relates to one of their flaws.

The main ingredient in opposition is an *opponent*: a character who attacks another character's weaknesses. Usually, although not always, that weakness is associated with how that character wants to be seen.

Usually, although not always, opponents are villains cast in the mold of Richard of Gloucester. They are what some critics call "Marlovian," meaning that they bear the signatures of Shakespeare's early-career rival playwright, Christopher Marlowe's, overreaching hero/villains: aware of their own villainy, driven by a malicious glee, and prone to overly intricate planning.

Shakespeare writes a lot of these characters. Sometimes they show up in the comedies, the way Don John does in *Much Ado About Nothing*. But the most well-known examples are from Shakespeare's tragedies: Aaron and Tamora (in *Titus Andronicus*), Richard of Gloucester (in *Richard III*), Iachimo (in *The Winter's Tale*), and—most famously—Iago (in *Othello*).

Samuel Taylor Coleridge once noted that Iago was "motiveless" (1987). That's a common mistake—both in Iago's case and in the case of Shakespeare's villains generally. Neither villains nor opponents are motiveless, or "motivated" by a desire to do evil for the sake of evil. They don't attack other characters for the sole purpose of ruining their lives or thwarting their happiness. Opponents are characters, driven by the need for validation, just like everybody else. They want to be seen in a specific way.

Opponents, however, think that they can achieve this by exploiting other characters' weaknesses for their own ends. This exploitation often involves a detailed plan, although some opponents (like Iago and Richard) improvise large pieces of it.

The simplest—and probably shortest—example of opposition is Richard's attack on (and wooing of) Anne. Anne's motivation is simple: she wants to be seen as a good person. Her flaw is that she thinks she can do this by consistently playing by a set of well-defined moral rules. Since this is Richard's play, he finds a way to turn that motivation into a weakness that he can attack.

The scene is I.ii. Anne is leading a funeral procession for her father (who Richard murdered). Enter Richard:

> GLOUCESTER
> Stay, you that bear the corpse, and set it down.
> LADY ANNE
> What black magician conjures up this fiend
> To stop devoted charitable deeds? [...]
> Avaunt, thou dreadful minister of hell!
> Thou hadst but power over his mortal body.
> His soul thou canst not have. Therefore, be gone.
> GLOUCESTER
> Sweet saint, for charity, be not so curst. (33–49)

Geez, says Richard. *You don't have to be so angry. I'm just interrupting your dad's funeral.* But Anne has none of it, and hits him with twenty lines of abuse—"lump of foul deformity" is about the worst of it. And Richard plays on this:

> GLOUCESTER
> Lady, you know no rules of charity,
> Which renders good for bad, blessings for curses. (68–69)

We've all seen this move before—if not in Shakespeare, then in life's rich pageant of dysfunctional relationships. Richard plays on Anne's desire to be seen as a good person by holding her to a totally unreasonable standard, which makes her ordinary human shortcomings seem just as bad as his outright crimes. *I killed your father, but you're calling me names. Really, we're both behaving badly.*

Anne lets him have it for a while longer (it's "hedgehog" this time). And then Richard attacks:

> LADY ANNE
> He is in heaven, where thou shalt never come.
> GLOUCESTER
> Let him thank me that holp to send him thither,
> For he was fitter for that place than earth.
> LADY ANNE
> And thou unfit for any place but hell.

> GLOUCESTER
> Yes, one place else, if you will hear me name it.
> LADY ANNE
> Some dungeon.
> GLOUCESTER
> Your bed-chamber. (102–9)

Is Richard hitting on Anne during her father's funeral? He is. And then he doubles down:

> [...] gentle Lady Anne,
> To leave this keen encounter of our wits
> And fall somewhat into a slower method,
> Is not the causer of the timeless deaths
> Of these Plantagenets, Henry and Edward,
> As blameful as the executioner?
> LADY ANNE
> Thou art the cause and most accursed effect.
> GLOUCESTER
> Your beauty was the cause of that effect.
> Your beauty, which did haunt me in my sleep,
> To undertake the death of all the world
> So I might live one hour in your sweet bosom. (111–19)

Richard's strategy is simple. He knows that Anne wants to be seen as a good person, so he reiterates that she isn't. She's been angry instead of forgiving, and—what's worse—she's been pretty. That practically forced Richard to kill her father. So if Anne's a good person, she'll prove how forgiving she is by marrying her father's murderer. That's how he drives the point home:

> GLOUCESTER
> Teach not thy lips such scorn, for they were made
> For kissing, lady, not for such contempt.
> If thy revengeful heart cannot forgive,
> Lo, here I lend thee this sharp-pointed sword,
> Which if thou please to hide in this true bosom. (166–70)

And there it is: *forgive me with a marriage or kill me in revenge. What you choose to do is how you tell the world who you are.* It might not be realistic, but—at least in the world of the play—it's sensible. Anne's weakness is that she's too caught up in public piety. Here, with Richard, she's too willing to go too far to show the world that she's forgiving.

But there's more. Maybe—just maybe—Anne thinks she's good enough to fix Richard. After that exchange, he asks for one more thing:

> GLOUCESTER
> That it would please thee leave these sad designs

> To him that hath more cause to be a mourner,
> And presently repair to Crosby Place
> Where, after I have solemnly interred
> At Chertsey monastery this noble king,
> And wet his grave with my repentant tears,
> I will with all expedient duty see you.
> For diverse unknown reasons, I beseech you,
> Grant me this boon.
> LADY ANNE
> With all my heart. And much it joys me too,
> To see you are become so penitent. (205–15)

The upshot: Richard implies that the promise of Anne's love has woken up a moral sensibility in him, and he vows to take poor Henry's body to the monastery and weep for what he's done. That way, Anne gets the moral satisfaction of having forgiven—and reformed—the worst man in Christendom.

And so Anne goes home, hardly believing what a good person she is, clearing a space in her bedroom for Richard, thinking about how much potential he has.

Other opponents mount more sustained campaigns. Iago's against Othello is the most famous, but others are differently excellent. Antonio's opposition to Bassanio in *The Merchant of Venice* is remarkable for its emotional subtlety. Lighthearted comedies—like *A Midsummer Night's Dream*—also feature opponents in the form of bickering couples: Titania and Oberon, for instance, spend the entire play in opposition to one another. Opposition doesn't require that one character be a cartoonish, Marlovian villain (although Oberon, with his inept sidekick, elaborate plans, and magic potions, looks a lot like one).

One excellent example of non-Marlovian opposition is between Hamlet and Claudius in *Hamlet*. It begins the first moment we see them on stage together.

You'll remember that Claudius's first speech tells us how he wants to be seen: as balanced, competent, patient, and just. We might speculate that this is important to Claudius because these are important qualities in a newly-elected king. Whether this is true or not, we can see how Claudius tries to present them with his first speech in I.ii.1–16:

> KING CLAUDIUS
> Though yet of Hamlet our dear brother's death
> The memory be green, and that it us befitted
> To bear our hearts in grief and our whole kingdom
> To be contracted in one brow of woe,
> Yet so far hath discretion fought with nature
> That we with wisest sorrow think on him
> Together with remembrance of ourselves.
> Therefore, our sometime sister, now our queen,
> The imperial jointress to this warlike state,

> Have we, as it were with a defeated joy —
> With an auspicious and a dropping eye,
> With mirth in funeral and with dirge in marriage,
> In equal scale, weighing delight and dole —
> Taken to wife. Nor have we herein barred
> Your better wisdoms, which have freely gone
> With this affair along.

This is just the introduction. He hasn't yet talked about his plan for thwarting Fortinbras's invasion by sending ambassadors to Norway. When he talks about it, notice how he does it: the message is clear. *I've got this handled*, his tone says. *This invasion might seem like something to panic over, but it's really no big deal*:

> Now follows that you know: young Fortinbras,
> Holding a weak supposal of our worth,
> Or thinking by our late dear brother's death
> Our state to be disjoint and out of frame,
> Colleagued with the dream of his advantage,
> He hath not failed to pester us with message
> Importing the surrender of those lands
> Lost by his father, with all bonds of law,
> To our most valiant brother. So much for him.
> Now for ourself, and for this time of meeting,
> Thus much the business is: we have here writ
> To Norway, uncle of young Fortinbras —
> Who, impotent and bed-rid, scarcely hears
> Of this his nephew's purpose—to suppress
> His further gait herein in that the levies,
> The lists and full proportions, are all made
> Out of his subject. And we here dispatch
> You, good Cornelius, and you, Voltimand,
> For bearers of this greeting to old Norway,
> Giving to you no further personal power
> To business with the king, more than the scope
> Of these delated articles allow. (17–38)

Claudius might have written *reassurance* over every word of his plan. Fortinbras is invading only because he underestimates Denmark's strength. He can't threaten Denmark, only "pester" it. And Claudius presents his plan as absolutely certain to succeed. There's no "and if this fails, we'll meet Fortinbras with arms." The message Claudius means to send is clear. *I have this handled. We can focus on other business.*

And focus on other business he does. There's Laertes's request to return to France, for instance. You'll remember that when Claudius hears Laertes's request, he again emphasizes that he is patient, fair, and just:

> KING CLAUDIUS
> And now, Laertes, what's the news with you?
> You told us of some suit. What is it, Laertes?
> You cannot speak of reason to the Dane
> And lose your voice. What wouldst thou beg, Laertes,
> That shall not be my offer, not thy asking? (42–46)

"You cannot speak of reason to the Dane," says Claudius, "and lose your voice." *If you're reasonable,* he means, *I'll hear you.*

So far in I.ii, Shakespeare has told us at least three times how Claudius means to present himself. This scene is a public moment, and so Claudius moves slowly and deliberately, demonstrating that he is in control, and that he intends to be fair and reasonable. That makes him the kind of king that Denmark can trust during a moment of crisis.

And then, after granting Laertes leave, Claudius turns to Hamlet. Here's how things unfold:

> KING CLAUDIUS
> Take thy fair hour, Laertes. Time be thine,
> And thy best graces spend it at thy will!
> But now, my cousin Hamlet, and my son —
> HAMLET
> A little more than kin and less than kind.
> KING CLAUDIUS
> How is it that the clouds still hang on you?
> HAMLET
> Not so, my lord. I am too much in the sun. (63–68)

This is Hamlet's first attack on Claudius. Hamlet knows how Claudius wants to be seen and—just as Richard does with Anne—Hamlet treats Claudius's desire to be seen as capable, just, and patient as a vulnerability. All he does is interrupt Claudius with a snide remark, but that's enough. If Hamlet's attack really works, Claudius will respond in a way that shows the assembled court that he isn't the just and patient king that he pretends to be.

Claudius doesn't snap at Hamlet, but the conversation does slip out of his control. Maybe because she thinks that things could get worse, Claudius's new wife (and Hamlet's mother) Queen Gertrude jumps in:

> QUEEN GERTRUDE
> Good Hamlet, cast thy nighted color off
> And let thine eye look like a friend on Denmark.
> Do not for ever with thy vailed lids
> Seek for thy noble father in the dust.
> Thou knowest it is common: all that lives must die,
> Passing through nature to eternity.
> HAMLET
> Ay madam, it is common.

> QUEEN GERTRUDE
> If it be,
> Why seems it so particular with thee?
> HAMLET
> Seems, madam! Nay it is. I know not "seems."
> It is not alone my inky cloak, good mother,
> Nor customary suits of solemn black,
> Nor windy suspiration of forced breath,
> No, nor the fruitful river in the eye,
> Nor the dejected behavior of the visage,
> Together with all forms, moods, shapes of grief,
> That can denote me truly. These indeed "seem,"
> For they are actions that a man might play.
> But I have that within which passeth show.
> These but the trappings and the suits of woe. (69–86)

This is a moment for Hamlet. He comes across as dramatic and self-indulgent, but Claudius comes across as unable to manage his family. He tries to re-take control of the conversation:

> KING CLAUDIUS
> It is sweet and commendable in your nature, Hamlet,
> To give these mourning duties to your father.
> But you must know your father lost a father.
> That father lost, lost his, and the survivor bound
> In filial obligation for some term
> To do obsequious sorrow. But to persever
> In obstinate condolement is a course
> Of impious stubbornness. It is unmanly grief.
> It shows a will most incorrect to heaven,
> A heart unfortified, a mind impatient,
> An understanding simple and unschooled.
> For what we know must be, and is, as common
> As any the most vulgar thing to sense.
> Why should we in our peevish opposition
> Take it to heart? Fie! It is a fault to heaven,
> A fault against the dead, a fault to nature,
> To reason most absurd, whose common theme
> Is death of fathers, and who still hath cried
> From the first corpse till he that died today,
> "This must be so." We pray you, throw to earth
> This unprevailing woe, and think of us
> As of a father. For let the world take note:
> You are the most immediate to our throne,
> And with no less nobility of love
> Than that which dearest father bears his son,
> Do I impart toward you. For your intent
> In going back to school in Wittenberg,
> It is most retrograde to our desire,

And we beseech you, bend you to remain
Here, in the cheer and comfort of our eye,
Our chiefest courtier, cousin, and our son. (87–117)

We see it there again: Claudius wants to come across as just, patient, and reasonable. We get a long speech, built on carefully balanced phrases that appeal to reason, that ought to pack this whole situation of Hamlet's back in the box. And then Hamlet scuttles it again:

QUEEN GERTRUDE
Let not thy mother lose her prayers, Hamlet.
I pray thee, stay with us. Go not to Wittenberg.
HAMLET
I shall in all my best obey you, madam. (118–20)

There it is. Hamlet is testing Claudius, ever so slightly, by promising to obey his mother. He's not promising to obey Claudius in either his capacity as Hamlet's stepfather or as the king of Denmark.

This is a subtle attack. If Claudius lets a slight like Hamlet's go entirely, he's letting his authority go disrespected. But if he takes the bait, he's going to look too reactive. If you're secure in your authority, you don't dole out punishment over every perceived slight. Luckily, Claudius walks the line:

KING CLAUDIUS
Why, it is a loving and a fair reply.
Be as ourself in Denmark. Madam, come.
This gentle and unforced accord of Hamlet
Sits smiling to my heart—in grace whereof,
No jocund health that Denmark drinks today
But the great cannon to the clouds shall tell,
And the king's rouse the heavens all bruit again
Re-speaking earthly thunder. Come away. (121–28)

He says he's happy with Hamlet's response—calls it both "loving" and "fair" when, in reality, it's neither—and leaves the scene before anyone can start dissecting Claudius's prematurely declared victory. He's also going to treat everybody to a round of recreational drinking and cannon firing. If Claudius wants them to forget about the last five minutes, this can't hurt.

As in Richard's scene with Anne, the conflict in this exchange involves what becomes the truth about a character. Claudius wants everybody else to see him as capable, patient, and judicious. Hamlet wants everyone to see Claudius as inept—as not in control, and probably as irritable, too.

This plays neatly into Hamlet's motivation. As we've discussed earlier, Hamlet himself wants to be seen as a loyal son to his dead father. This early in the play, he thinks that he can do this by making Claudius look bad. Hamlet doesn't attack Claudius in this scene out of motiveless malignity. He attacks

Claudius because he thinks it will help him be seen in the way that he wants to be seen.

In these two scenes, Richard and Hamlet aren't in opposition to Anne and Claudius just because they attack Anne's and Claudius's weaknesses. They're in opposition because these attacks are part of a sustained, coordinated plan that they'll use to get what they want. This is truer of Hamlet than of Richard. Anne disappears the moment she's done being wooed, but Hamlet's attacks on Claudius (and Claudius's attacks on Hamlet) drive the action of *Hamlet* from this opening moment until Hamlet's final, fatal swordfight in Act V. If Hamlet and Claudius stopped plotting against each other, *Hamlet* would grind to a halt.

In summary, opposition has a few salient features:

1. An opponent plots against another character by attacking their weaknesses. These weaknesses, like flaws, are intimately related to that character's motivation.
2. Opposition involves a series of attacks. A character isn't an opponent just because they do something mean. They're an opponent because their attacks against another character are part of a coordinated plan.
3. This coordinated plan is not simply malicious. Opponents have motivations and goals, just like other characters. They attack other characters because they think that this will help them be seen the way they want to be seen.
4. Opposition is a form of conflict. Characters end up in opposition to one another because they both want the same thing, and only one of them can get it.

Conflict—whether in its ordinary form or in the form of opposition—defines and highlights differences between characters. In the opening scene of *Hamlet*, for example, Marcellus and Horatio are in conflict over the nature of the world: whether ghosts really exist, and whether they've been seen more recently in Denmark. This tells us about who Marcellus and Horatio are. We might say that Marcellus is superstitious while Horatio is skeptical.

It also tells us about Shakespeare's Denmark. In that Denmark, whether ghosts actually exist is not a settled issue. However, the dialogue between Marcellus and Horatio in I.i tells us that the superstitions surrounding ghosts are widely agreed on. Ghosts have been known to speak, and to drive their listeners to madness. They disappear at sunrise, and their appearance suggests that some kind of injustice is afoot. In other words: Conflict tells us how characters are similar and different. These similarities and differences also tell us about the rules that characters play by, or the rules of their world.

This storytelling strategy takes on a more abstract and coordinated form in the subject of our next chapter: character webs.

4.3 Character Webs

While Shakespeare uses conflicts between characters to help us understand who they are, he also differentiates his characters by creating abstract, structural relationships between them. The trope that people commonly use to talk about these relationships is a "foil." That term is Shakespeare's own, and used immediately before the fencing match between Hamlet and Laertes begins in V.ii.240–42:

> HAMLET
> I'll be your foil, Laertes. In mine ignorance
> Your skill shall, like a star in the darkest night,
> Stick fiery off indeed.

Foil is a jeweler's term for setting a gem in metal to make it appear brighter, and that's how Hamlet uses it here. He's going to make Laertes sparkle.

The problem with a term like "foil" is that it focuses on simple, contrasting relationships between individual characters, like Hamlet and Laertes. Really, Shakespearean storytelling is built on complex systems of abstract relationships between several characters whose qualities mutually define each other. We'll call this system of mutual definition a *character web*.

Character webs invite the audience to compare characters to one another. Usually, this involves putting different characters in similar situations, or facing them with similar questions. How the characters behave differently, or how they answer the question differently, tells the audience two things: how the characters are different, and which differences their world allows. Sometimes, a character web can also tell an audience what kind of behavior is normal, expected, or ordinary in the world of the story. They help establish what I loosely call *situation*: the set of choices available to a character at a specific moment in their story, and what those choices mean.

Probably no Shakespearean storytelling technique has been so widely adopted by later writers. Once you know how to look for character webs, you can't stop seeing them. They're everywhere. We'll start by looking at modern webs from *Sex and the City* (2008), *Beloved* (1987), *Fences* (1986), *Great Expectations* (1861), *IT* (1986), and *The Fifth Season* (2015).

The simplest web we'll look at—the flint axe of character webs—is from *Sex and the City* (the movie). It's typical of the *Sex and the City* franchise in two ways:

1. The four principal characters (mutual friends Carrie, Miranda, Samantha, and Charlotte) are at brunch. (This happens a lot.)
2. Carrie asks a question that prompts Miranda, Samantha, and Charlotte to each respond differently.

If you've never seen *Sex and the City*, don't worry. The character web-building tool we're about to look at gets used all over the place. In it, one character asks a question, and several other characters answer it. Each character's answer tells you how each character is different from the others and what kinds of answers are possible.

The occasion for this scene is that Miranda has left her boyfriend, Steve, after he confessed that he cheated on her. Miranda has consequently convened a brunchtime meeting of her friends (Carrie, Charlotte, and Samantha) so that they can advise her about what to do next.

Here's the scene:

> CARRIE
> I don't know if this question is allowed—but how is Steve handling this?
> MIRANDA
> Says he's devastated—begs me to forgive him. Not going to happen. I can barely even look at him.
> CHARLOTTE
> Steve—I can't believe it.
> CARRIE
> That's what I said.
> SAMANTHA
> Miranda, honey—are you sure you want to do this? It's just one time. Anyone can have a slip.
> MIRANDA
> Well, even if I could get my head around that justification—it's the cheating part—the behind my back part … the violation of the trust—that's the thing that's killing me.

This is pretty straightforward, right? Carrie (author of a weekly column called "Sex and the City") asks how Steve is doing. For Carrie, there's complexity behind everything and emotional context matters a great deal.

In contrast: Charlotte (the Connecticut prep-school blue-blood) is wide-eyed and baffled by the seedy reality of infidelity. It's the kind of thing that happens, but not to anybody you know. Sort of like dying in a plane crash or a tornado.

To Samantha (a sexually nonchalant veteran of Studio 54) that same seedy sexual reality is a road well traveled. On a long enough timeline, her thinking goes, infidelity just happens. It's inconvenient. You deal with it.

For Miranda (the Harvard Law Voice of Reason) the issue is less about sex and more about the end of the genuine, unforced compatibility that is the foundation for any functional, long-term relationship. The issue isn't infidelity, but what infidelity means. For instance: Does it mean that she and Steve can't trust each other?

You get it. Carrie is curious, Charlotte is naive, Samantha is cynical, and Miranda is philosophical. This brunchtime exchange tells us who each character is in a clear, economical way. A well-executed moment does this in a way that the audience understands intuitively, and that looks and feels natural.

There's a little bit more to this web, but not much. You'll notice, for instance, that this brunch exchange is also a piece of multi-point conflict (which we'll discuss in detail later on): Each character around the table is trying to decide what Miranda ought to do about Steve. But there's one more thing. Let's revisit two lines of dialogue:

CHARLOTTE
Steve—I can't believe it.
CARRIE
That's what I said.

In these lines, Carrie agrees with Charlotte's surprise at Steve's infidelity. This agreement centers the situation: Steve is—or to this point has been—a decent guy. In the world of this story, a reasonable person would be surprised that Steve cheated on Miranda. Carrie's agreement with Charlotte tells us that Charlotte's surprise isn't down solely to her naiveté.

Also: these characters' responses tell us something else about the world of their story. Nobody says, "So how should we kill Steve?" or, "It's payback time." The city in *Sex and the City* is New York, and if it were the New York of *Cruising* (1980), *New Jack City* (1991), or even *Ghostbusters* (1984), revenge might be a real possibility. But this is *Sex and the City*. Well-scrubbed, sophisticated banter is the only thing on the brunch menu. Miranda, Carrie, Samantha, and Charlotte can't revenge-murder Steve for the same reasons they can't get chlamydia: these possibilities are unwritten, or outside the scope of expectations that this piece of storytelling enumerates.

A similarly concise piece of character webbing opens Toni Morrison's *Beloved*. Here are the novel's first lines:

124 was spiteful. Full of a baby's venom. The women of the house knew it and so did the children. For years each put up with the spite in his own way, but by 1873 Sethe and her daughter Denver were its only victims. The grandmother, Baby Suggs, was dead, and the sons, Howard and Buglar, had run away by the time they were thirteen years old [...]

This web is as simple as the one from *Sex and the City*, but built to a different purpose. Characters' responses to the haunting at 124 set up a pattern that defines the world of *Beloved*: When confronted with adversity, *Beloved*'s men (like Howard and Buglar) deal with it by running away. The women (like Sethe and Denver) deal with it by persisting—staying put—until, like Baby Suggs, they die in place.

This web, in other words, sets our baseline expectations for how different types of characters will behave. When Sethe eventually takes a lover, Paul D, we wonder whether she'll leave her house at 124, and we wonder whether Paul D will stick around.

This technique, differentiating characters from one another using a single reference point, doesn't have to be confined to a single moment in a piece of storytelling. Consider *Fences*, which is a well-grounded piece of storytelling in the tradition of *King Lear*. *Fences* presents a family of adults. There's Troy Maxson (an overbearing father and one-time aspiring baseball player), Rose (Troy's long-suffering wife), Lyons (Troy's adult son, a jazz musician), and Gabe (Troy's brother, an ex-soldier who's sustained delusion-inducing head trauma).

Gabe believes he's the archangel Gabriel, sometimes makes a public nuisance of himself, and once received a government payout thanks to his head injury. Gabe does a lot of things in *Fences*—he's a vehicle for the play's moral vision, which has something to do with the redemptive power of acceptance. He also helps establish a character web by showing us how the other adults in the Maxson family are different from one another.

Troy, for instance, takes advantage of Gabe—or, more specifically, of Gabe's payout. It's what bought the house that Troy, Rose, and their son (Cory) live in. Later in the play, Troy has Gabe committed. He feels bad about that, but not so bad that he's willing to fix it. That's classic Troy. He feels the same way about cheating on his wife.

Troy's wife Rose, in contrast, nurtures and protects Gabe, mostly by giving him food. That's classic Rose. Gabe's an innocent, so Rose takes responsibility for him. She does the same thing with Troy's illegitimate daughter, Raynell.

Lyons, Troy's adult son and not-really-aspiring jazz musician, plays into Gabe's delusions the way you might play into a child's stories about an imaginary friend. At the same time, he doesn't help Gabe get anything he needs. That's classic Lyons. He might be friendly, but that doesn't make him good.

Although *Fences* is a very different piece of storytelling from *Sex and the City* or *Beloved*, these character webs are similar. Both focus on a handful of individual characters whose different approaches to common problems are starkly defined. Nobody is going to confuse Miranda with Charlotte, or confuse Troy with Lyons, or confuse men's and women's behavior in *Beloved*.

But character webs can also get more complicated. One common form of complex character web uses pairs of characters to represent variations of the same kind of relationship. In *Great Expectations*, for instance, Charles Dickens builds webs out of different mentor/mentee (or, if you prefer, student/teacher) pairs. Each pair presents a different way of thinking about love, kindness, and fairness in Dickens's version of nineteenth-century London.

At one end of the spectrum are Abel Magwitch and an orphan, Pip. In recognition of Pip's kindness, Magwitch becomes his anonymous benefactor, providing the adult Pip with an allowance that eventually allows him to become a gentleman. Both Pip and Magwitch, whatever other bad decisions they make, are capable of love and compassion even though the world has treated them unfairly.[2]

---

[2] Pip is an orphan and Magwitch has been exiled from England on pain of death.

At the other end are Miss Havisham and Estella. Miss Havisham is a wealthy spinster who, after being left at the altar, still wears her wedding dress. She has vowed revenge and plans to get it by teaching her beautiful ward, Estella, to torment and spurn men. (This includes Pip, who unfortunately loves Estella.) Both Miss Havisham and Estella are comparatively lucky. Unlike Pip and Abel, they have never had to skip meals. At the same time, they use things that look like love and compassion to hurt other people.

Dickens highlights Miss Havisham and Estella's damage by building other characters into the *Great Expectations* web. Biddy, for instance, is a foil for Estella: kindhearted, smart, and interested in Pip. But Pip ignores her. Every time we hear something good about Biddy, we're reminded that Pip's doubling down on a bad decision by going after Estella instead. Pip and Biddy end up together, but only after a lot of suffering and reform.

The point: *Great Expectations* builds a character web by inviting the audience to compare relationships between characters (like Abel/Pip and Miss Havisham/Estella). Each of these relationships is clarified and defined by satellite characters like Biddy, who help us remember how each principal character is flawed. Biddy is the girl Pip ought to want and the girl Estella ought to be.

It can get more complicated. In *IT*, Stephen King tells two sets of stories simultaneously—one set in 1958, the other in 1985. Each set of stories involves the same cast of characters, who are budding adolescents in 1958 and thirtysomething adults in 1985. In the 1958 storyline, each of the child characters encounters a shapeshifting, child-killing creature that (mostly) appears to them as a clown, Pennywise. The child characters eventually unite—under the banner of the "Losers' Club"—to kill it. In the 1985 stories, the now-adult Losers learn that Pennywise has returned and reunite to take it on again.

This means we get three sets of character webs. The simplest two webs differentiate the members of the Losers' Club from one another as children (in 1958) and then as adults (in 1985). The more complicated web involves pairs of characters, just like in *Great Expectations*. Except this time, the pairs are the child and adult versions of the same character. Instead of mentor/mentee, or student/teacher, we get Beverly Marsh the Child/Beverly Marsh the Adult. And just as in Dickens, each of these pairs is built around a theme.

Every member of the Losers' Club had some kind of childhood struggle. I'll call it trauma, even though not all trauma is created equal. For instance, Beverly had an abusive, controlling father. Ben got an *H* carved into his belly by school bully Henry Bowers. Mike was one of the few black kids in Derry—a town that has a grisly history of racial violence, complete with a local version of the Klan. Others of the Losers have overprotective parents or stutters. All of them also deal with the predations of Pennywise, the shapeshifting, child-killing, sewer-dwelling clown demon.

Some characters—Bill and Ben, for instance—process their childhood trauma in ways that make them capable adults. Come 1985, when Pennywise shows up in their adult lives, they're successful authors and architects, and ready to fight it again.

Other characters don't manage as well. One kills himself when he learns that Pennywise has come back to Derry. Others are just treading water. Eddie's married a second edition of his hypochondriac mother, for instance, just as Beverly's married a richer, more successful, and more violent version of her father.[3] They're just reliving their childhoods as adults, tripping over the same mistakes they made when they were teenagers. The character webs in *IT* let the audience compare the ways that each character has dealt with their childhood trauma. Some process it, some relive it, and some eventually die of it.

In other words, King uses character webs to help define how each character's transition from childhood to adulthood contributes to who they are. The result is that *IT* draws its characters in incredible detail and with stunning economy, even though—like *Great Expectations*—*IT* is also a very thick book.

Complex webs can also focus our expectations in the same ways that *Beloved*'s men-and-women web does. In *The Fifth Season* (2015), for instance, N. K. Jemisin tells the story of a single character (alternately known as Damaya, Syenite, and Essun) by jumping between three storylines that focus on her girlhood (when she's known as Damaya), her young adulthood (when she's Syenite), and her middle age (when she's Essun). In each of these storylines, Jemisin places Damaya/Syenite/Essun—who we'll just call "Essun"—in an intimate relationship with a man (Schaffa, Alabaster, and Jija, respectively) who loves, manipulates, and attacks her. Essun, for her part, loves, manipulates, and attacks each of these men as well. Essun's intimate relationships are all relationships of opposition.

The baseline expectation in *The Fifth Season*, in other words, is that characters who love one another will also attack one another. As Essun's story unfolds across *The Fifth Season* and its sequels (since this is the first book in a trilogy), the central question becomes whether she can break free from this pattern of intimate opposition and discover a way to love other characters—her romantic partners, her friends, and her estranged daughter—differently.

This is especially important because *The Fifth Season* and its sequels are complex pieces of storytelling. They include storylines set in multiple times and civilizations, and carry a heavy burden of exposition: Characters include animate statues and different kinds of psychics all fighting for survival on a moonless, volcanically active Earth orbited by giant, magic crystals, and riven by complex forms of oppression and bigotry. In the midst of all this, its central

---

[3]This character web in *IT* is established in some unusual ways. For example, the shapeshifting creature Pennywise attacks each member of the Losers' Club by choosing a different form. That form is tailored to each Loser's weaknesses, and—consequently—helps establish each Loser's flaws.

IT is also brimming with symbols that aren't Pennywise. The most unusual may be the glass corridor that connects two library buildings (the children's library and the adults' library) in Derry. This represents the passage from childhood to adulthood. Characters' responses to the glass corridor indicate how successfully they've managed this passage. For example: Ben, a successful architect, has designed a skyscraper inspired by it.

character web keeps us focused on the issue that really matters: whether Essun will learn a better way to love other people.

That's a lot of modern-day character webs. Let's step back for a moment.

Here's what we've seen so far: Character webs help us understand who characters are. In Shakespearean stories, this also means understanding how characters change or—in some cases—fail to change. Character webs also help us understand the rules of the world in which characters live by defining what's normal. This is true even when the webs are complicated. In *Great Expectations*, it's normal to fall in love. In *The Fifth Season,* it's normal for lovers to attack one another. In *IT*, it's normal for children to experience horrific trauma. In *Beloved,* it's normal for men to leave a difficult situation and normal for women to stick around.

Character webs also tell us about what's possible. In *Fences*, it's possible to be kind without being good. In *Great Expectations*, it's possible to be anything from vengeful to loving. In *IT*, it's possible for childhood trauma to be a source of strength, of terror, or of confusion.

In doing this, character webs also focus our attention. In *Great Expectations*, we wonder whether Estella will end up vengeful (like Miss Havisham) or loving (like Biddy). In *Beloved*, we wonder whether Paul D will follow the pattern set by *Beloved*'s other men and walk away from Sethe, or whether he'll break that pattern and stick with her. In *The Fifth Season*, we wonder whether Essun will overcome the cycle of opposition that has characterized her past relationships. Because they help define characters' flaws, and because they show us what is normal and what is possible in characters' worlds, character webs can also show us where to look for a character's revelation, and what form that revelation is likely to take.

Character webs, like relationships of opposition, aren't contained in a single scene, a single exchange, or a single moment. Instead, they are built over the course of a piece of storytelling. Sometimes, they're built out of things that characters say (like how they answer a question—for instance, "how should my friend deal with her cheating partner?"). At other times, webs are built out of things that characters do (like how they respond to a problem—for instance, the child-killing demon clown of your youth rising from the dead).

Finally, character webs range from the simple to the complex. Simple webs involve individual characters' relationships to one another and are mostly built around differentiation. How each of the members of the Maxson family treat Gabe, for instance, tells us how each of them is different.

Complex character webs, in contrast, often compare relationships between characters. In the process they also outline a spectrum of behavior. Characters in *IT*, for instance, are differently capable of turning childhood trauma into adult competence. Characters in *Great Expectations* are differently capable of emotional generosity. Characters in *The Fifth Season* attack, and hurt, the people they love.

Shakespeare uses both simple and complex character webs, built on everything from dialogue, action, and conflict and opposition (which we've read about in this chapter) to scene weave, symbols, and moral vision (which we'll read about in the next chapter). If you can understand what a play's character webs look like, and how Shakespeare builds them, you're more than halfway to understanding Shakespeare's storytelling.

Let's look at one of Shakespeare's most complicated early character webs, from *A Midsummer Night's Dream*. This is a romantic comedy, but unusual. Many of Shakespeare's best-known plays have only one plot. A few—like *Romeo & Juliet* and *King Lear*—feature a single subplot. *A Midsummer Night's Dream* has four subplots, which is a lot for any piece of storytelling. *The Lord of the Rings* only has two subplots,[4] and it's thick enough to prop open a bank vault.

A Midsummer Night's Dream, being a short play, has to manage each plot and its associated characters efficiently. It does this by approaching its character webs in the same way as *IT* and *Great Expectations*: by working with characters in pairs. In *A Midsummer Night's Dream*, these pairs are almost all romantic couples, and—depending on how you count—there can be as many as eight of them. What differentiates each couple from the others is how they approach what modern readers would call *consent*.

A Midsummer Night's Dream opens with our first couple, Theseus and Hippolyta. They're about to be married, and Theseus is more enthusiastic about the prospect than Hippolyta. Here's the beginning of I.i:

> THESEUS
> Now, fair Hippolyta, our nuptial hour
> Draws on apace. Four happy days bring in
> Another moon—But O, methinks, how slow
> This old moon wanes! She lingers my desires,
> Like to a step-dame or a dowager
> Long withering out a young man's revenue.
> HIPPOLYTA
> Four days will quickly steep themselves in night.
> Four nights will quickly dream away the time.
> And then the moon, like to a silver bow
> New-bent in heaven, shall behold the night
> Of our solemnities. (1–11)

Theseus, to his credit, isn't obtuse enough to miss how Hippolyta feels about their impending marriage, and—after a brief bit of Duke-ing—he makes Hippolyta a promise:

> THESEUS
> Hippolyta, I wooed thee with my sword,
> And won thy love doing thee injuries.

---

[4]Frodo taking the Ring to Mt. Doom is the plot. The first subplot involves Legolas and Aragorn fighting the orcs, and the second subplot involves Merry, Pippin, and the Ents.

> But I will wed thee in another key,
> With pomp, with triumph, and with reveling. (16–19)

If we were wondering why Hippolyta was marrying Theseus, we have our answer: she doesn't have a choice. Theseus has conquered her people and taken Hippolyta as a prize. While Theseus isn't going to give her a choice about marrying him, he does seem to care about her happiness.

We then meet our next two relationship pairs: Lysander and Hermia, and Demetrius and Hermia. That's not a typo: Hermia shows up twice because both Lysander and Demetrius want to marry her. This conflict gets introduced by Hermia's father, Egeus, who asks Theseus to help sort things out:

> EGEUS
> Full of vexation come I, with complaint
> Against my child, my daughter Hermia.
> Stand forth, Demetrius. My noble lord,
> This man hath my consent to marry her.
> Stand forth, Lysander. And my gracious duke,
> This man hath bewitched the bosom of my child [...] (22–29)

Both Lysander and Demetrius want to marry Hermia, but only Demetrius has Hermia's father's permission, and only Lysander has Hermia's love. This is more than a family squabble. Egeus is willing to take the matter all the way to the gallows:

> EGEUS
> [If Hermia] will not here before your grace
> Consent to marry with Demetrius,
> I beg the ancient privilege of Athens.
> As she is mine, I may dispose of her,
> Which shall be either to this gentleman [Demetrius]
> Or to her death, according to our law
> Immediately provided in that case. (39–45)

Hermia either marries Demetrius, or she dies. Theseus, however, gives Hermia a third option: she can become a nun. Hermia lays out her thinking:

> HERMIA
> So will I grow, so live, so die, my lord,
> Ere I will yield my virgin patent up
> Unto his lordship [Demetrius], whose unwished yoke
> My soul consents not to give sovereignty.
> THESEUS
> Take time to pause and, by the next new moon —
> The sealing-day betwixt my love and me,
> For everlasting bond of fellowship —
> Upon that day either prepare to die

> For disobedience to your father's will,
> Or else to wed Demetrius, as he would,
> Or on Diana's altar to protest
> For aye austerity and single life. (79-90)

The similarity between the Theseus/Hippolyta and Demetrius/Hermia relationship ought to be clear: these are both forced marriages, with Theseus and Demetrius doing the forcing.

That overall similarity highlights a difference between Hippolyta and Hermia. While Hippolyta is willing, however unhappily, to go along with her marriage to Theseus, Hermia isn't willing to do the same with Demetrius. She'd rather spend the rest of her life celibate, or die.

There's also a difference between Theseus and Demetrius. Theseus cares about whether Hippolyta is happy. That doesn't involve giving her a choice, but he does promise Hippolyta that the marriage will be better than a battle. There's no such promise from Demetrius. His only words to Hermia are:

> DEMETRIUS
> Relent, sweet Hermia: and, Lysander, yield
> Thy crazed title to my certain right. (91-92)

This tells us something about the world of *Midsummer*. Forced marriage is common practice in Athens. However distasteful that might seem to us, there are (in the world of *Midsummer*) better and worse kinds of forced marriage. Theseus may not give Hippolyta a choice about who (or whether) to marry, but he at least understands that she has feelings. Demetrius doesn't seem to understand, or care about, Hermia's feelings at all.

Likewise, there are degrees of acceptance. Given the reality of a forced marriage, it's possible to unhappily consent (as Hippolyta does) or opt for death or chastity (as Hermia does). It's not a great choice, but it's what the play offers its would-be brides.

After this—and still in I.i—we meet our next couple: Demetrius and Helena. Helena doesn't appear on stage quite yet, but Lysander introduces them:

> LYSANDER
> Demetrius, I'll avouch it to his head,
> Made love to Nedar's daughter, Helena,
> And won her soul. And she, sweet lady, dotes,
> Devoutly dotes, dotes in idolatry,
> Upon this spotted and inconstant man. (106-10)

This is different from what we've seen before. Helena is in love with Demetrius, just as Hermia is in love with Lysander. At some point, Demetrius was interested in Hermia. But now he's not.

If you're keeping score, this means that we have two kinds of couples: one kind (the Theseus/Hippolyta and Demetrius/Hermia kind) is built on forced marriage. The second kind of couple (the Lysander/Hermia and Demetrius/Helena kind) is unforced. Partners can marry for love.

In Athens, however, there are problems with love. One set of problems involves resistant fathers and a liberally applied death penalty. And as the Demetrius/Helena couple shows us, another set of problems involves feelings. Characters can lose interest in one another. Lovers in this play can change their mind. The course of true love never does run smooth.

If we wanted to organize the relationships we've seen so far—even though we're hardly a hundred lines into the play—we could say that there are both good and bad versions of both forced and unforced marriages. They look like this:

Good and Forced: Theseus and Hippolyta.
Bad and Forced: Demetrius and Hermia.
Good and Unforced: Lysander and Hermia.
Bad and Unforced: Demetrius and Helena.

What seems to make a good relationship in *A Midsummer Night's Dream* is how much—or to what degree—partners care about each other's happiness. The common ingredient in both bad relationships is Demetrius, who seems to alternately believe that he can (a) ignore other people's feelings or (b) argue them into feeling differently.

The next couple we meet underscores this point. They're the king and queen of fairies, Titania and Oberon, and boy howdy are they a mess. Here's our introduction to them in II.i.60–81:

> OBERON
> Ill met by moonlight, proud Titania.
> TITANIA
> What, jealous Oberon! Fairies, skip hence.
> I have forsworn his bed and company.
> OBERON
> Tarry, rash wanton. Am not I thy lord?
> TITANIA
> Then I must be thy lady. But I know
> When thou hast stolen away from fairy land
> And, in the shape of Corin, sat all day
> Playing on pipes of corn and versing love
> To amorous Phillida. Why art thou here,
> Come from the farthest Steppe of India?
> But that, forsooth, the bouncing Amazon,
> Your buskined mistress and your warrior love,
> To Theseus must be wedded, and you come
> To give their bed joy and prosperity.

OBERON
How canst thou thus for shame, Titania,
Glance at my credit with Hippolyta
Knowing I know thy love to Theseus?
Didst thou not lead him through the glimmering night
From Perigenia, whom he ravished?
And make him with fair AEgle break his faith,
With Ariadne, and Antiopa?
TITANIA
These are the forgeries of jealousy!

The moment they run into each other, Titania and Oberon start confessing each other's sins. Oberon's been tangling beards with the pasture girls. Titania's been playing fairy godmother to Theseus. It has All Gone Wrong for Titania and Oberon. They, like Demetrius, are bent on thinking of their relationship conflicts as arguments that they can win. If there's one rule for relationships that's shared among Shakespeare's plays—other than that lovers need to be authentic, honest, and vulnerable—it's that good relationships aren't competitions.

But we don't need to know that. We've already seen the difference between good and bad relationships in *A Midsummer Night's Dream*, and we know that Titania and Oberon's relationship is one of the bad ones. Neither of them cares about the other's happiness.

Immediately after this (II.i.188–210) we meet Demetrius and Helena again. Here's how they enter:

DEMETRIUS
I love thee not, therefore pursue me not.
[...] get thee gone and follow me no more.
HELENA
You draw me, you hard-hearted adamant.
[...] leave you your power to draw
And I shall have no power to follow you.
DEMETRIUS
Do I entice you? Do I speak you fair?
Or, rather, do I not in plainest truth
Tell you I do not, nor I cannot, love you?
HELENA
And even for that do I love you the more.
I am your spaniel and, Demetrius,
The more you beat me, I will fawn on you.
Use me but as your spaniel, spurn me, strike me,
Neglect me, lose me—only give me leave,
Unworthy as I am, to follow you.
What worser place can I beg in your love —
And yet a place of high respect with me —
Than to be used as you use your dog?

Yikes. So far, we've seen a lot of evidence that—in the world of *A Midsummer Night's Dream*—you can't argue someone into loving you. Here, we see a funhouse mirror reflection of the same idea: you can't argue them out of loving you, either. No matter how terribly Demetrius acts, Helena is still bound to him. To drive the point home, Shakespeare has Demetrius act worse:

> DEMETRIUS
> Tempt not too much the hatred of my spirit,
> For I am sick when I do look on thee.
> HELENA
> And I am sick when I look not on you.
> DEMETRIUS
> You do impeach your modesty too much
> To leave the city and commit yourself
> Into the hands of one that loves you not,
> To trust the opportunity of night
> And the ill counsel of a desert place
> With the rich worth of your virginity.
> HELENA
> Your virtue is my privilege [...]
> DEMETRIUS
> I'll run from thee and hide me in the brakes,
> And leave thee to the mercy of wild beasts.
> HELENA
> The wildest hath not such a heart as you.
> [...]
> DEMETRIUS
> I will not stay thy questions. Let me go.
> Or, if thou follow me, do not believe
> But I shall do thee mischief in the wood. (211–37)

It's a bad look for everyone. But the similarities and differences between these couples do a sophisticated job of delineating what makes relationships work—or not work—in *Midsummer*. On the one hand, good relationships are built on consideration of other people's feelings. On the other, nothing can stop someone from chasing you if they've come down with a case of love. It's a lot like rabies.

This character web in *A Midsummer Night's Dream* uses a comparison between several different relationships to set up a complex romantic thesis that governs the rest of the play. It goes like this: Relationships aren't good (or bad) because people get to choose who they're in relationships with. They're good (or bad) based on people's attentiveness to one another's feelings. While there are cosmetic differences between forced and unforced marriages in the world of *A Midsummer Night's Dream*, the idea that people enter into relationships voluntarily is an illusion. Nobody gets a choice about who they love.

A Midsummer Night's Dream sets all of this up early, since the vehicle for much of the play's comedy is a love potion. In the end—with the exception of Theseus and Hippolyta—at least one person in each of these relationships gets a dose. Hilarity ensues. Demetrius and Lysander end up fighting over Helena (rather than Hermia) and Titania finds romantic bliss with an egotistical doofus (and aspiring actor) who has the head of a donkey.

A second set of love potion doses sets everything to rights, and the play's mortal couples (that is, Theseus and Hippolyta, Demetrius and Helena, and Lysander and Hermia) end their stories by heckling an inept production of *Pyramus and Thisbe*.

It's a nice moment. *Pyramus and Thisbe* presents itself as a *Romeo and Juliet*-style tragedy in which two young people—who can't choose but to love each other—end up dead by mutual suicide (Pyramus, thinking that Thisbe has been eaten by a lion, stabs himself; Thisbe, discovering Pyramus's body, does the same). But the play is hilariously terrible. The experience of not being able to choose your partner is, in *A Midsummer Night's Dream*, ostensibly a tragedy but actually a comedy.

This is all very complicated, but audiences understand it intuitively. Shakespeare doesn't need some moralizing character to tell the audience that love is never a choice, and so the recipe for happiness is to try to understand the needs of whomever you happen to marry. Instead, Shakespeare lays out *Midsummer*'s romantic thesis, in all its head-spinning detail, by inviting the audience to compare characters' relationships to one another.

As he does that, *Midsummer*'s character webs focus our attention on certain characters' development. We watch *A Midsummer Night's Dream* partly to see whether Demetrius will learn to care about other people's feelings (the way that Lysander and Theseus do), or whether Helena will learn to set romantic boundaries (the way that Hermia does), or whether Oberon and Titania will learn to enjoy each other's company (the way that Theseus and Hippolyta do).

The good news: While many of Shakespeare's plays end up with very complicated character webs, most are simpler than those of *A Midsummer Night's Dream*. This is especially true at the moment we first meet characters, since that's when the differences between them get drawn in the starkest terms.

Let's return to *Hamlet*. Over the course of *Hamlet*, we see several different characters (Hamlet, Laertes, Fortinbras, and Ophelia) respond differently to the same basic question: How do I deal with my father's murder? It's the same basic setup as brunch in *Sex and the City*, except that Hamlet, Laertes, Fortinbras, and Ophelia don't get asked the question over mimosas. Instead, each of their fathers (Old Hamlet, Old Fortinbras, and Polonius) are actually murdered, and the characters answer the murder question with actions as well as words.

How do you deal with your father's murder? For some characters—like Laertes and Fortinbras (and, to a lesser extent, Hamlet)—the answer is that you deal with your father's murder by overthrowing the government that allowed it to happen. For others (like Hamlet and Ophelia), you process your grief in ways that threaten your sanity. For some (like Hamlet and Laertes), dealing with your father's murder means making sure that everybody understands how it happened and why you avenged it.

For some characters (like Laertes and Hamlet) the answers to this question change as their stories progress. For others (like Ophelia and Fortinbras) they stay the same. Regardless, the fact that all four of these characters get put in the same basic situation, and respond to it differently, helps us understand both how these characters are different and what kinds of responses the world of *Hamlet* allows. Nobody in *Hamlet* files a wrongful death suit, or demands wergild, even though some version of either one might have been possible in some version of historical Denmark.

But there's another character web that gets built as Shakespeare introduces his principal characters in *Hamlet*: Claudius and Polonius. In Act II, after we've seen both these fathers in action, Shakespeare elaborates on each of them by showing us how they spy on their son (or, in Claudius's case, stepson). Here's how Polonius does it in II.i.1–16:

> LORD POLONIUS
> Give him this money and these notes, Reynaldo.
> REYNALDO
> I will, my lord.
> LORD POLONIUS
> You shall do marvellous wisely, good Reynaldo,
> Before you visit him, to make inquire
> Of his behavior.
> REYNALDO
> My lord, I did intend it.
> LORD POLONIUS
> Marry, well said. Very well said. Look you, sir,
> Inquire me first what Danskers are in Paris
> And how, and who, what means, and where they keep,
> What company, at what expense, and finding
> By this encompassment and drift of question
> That they do know my son, come you more nearer
> Than your particular demands will touch it.
> Take you, as it were, some distant knowledge of him
> As thus, "I know his father and his friends,
> And in part him." Do you mark this, Reynaldo?
> REYNALDO
> Ay. Very well, my lord.

This exchange goes on. Polonius is wordy and detailed and forgets (or pretends to forget) what he was talking about, and so has to repeat himself. But two things are clear. First, Laertes might know Reynaldo, but only as a servant. Second, Polonius feels the need to tell Reynaldo how to do his spying.

This is different from how Claudius sends Rosencrantz and Guildenstern after Hamlet in the next scene (II.ii.1–33):

> KING CLAUDIUS
> Welcome, dear Rosencrantz and Guildenstern!
> Moreover that we much did long to see you,
> The need we have to use you did provoke
> Our hasty sending. Something have you heard
> Of Hamlet's transformation [...]
> What it should be,
> More than his father's death, that thus hath put him
> So much from the understanding of himself,
> I cannot dream of. I entreat you both
> That, being of so young days brought up with him,
> And sith so neighboured to his youth and havior,
> That you vouchsafe your rest here in our court
> Some little time, so by your companies
> To draw him on to pleasures, and to gather
> So much as from occasion you may glean,
> Whether aught to us unknown afflicts him thus
> That, opened, lies within our remedy.
> QUEEN GERTRUDE
> Good gentlemen, he hath much talked of you,
> And sure I am two men there are not living
> To whom he more adheres. [...]
> ROSENCRANTZ
> Both your majesties
> Might, by the sovereign power you have of us,
> Put your dread pleasures more into command
> Than to entreaty.
> GUILDENSTERN
> But we both obey,
> And here give up ourselves, in the full bent,
> To lay our service freely at your feet
> To be commanded.
> KING CLAUDIUS
> Thanks, Rosencrantz and gentle Guildenstern.

Claudius takes a different approach to spying than Polonius, one that seems both more subtle and more threatening. He's chosen Hamlet's friends, rather than some distant professional, to spy on him. He's not about to tell them how to do the job, either. Instead, he and Gertrude are going to rely on their spies' acquaintance with Hamlet, and Hamlet's genuine, unforced trust in Rosencrantz and Guildenstern, to discover whatever it is they want to know.

The difference between Polonius's spying and Claudius's, in other words, tells us something specific about Claudius's threat to Hamlet. While Polonius is interested only in what other people think about Laertes, Claudius seeks out the secrets of Hamlet's character, and the inner matter of Hamlet's thoughts. And he'll use Hamlet's friends—and even Hamlet's own mother—to do it by fooling them into thinking that their spying is being done for Hamlet's own good. With Claudius around, in other words, no relationship of Hamlet's is safe.

There are other techniques that Shakespeare uses to build character webs, and we'll look at some of them (like *scene weave* and *symbols*) later on. But there's one more that's worth returning to: conflict.

So far, the conflicts that we've looked at—between Sampson and Gregory, Horatio and Marcellus, Richard and Anne, or Hamlet and Claudius—have involved only two characters. But one technique that Shakespeare uses to great effect, and usually to build character webs, is *multi-point* conflict. That's a conflict where, in the space of a single scene, every speaking character is in conflict with every other one.

Consider Ophelia's funeral in *Hamlet* V.i. In this scene, Laertes has just leaped into Ophelia's grave to hold her one last time when Hamlet shows up and leaps into the grave after him. Then Hamlet and Laertes start fighting. Here's how everybody tries to determine what will happen next:

> LAERTES
> The devil take thy soul!
> *Grappling with him*
> [...]
> KING CLAUDIUS
> Pluck them asunder.
> QUEEN GERTRUDE
> Hamlet, Hamlet!
> ALL
> Gentlemen —
> HORATIO
> Good my lord, be quiet. (244–51)

A handful of lines, and look how much we learn. First: The normal, baseline response to this fight is to remind Hamlet and Laertes to behave like "gentlemen"—that's the line given to everyone who isn't a well-established character. The well-established characters, however, all react differently:

1. Laertes forgets about Ophelia, curses Hamlet, and then attacks him. Another, more empathetic character might say something like "I see you loved her too." A more patient one might step aside, knowing he'll have a chance to pay back Hamlet in a lethally rigged fencing match.
2. Claudius wants to separate Laertes and Hamlet immediately. Instead of doing it himself, he orders it done. (Old Hamlet, the warrior king, might have jumped into the grave himself to part the fighters.)
3. Gertrude calls out Hamlet's name. Why she does this isn't totally clear: Maybe she thinks Hamlet might get hurt, or maybe she's appalled that he's acting so badly. Maybe both. Gertrude doesn't say "oh, poor Ophelia!" or order Hamlet out of the grave, or join Claudius in marshaling the other funeral-goers into parting Hamlet and Laertes.

As has been the case since the beginning of the play, her response to Hamlet's terrible behavior involves simultaneously protecting Hamlet while bewailing the harm he does to other people.
4. Horatio tells Hamlet to be quiet. He thinks that the only way that Hamlet and Laertes will actually stop fighting is if Hamlet keeps his mouth shut. Even if the attendants part Hamlet from Laertes, Hamlet will almost certainly keep goading him. As always, Horatio's actions remind us of Hamlet's flaws: Even though Hamlet is thoughtful, he is also inclined to petty viciousness.

This is late in the play—well after we've learned these characters' motivations and flaws. But these five lines remind us that, although the conditions of the play have changed, the characters themselves have not.

Character webs are important, so it's worth reviewing what we've learned about them:

1. Stories are about characters, but pieces of storytelling (like plays) are about relationships between characters.
2. Sometimes, those relationships emerge from conflict (in its ordinary or multi-point varieties). At other times, those relationships are abstract: built out of the ways that characters respond differently to similar situations.
3. Character webs highlight and refine the qualities of characters—generally by showing us how characters are different from one another.
4. Character webs also help us understand the world of a story by telling us which actions, attitudes, or responses are possible.

Just as characters are the heart of stories, so are character webs the heart of storytelling. In the next section, we'll examine more of the techniques that Shakespeare uses to establish character webs: situation, symbols, scene weave, and moral vision.

Points of Review

In this chapter, we've learned how Shakespeare crafts a piece of storytelling by using three different tools: conflict, opposition, and character webs. You may have noticed that these three tools travel in packs. Where you have opposition or conflict you also have material for a character web.

Conflict is everywhere. Stories, and storytelling, are built on it. In the universe of stories, conflict takes a surprising number of forms: characters are in conflict with themselves, with their societies, with their fates. But in Shakespeare, the only kind of conflict you'll find is conflict between characters. This takes a specific form: characters are in conflict when they all want the same thing.

Sometimes, the thing they want is tangible: In *A Midsummer Night's Dream*, Demetrius and Lysander begin their stories both wanting to marry Hermia. Many times, the thing characters want is intangible: Theseus, Egeus, Demetrius, Lysander, Oberon, Puck, and Hermia aren't in conflict over who Hermia will marry, but over who gets to decide.

As a rule: overt conflict—that is, conflict in which characters are all equally aware of the conflict's nature—will bring characters together. Covert conflict—that is, conflict in which characters believe they are in conflict over different issues—will drive them apart.

While conflict between characters propels a play from line to line and from scene to scene, Shakespeare's plays also include structural conflicts. These are conflicts that run the course of an entire play. In *Hamlet*, for instance, there is a structural conflict over which version of the story about Old Hamlet's death will become the truth. In *A Midsummer Night's Dream*, the conflict over who decides Hermia's marriage drives much of the play's first four acts—it's not until late in Act IV, and six collective doses of love potion, that Theseus decides to overbear Egeus's will and allow Hermia to marry Lysander.

A special case of prolonged conflict is opposition. While characters are always in conflict with one another, opponents negotiate conflict by attacking other characters' weaknesses. Shakespeare's villains are often opponents, using a combination of deceit and trickery to manipulate characters into hurting themselves or one another.

Opposition, like structural conflict, is durable. A relationship of opposition is likely to last for most of a play, and involve some amount of planning and (in the case of mutual opposition) counter-planning. Hamlet and Claudius are mutual opponents, for instance. But it would be hard to call Iago's opposition to Othello mutual. Iago attacks Othello's weaknesses, but Othello never attacks Iago's.

Conflict and opposition tell us how characters compare to one another, and are one way that Shakespeare builds character webs—abstract relationships between characters that define and highlight those characters' important attributes.

Some character webs involve putting different characters in similar situations, so that the characters' reactions tell the audience how characters are different from one another. Other, more complex, character webs will place characters on a spectrum of behavior. These more complex webs may also highlight differences in relationships between characters, rather than focusing solely on the attributes of individual characters themselves. *A Midsummer Night's Dream*, for instance, compares different types of romantic relationships to one another by contrasting several romantic couples.

Character webs do more than tell us who characters are, though. They also help us learn about the world of the story.

There are implicit rules in every piece of storytelling. Sometimes, there are things that we can expect to happen: a bachelor or bachelorette might fall in love. There are also limits to the choices that we can expect characters to make. History might tell us that a merchant like Antonio would have insured his ships if he lived in Early Modern Venice. But the Venice of *Merchant* is not our historical Venice any more than *Hamlet*'s Denmark is history's Denmark. We don't make sense of Hamlet's actions by pointing out that ghosts don't exist and, therefore, that the ghost must have been some plotter—Polonius, maybe—in an elaborate disguise all along.

Instead, because all the characters—including the skeptic, Horatio—declare that they have seen a ghost, we can conclude that ghosts exist in *Hamlet*'s Denmark. Because nobody scolds Antonio for rashly letting his ships travel uninsured, we can conclude that, in *Merchant*'s Venice, maritime insurance is not an expected method of risk mitigation.

Character webs, in other words, tell us what is possible. They also tell us what is normal. The guards in *Hamlet*, on seeing the ghost, attempt to make it speak. Because the characters largely agree on that course of action, we can infer that it seems reasonable, or normal, to them. You see a ghost, you get it to say something. Other courses of action that might seem reasonable to us—running away, taking a picture, waving a cross, or drinking less—aren't reasonable in the world of the story.

You can check your understanding of conflict, opposition, and character webs by answering the questions in Chapter 7. Once you understand these concepts, you'll be ready to learn about the other techniques Shakespeare uses to weave his stories together.

4.4 Further Reading

Relationships Between Characters

These anthologies and monographs present several different ways of thinking about how characters interact with one another, and about how their interactions contribute to Shakespeare's plays' shapes, structures, and progressions.

Conflict and Opponents

Ball, David. *Backwards and Forwards: A Technical Manual for Reading Plays*. Southern Illinois University Press, 1983.

Backwards and Forwards is a concise, readable book that deals comprehensively with dramatic structure, and its short chapter on conflict ("Obstacle, Conflict") presents a four-type theory of conflict which has been widely used in other articles and books on script analysis.

Charney, Maurice. *Shakespeare's Villains.* **Fairleigh Dickensen University Press, 2011.**

Shakespeare's Villains is a guide to the plotting, secretive, and malevolent characters in Shakespeare's plays. In addition to naming the villains' salient qualities, he divides them into useful categories, like *tyrants* (including Julius Caesar and Duke Frederick) and *calumniators* (like Don John, Iachimo, and Lucio). While Charney doesn't recognize conflict and opposition as concepts in the same way that we do here, his selection of villains includes most of the major Shakespearean characters who spend their stories in opposition with others.

Thomas, James. *Script Analysis for Actors, Directors, and Designers.* **Focal Press, 2013.**

Script Analysis is a textbook, and like *Backwards and Forwards* it is comprehensive. Its chapter on character ("Characters") presents a multi-factor model of conflict that draws from a variety of critics, including Stanislavski and Brunetière, and uses a grammar that may be more familiar to readers who have a deeper grounding in dramatic theory.

Character Webs

Brennan, Anthony. *Shakespeare's Dramatic Structures.* **Routledge & Kegan Paul, 1986.**

Few writers make use of the term "character web" to describe the concept as it is used in this book. *Shakespeare's Dramatic Structures* subsumes it, and other concepts from this book, in its broader focus on pattern and variation in Shakespeare's plays. The chapters on interaction and separation, for instance, discuss matters like conflict, opposition, plans, and battles in perceptive ways that are also remarkable models of close reading. *Shakespeare's Dramatic Structures* is part of the excellent *Critical Studies* series from Routledge.

References

Atwood, Margaret. (1985) 1998. *The Handmaid's Tale.* New York: Anchor Books.
Camus, Albert. (1942) 1989. *The Stranger.* Trans. Matthew Ward. Vancouver: Vintage.
Cassavetes, Nick. *The Notebook.* Directed by Nick Cassavetes. 2004; Burbank: Warner Brothers, 2018. Blu-Ray.
Chandor, J.C. *All Is Lost.* Directed by J.C. Chandor. 2013; Santa Monica: Lionsgate, 2014. Blu-Ray
Coleridge, Samuel Taylor, and R.A Foakes (ed.). 1987. *Lectures 1808–1819 On Literature, Volume 2.* Princeton: Princeton University Press.
Dickens, Charles. (1861) 2002. *Great Expectations.* New York: Penguin Classics.
Friedkin, William. *Cruising.* Directed by William Friedkin. 1980; Shenley: Arrow Films, 2019.

Hanson, Curtis. *Never Cry Wolf*. Directed by Carroll Ballard. 1983; Burbank: Walt Disney Pictures, 2004. DVD.
Jemisin, N.K. 2015. *The Fifth Season*. London: Orbit Books.
King, Michael Patrick. *Sex and the City*.Directed by Michael Patrick King. 2008; Burbank: Warner Brothers, 2019.
King, Stephen. 1986. *IT*. New York: Signet.
London, Jack. (1902) 1986. "To Build a Fire." In *"To Build a Fire" and Other Stories*, 17–28. New York: Bantam Books.
Morrison, Toni. 1987. *Beloved*. New York: Plume.
Ramis, Harold, and Dan Ackroyd. *Ghostbusters*. Directed by Ivan Reitman. 1984; Culver City: Sony Pictures Home Entertainment, 2016.
Tolkien, J.R.R. (1956) 1987. *The Lord of the Rings*. New York: Houghton Mifflin Harcourt.
Wilson, August. 1986. *Fences*. New York: Plume.
Wright, Thomas Lee. *New Jack City*. Directed by Mario Van Peebles. 1991; Burbank: Warner Brother, 2012. Blu-Ray.

CHAPTER 5

Structure

In the last chapter, we looked at several techniques that Shakespeare uses to connect stories to one another in order to produce a piece of storytelling like a play. The most comprehensive of these techniques is the character web, which is a system of relationships between characters that shows us how each character is different from the others. Sometimes, character webs do this by having different characters respond to similar situations, or by having them answer similar questions. At other times, they do this by putting characters in conflict with one another. Characters who want the same thing (like to decide who Juliet will marry) will use different strategies to get it. Those different strategies tell us what each character values, what kinds of validation they're seeking, how they hurt themselves and other people, and how those qualities differ from character to character.

If a story is about a character, a piece of storytelling is about relationships between characters. In this chapter, we'll learn more about some of the techniques that Shakespeare uses to build those relationships: *scene weave*, *symbols*, and *moral vision*.

Up to this point, we've talked about stories as a simple recounting of what a character wants and how they try to get it. In the process, we've ignored much of how stories work from moment to moment. A story doesn't tell us everything. Between the time Hamlet sees his father's ghost and the time he murders Claudius, Hamlet probably uses the bathroom at least once. But we don't see this happen because *Hamlet* isn't a continuous portrayal of events. Instead, stories are collections of moments that connect to one another. These connections help tell the story.

Sometimes, for instance, what happens in one scene will cause, or allow, something to happen in the next. At other times, what happens in one scene has an abstract logical relationship to what happens in the next, and that relationship helps the audience learn something about the characters and their world. In *Hamlet*, we see consecutive scenes in which Hamlet and Laertes both ask permission to leave Denmark; Laertes's request is granted, and Hamlet's is not. This tells us that Hamlet's request to leave Denmark is not, on the face of it, unreasonable, and that Claudius's wish that Hamlet remain in Denmark has specific reasoning behind it.

In *King Lear*, we get two stories about two fathers (Lear and Gloucester) who both have good and evil children. In each of their stories, the fathers at first misjudge and mistreat the good child and later, as part of their revelations, reconcile with them. *King Lear* presents each of these moments in Lear and Gloucester's stories—the initial mistreatment, the recognition of wrongdoing, the reconciliations—side by side, so that each moment highlights and defines qualities of the moment from the other father's story.

This technique, of arranging moments in a story so that their logical relationships are clear to the audience, is *scene weave*. In a piece of storytelling with multiple plots (like *King Lear* or *A Midsummer Night's Dream*) we'll see Shakespeare weave the plots together like a tapestry, alternating between one thread and another to form a coherent, overarching pattern.

Symbols help this pattern take shape. You might have left your high school English class never wanting to talk about symbols again. But symbols are a delight when they're well used. They don't just represent an abstract idea (or set of ideas) for the sake of keeping high school English departments in business. Symbols develop characters. Like characters, they also form webs of mutual reference and definition.

In *Star Wars* (1977), for instance, the light saber is a symbol. So is the blaster. So is the Death Star, and so is the Millennium Falcon. Each one of them represents a different way of managing conflict: directly and personally (the light saber), less intimately and discriminately (the blaster), with a campaign of intentionally terrifying, indiscriminate force (the Death Star), and by running away (the Millennium Falcon). The meaning of each symbol is established early on, and while these meanings evolve as *Star Wars* progresses, each character's first reaction to each symbol tells us something about the character's attitude toward conflict. When Luke calls the Falcon a "piece of junk," we're given to understand that he doesn't think much of running away. When Han says, "hokey religions and ancient weapons are no match for a good blaster at your side," he's talking about the light saber, but he's also telling us about the method of conflict resolution he feels most comfortable with.

Shakespeare uses symbols in the same way. *Hamlet*, like *Star Wars*, offers its characters a choice of weapons, and these tell us how they prefer to approach conflict. There's poison for duplicitous people like Claudius, and swords for more honorable people who, like Old Hamlet, prefer to settle their deadly quarrels openly. When—in the closing duel—Hamlet grabs a sword that he doesn't know is poisoned, and unwittingly kills Laertes with it, we understand how the moral scoreboard is being tallied: poison and treachery are responsible for Laertes's (probably wrongful) death, just as they are responsible for Old Hamlet's, Hamlet's, and Gertrude's. When Claudius dies—a victim of his own poison and a few energetic sword thrusts from Hamlet—we're to understand that he has been killed by a combination of Hamlet's boldness and his own chicanery. At the end of *Hamlet*, direct action wins the day.

That favoring of direct action over plotting is part of *Hamlet*'s moral vision, or the baseline set of values that inform a piece of storytelling. As a play progresses, characters' revelations tend to converge on a statement about the ways that people ought to think and behave. In the universe of stories—that is, in all stories everywhere—these moral visions can concern people's relationships with their religion, nature, or the cosmos. Sometimes, those moral visions are meant to speak directly to the audience. It's hard to read a novel like *Atlas Shrugged* (1957), *Uncle Tom's Cabin* (1852), or *Native Son* (1940) without hearing a clear message about the values that real people in the real world ought to hold.

This isn't Shakespearean territory. Shakespeare's moral visions are relentlessly human, focusing on how people ought to behave toward one another. While gods are invoked in Shakespeare, and even show up occasionally, they don't occupy the moral center of Shakespeare's storytelling. Shakespeare's moral visions are also very much confined to the world of the story. They differ a great deal from play to play. They are not guides to real life, although some of them are sensible.

Shakespeare's most common moral vision—common to nearly all the comedies and to nearly every romantic relationship that Shakespeare presents—is that characters ought to be authentic, honest, and vulnerable. Successful Shakespearean characters know what they want and declare it openly, even when they run the risk of being hurt.

This takes some learning. In *Much Ado About Nothing*, Beatrice and Benedick begin their stories as inauthentic and dishonest. They are both clearly interested in each other but aren't willing to admit it, and consequently spend a lot of words explaining why love is not for them. Eventually, Beatrice and Benedick drop their pretense of voluntary celibacy and admit their feelings to one another, even though by doing this they each risk rejection and ridicule from the other.

Another lover in *Much Ado*, Claudio, has a similar revelation. Even though he's interested in Hero from the moment he sees her, he's afraid to approach her himself. He asks his friend Don Pedro to woo Hero on his behalf—a scheme that's abetted by a conveniently timed masked ball. After some chicanery by Don John (*Much Ado*'s bastard villain) Claudio finally takes ownership of, and responsibility for, his feelings, publicly declaring his devotion to Hero after he (mistakenly) thinks he's killed her.

Authenticity, honesty, and vulnerability aren't bad ideas, but some of Shakespeare's other moral visions are less at home in polite company. As far as justice in *Titus Andronicus* goes, burying criminals up to their necks and starving them to death is just another day in court. That moral logic makes a lot of sense in *Titus*, but don't try it at the coffee shop.

By the end of this chapter, you should be able to discover and describe how moral vision and other storytelling tools—like symbols and scene weave—help produce a piece of storytelling. These techniques have also been widely used by modern-day storytellers. If you understand symbols, scene weave, and moral vision, you'll see them at work everywhere.

5.1 Scene Weave

Like most of Shakespeare's storytelling tools, you've probably seen a scene weave before—even if you didn't know what it was called. It's so gracefully integrated into the art of modern storytelling that it's hard to imagine a world where it didn't exist.

Let's look at one of the most famous scene weaves in modern storytelling: the ending of *The Godfather* (1972). If you haven't seen *The Godfather*, it goes like this:

The anchor story in *The Godfather*—that is, the story that *The Godfather* focuses on in the same way that *Hamlet* focuses on Hamlet—is Michael Corleone's. Michael is the son of Vito Corleone, the head of a New York crime family. Michael's a straight shooter, like Johnny Smith in *The Dead Zone* (1979), and at the beginning of his story he's fresh out of the Marines. He and his wide-eyed fiancée, Kay, they're as wholesome as Wonder Bread.

In Michael's first scenes with Kay, he is authentic, honest, and vulnerable. He doesn't pretend to be anybody other than he is, and tells Kay about his family's criminal interests even though this is, relationship-wise, risky business. And so when Michael tells Kay that he wants no part of his family's criminal enterprises, we believe him.

But fate says otherwise. Michael gets entangled in his family's business while protecting his hospitalized father, Vito, from an assassination attempt. In the aftermath, Michael becomes increasingly strategic, calculating, and savage, first killing rivals and then ordering them killed—the way you do when you rise to leadership of a crime family. During this, Michael keeps Kay (who's now his wife) at arm's length. Not literally—they have a couple kids—but in the sense that he gradually, but consistently, maintains a boundary between his personal and professional lives that she is not allowed to cross.

Michael might have started his story as authentic, honest, and vulnerable, but by the end he's become an entirely different person—violent, calculating, and secretive. This is where *The Godfather*'s famous scene weave comes in.

In the final movement of his story, Michael orders that the heads of several other crime families be assassinated. This happens on the same day that he is to become godfather to his sister, Connie's, child. During the assassinations,

The Godfather alternates between showing us the baptism—where Michael becomes godfather to Connie's kid—and showing us the murders that Michael has ordered. You see a cute baby, surrounded by family, and the movie cuts to an assassin loading a gun. Cut back to the cute baby, and back to another assassin. Cut to Michael affirming his belief in Christ as part of his baptismal vows, and then to his men shooting people down in elevators, in massage parlors, in the street. It's not very Wonder Bread at all.

That's scene weave. When it's well-constructed, scene weave makes the relationship between scenes matter just as much as the content of the scenes themselves. In *The Godfather*, we don't just understand that Michael has changed because he's ordered a half-dozen murders, or—for that matter— because he's attending a baptism. Instead, the juxtaposition of those moments highlights the difference between Who Michael Is and Who Michael Pretends to Be. The separation of his personal and professional lives is complete and— from the standpoint of his relationship with Kay—terrifying. When, at the end of *The Godfather*, Michael shuts the door to his office on Kay, we understand what's been lost. Michael has achieved power, but at the cost of human intimacy.

Shakespeare does the same thing. He didn't have the dubious advantage of a camera, or of filmmaking techniques like jump cuts, but he did have a stage. In Shakespeare's early scene weaves, he divides the stage in half. That way, the audience's attention can switch easily from one side of the stage to the other, from one scene to the next, without a lot of entrances and exits. If you imagine *The Godfather* as a stage play rather than a movie, you'd think of the assassinations playing out on the left side of the stage while the baptism happens on the right.

Here's one example from *Richard III*. Near the end of the play (V.iii), Richard (Shakespeare's energetic villain) prepares to battle Henry (the boring, nominal hero). Like all well-fought battles, this one begins with a good evening of rest, camaraderie, and strategy, and so Shakespeare has Richard and Henry pitch their tents—which operate both as personal quarters and command centers—at opposite ends of the stage.

The scene begins:

> KING RICHARD III
> Here pitch our tents, even here in Bosworth field.
> My Lord of Surrey, why look you so sad?
> SURREY
> My heart is ten times lighter than my looks.
> [...]
> KING RICHARD III
> Up with my tent there! Here will I lie tonight.
> But where to-morrow? Well, all's one for that.
> Who hath descried the number of the foe?
> NORFOLK
> Six or seven thousand is their utmost power.

KING RICHARD III
Why, our battalion trebles that account.
Besides, the king's name is a tower of strength
Which they, upon the adverse party, want.
Up with my tent there! Valiant gentlemen,
Let us survey the vantage of the field.
Call for some men of sound direction.
Let's want no discipline, make no delay,
For lords, tomorrow is a busy day. (1–19)

Richard is confident, since he has three times as many soldiers as Henry (a.k.a. Richmond). Despite this, Richard's officer Norfolk doesn't seem happy at all. He's on the wrong side of this battle and he knows it.

After this (V.iii.20–46)[1] we get some action from Henry's camp:

Enter, on the other side of the field, RICHMOND, Sir William Brandon, OXFORD, and others. Some of the Soldiers pitch RICHMOND's tent
RICHMOND
The weary sun hath made a golden set,
And by the bright track of his fiery car
Gives signal of a goodly day to-morrow.
Sir William Brandon, you shall bear my standard.
Give me some ink and paper in my tent.
I'll draw the form and model of our battle,
Limit each leader to his several charge,
And part in just proportion our small strength.
My Lord of Oxford, you, Sir William Brandon,
And you, Sir Walter Herbert, stay with me.
The Earl of Pembroke keeps his regiment.
Good Captain Blunt, bear my good night to him
And by the second hour in the morning
Desire the earl to see me in my tent.
Yet one thing more, good Blunt, before thou goest:
Where is Lord Stanley quartered, dost thou know?
BLUNT
Unless I have mistaken his colors much,
Which well I am assured I have not done,
His regiment lies half a mile at least
South from the mighty power of the king.
RICHMOND
If without peril it be possible,
Good Captain Blunt, bear my good night to him,
And give him from me this most needful scroll.
BLUNT
Upon my life, my lord, I'll undertake it.

[1] A note on nomenclature: the "scene" in "scene weave" does not mean the same thing as "scene" as it is used in Act/Scene divisions (e.g. "Act V Scene i"). Instead, think of the "scene" in "scene weave" as a single exchange between characters.

And so, God give you quiet rest tonight!
RICHMOND
Good night, good Captain Blunt. Come gentlemen,
Let us consult upon tomorrow's business
Into our tent. The dew is raw and cold.

Henry's field behavior is a stark contrast to Richard's. Henry seems more like a commander: issuing orders, planning a battle, and compensating for the relatively meager strength of his forces. Compared to Henry's, Richard's planning looks slipshod.

Let's see what comes next:

KING RICHARD III
So, I am satisfied. Give me a bowl of wine.
I have not that alacrity of spirit
Nor cheer of mind that I was wont to have.
Set it down. (73–77)

Richard has a case of pre-battle anxiety and decides that drinking is the best thing for it. Henry, on the other hand, turns to prayer:

RICHMOND
I'll strive with troubled thoughts to take a nap,
Lest leaden slumber peise me down to-morrow
When I should mount with wings of victory.
Once more, good night, kind lords and gentlemen.
Exeunt all but RICHMOND
O Thou, whose captain I account myself,
Look on my forces with a gracious eye.
Put in their hands thy bruising irons of wrath
That they may crush down with a heavy fall
The usurping helmets of our adversaries!
Make us thy ministers of chastisement
That we may praise thee in the victory!
To thee I do commend my watchful soul,
Ere I let fall the windows of mine eyes.
Sleeping and waking, O, defend me still! (105–18)

This is a basic character web, in the sense that two different characters (Richard and Henry) have the same problem (pre-battle anxiety) and decide to deal with it differently: Richard drinks, and Henry prays. We don't need to be military geniuses to know the right choice from the wrong one.

The same thing is true for their pre-battle planning: Richard trusts in the size of his army, and respect for the name of the king, to lead him to victory. Henry, on the other hand, trusts in things like strategy and planning.

But then it gets worse for Richard. After he and Henry fall asleep (still in V.iii), ghosts start showing up:

> *Enter the Ghost of Prince Edward, son to King Henry VI*
> GHOST OF PRINCE EDWARD [To KING RICHARD III]
> Let me sit heavy on thy soul tomorrow!
> Think, how thou stabbedst me in my prime of youth
> At Tewksbury. Despair, therefore, and die!
> *To RICHMOND*
> Be cheerful, Richmond, for the wronged souls
> Of butchered princes fight in thy behalf.
> King Henry's issue, Richmond, comforts thee.
> *Enter the Ghost of King Henry VI*
> GHOST OF KING HENRY VI [To KING RICHARD III]
> When I was mortal, my anointed body
> By thee was punched full of deadly holes.
> Think on the Tower and me. Despair and die!
> Harry the Sixth bids thee despair and die!
> *To RICHMOND*
> Virtuous and holy be thou, conqueror!
> Harry, that prophesied thou shouldest be king,
> Doth comfort thee in thy sleep. Live and flourish! (119–31)

You get the idea. The ghosts of the people that Richard has murdered show up one after another, each of them recounting Richard's crimes before they curse him and bless Henry. Richard's been doing a lot of murder, so there are a lot of ghosts in this scene—eleven more, after Edward and Henry—and all of them follow this same basic pattern.

These aren't jump cuts, like we see in *The Godfather*, but the principle is the same: we shift our attention from Richard to Henry, and back again, in a sequence of scenes. This process of shifting our attention draws our focus to the relationships between these characters and their situations.

Here's another example from another of Shakespeare's Histories, *Henry VI Part 3*. In the *Henry VI* plays, Henry VI's story is only one of many. In it, Henry is painted as a well-intentioned but inept ruler, placed in a political situation that outmatches his abilities as a leader. We first see him lose control of England's nobles, whose squabbling abandons the noble Lord Talbot to death at the hands of the French army. Later, England descends into a civil war between those same squabbling nobles. Through *Henry VI* parts 2 and 3, this war becomes increasingly petty and savage. Henry's ordinary, decent subjects suffer because of it.

While Henry appreciates their suffering, he's powerless to stop it. The scene we're about to see, II.v, is typical. In it, Henry looks down at a battlefield, wishing that he'd been born a shepherd instead of a king so that he wouldn't have to deal with court politics:

> KING HENRY VI
> This battle fares like to the morning's war,
> When dying clouds contend with growing light,
> What time the shepherd, blowing of his nails,

Can neither call it perfect day nor night.
Now sways it this way, like a mighty sea
Forced by the tide to combat with the wind.
[...]
Here on this molehill will I sit me down.
To whom God will, there be the victory!
[...]
Would I were dead, if God's good will were so!
For what is in this world but grief and woe?
O God! Methinks it were a happy life
To be no better than a homely swain,
To sit upon a hill, as I do now,
To carve out dials quaintly, point by point,
Thereby to see the minutes how they run,
How many make the hour full complete;
How many hours bring about the day;
How many days will finish up the year;
How many years a mortal man may live.
[...]
So minutes, hours, days, months, and years,
Passed over to the end they were created
Would bring white hairs unto a quiet grave.
Ah, what a life were this! How sweet! How lovely!
Gives not the hawthorn-bush a sweeter shade
To shepherds looking on their silly sheep,
Than doth a rich embroidered canopy
To kings that fear their subjects' treachery?
O, yes, it doth; a thousand-fold it doth. (1–46)

Henry is one of Shakespeare's whiniest kings—it's a close race between him and Richard II. While we can admire his empathy, it's hard to admire his hand-wringing.

And then we get our scene weave. As if on cue, a soldier enters dragging a dead body. One of Shakespeare's rare stage directions tells us that this is a son, dragging the body of his dead father. The scene goes like this:

SON
Ill blows the wind that profits nobody.
This man, whom hand to hand I slew in fight,
May be possessed with some store of crowns
And I, that haply take them from him now,
May yet ere night yield both my life and them
To some man else, as this dead man doth me. (55–60)

The son doesn't know that the dead man he plans to rob is his father. But once he starts to strip the body, he finds out:

> SON
> Who's this? O God! it is my father's face,
> Whom in this conflict I unwares have killed.
> O heavy times, begetting such events!
> From London by the king was I pressed forth.
> My father, being the Earl of Warwick's man,
> Came on the part of York, pressed by his master
> And I, who at his hands received my life, him
> Have by my hands of life bereaved him.
> Pardon me, God, I knew not what I did!
> And pardon, father, for I knew not thee!
> My tears shall wipe away these bloody marks;
> And no more words till they have flowed their fill. (61–72)

And we get Henry's reaction:

> KING HENRY VI
> O piteous spectacle! O bloody times!
> Whiles lions war and battle for their dens,
> Poor harmless lambs abide their enmity.
> Weep, wretched man, I'll aid thee tear for tear.
> And let our hearts and eyes, like civil war,
> Be blind with tears, and break overcharged with grief. (73–78)

But we're not finished. As the son and his dead father remain on stage, another soldier enters. This time, it's a father with his dead son.

> FATHER
> Thou that so stoutly hast resisted me,
> Give me thy gold, if thou hast any gold.
> For I have bought it with a hundred blows.
> But let me see. Is this our foeman's face? (79–82)

Here it comes. Just like the son who killed his father, the father who killed his son only finds out what he's done when it's time to strip the body for loot:

> Ah, no, no, no, it is mine only son!
> Ah, boy, if any life be left in thee
> Throw up thine eye! See, see what showers arise,
> Blown with the windy tempest of my heart,
> Upon thy wounds, that kill mine eye and heart!
> O pity, God, this miserable age!
> What stratagems, how fell, how butcherly,
> Erroneous, mutinous and unnatural,
> This deadly quarrel daily doth beget!
> O boy, thy father gave thee life too soon,
> And hath bereft thee of thy life too late! (83–93)

And, just like last time, Henry looks on and laments the state of his kingdom:

> KING HENRY VI
> Woe above woe! Grief more than common grief!
> O that my death would stay these ruthful deeds!
> O pity, pity, gentle heaven, pity!
> The red rose and the white are on his face,
> The fatal colors of our striving houses.
> The one his purple blood right well resembles.
> The other his pale cheeks, methinks, presenteth.
> Wither one rose, and let the other flourish.
> If you contend, a thousand lives must wither. (94–102)

And—in case we hadn't had enough by now—there's a circle of grief: the son grieves for his father, the father for his son, and Henry for himself:

> SON
> How will my mother, for a father's death,
> Take on with me and never be satisfied!
> FATHER
> How will my wife, for slaughter of my son,
> Shed seas of tears and never be satisfied!
> KING HENRY VI
> How will the country, for these woeful chances,
> Misthink the king and not be satisfied!
> SON
> Was ever son so rued a father's death?
> FATHER
> Was ever father so bemoaned his son?
> KING HENRY VI
> Was ever king so grieved for subjects' woe?
> Much is your sorrow. Mine, ten times so much. (103–12)

This is a simple scene weave and—let's be frank—it's not one of Shakespeare's best moments. Henry is a hard king to like, and the symmetry of this scene weave, with its alternating inadvertent father/son murders, its wooden prose, overwrought dialogue, and self-centered laments from Henry, goes on a bit too long. It's like the parade of ghosts in *Richard III*. We get the message after the first couple. The next eleven are a good time to hit the bathroom and get some more popcorn.

But, however tedious it is, the relationship between the son/father and father/son scenes tells us something that neither scene could tell us by itself: the violence of *Henry VI Part 3*'s civil wars is universal and indiscriminate. Good people on either side—represented by the red and white roses—end up doing equally terrible things. Henry's laments make more sense in this context: they're about the state of his kingdom generally, and not these people in particular. If you want to get way into it, you could say that the relationship between these moments presents each father/son pair as a synecdoche. Each is a stand-in for a thousand tragedies, small and large, that befall families as a consequence of England's civil war.

Both the *Henry VI* trilogy and *Richard III* are pieces of Shakespeare's early work. As Shakespeare's storytelling matures, his scene weaves become more naturally integrated into the practice of storytelling.

Take this weave from *King Lear*. This is one of the few Shakespearean plays that includes a subplot, and this creates an interesting practice of scene weave. Generally speaking, subplots highlight and define aspects of the main plot's characters and relationships. A piece of storytelling will draw attention to these moments of definition by jumping from the main plot to the subplot and back again. That way, the play can—for instance—establish character webs that include characters from each plotline, or use characters from each plotline to define, or elaborate on, the situations of every character in the play.

That sounds complicated, but when Shakespeare does it well the whole process looks and feels natural. *King Lear* is about fathers and their children. King Lear is the parent in the main plot; his subplot counterpart is Gloucester. In the main plot, Lear has three daughters: Regan, Goneril, and Cordelia. Gloucester, in contrast, has two sons: Edgar and Edmund. The opening scene weave in *Lear* does a remarkable job of showing us how Cordelia (Lear's youngest daughter) and Edmund (Gloucester's younger, illegitimate son) are different, both by contrasting their actions to one another (and to Regan and Cordelia's), and by defining Cordelia and Edmund's situations in ways that make it clear which choices they can choose to make, and what each of those choices means. It's really pretty neat.

Let's start with the first scene (I.i) in *King Lear*. In it, Gloucester sets up a potentially embarrassing situation for his bastard son, Edmund, by explaining the details of his (Edmund's) conception to another character, Kent.

> KENT
> Is not this your son, my lord?
> GLOUCESTER
> His breeding, sir, hath been at my charge. I have
> so often blushed to acknowledge him that now I am
> brazed to it.
> KENT
> I cannot conceive you.
> GLOUCESTER
> Sir, this young fellow's mother could, whereupon
> she grew round-wombed and had, indeed sir, a son
> for her cradle ere she had a husband for her bed.
> Do you smell a fault?
> KENT
> I cannot wish the fault undone, the issue of it
> being so proper.
> GLOUCESTER
> But I have, sir, a son by order of law, some year

elder than this, who yet is no dearer in my account. Though this knave came something saucily into the world before he was sent for, yet was his mother fair. There was good sport at his making, and the whoreson must be acknowledged. Do you know this noble gentleman, Edmund?
EDMUND
No, my lord.
GLOUCESTER
My lord of Kent. Remember him hereafter as my honorable friend.
EDMUND
My services to your lordship.
KENT
I must love you, and sue to know you better.
EDMUND
Sir, I shall study deserving. (9–32)

To recap: Gloucester, with minimal prompting, tells Kent that he loves both his sons, Edgar and Edmund, equally—even though he's embarrassed to acknowledge that Edmund is actually his son. He also mentions how much fun he had conceiving Edmund ("there was good sport at his making," Gloucester says, as Edmund stands quietly by). In the face of this awkwardness, Edmund gives short, polite answers.

And then we shift to the main plot. Lear, like Gloucester, has created a difficult situation for his children: he's abdicating the throne, and dividing his kingdom among his three daughters. But there's a catch: in order to claim their piece of Lear's kingdom, each of Lear's daughters will have to publicly proclaim how much they love him. What's more, although Lear says that he'll reward each daughter according to the quality of their speech, we learn that Lear has actually pre-divided his kingdom in order to give the best portion to his youngest daughter, Cordelia. They begin:

LEAR
Which of you shall we say doth love us most,
That we our largest bounty may extend
Where nature doth with merit challenge? Goneril,
Our eldest-born, speak first.
GONERIL
Sir, I love you more than words can wield the matter.
Dearer than eyesight, space, and liberty.
Beyond what can be valued, rich or rare.
No less than life, with grace, health, beauty, honor.
As much as child ever loved, or father found,
A love that makes breath poor, and speech unable.
Beyond all manner of so much I love you.
CORDELIA

> [*Aside*] What shall Cordelia do?
> Love, and be silent. (52–63)

Let's pause this for a moment. At Lear's prompting, Goneril makes an ornate speech about her love for Lear. Then, Cordelia's response shows us that we're in for something. Cordelia isn't comfortable with making a speech like Goneril's. Instead, her version of good behavior in the face of enforced awkwardness is something like Edmund's: be silent.

After awarding Goneril her piece of the kingdom, Lear continues to his second daughter, Regan:

> LEAR
> What says our second daughter,
> Our dearest Regan, wife to Cornwall? Speak.
> REGAN
> Sir, I am made
> Of the self-same metal that my sister is
> And prize me at her worth. In my true heart
> I find she names my very deed of love —
> Only she comes too short. That I profess
> Myself an enemy to all other joys,
> Which the most precious square of sense possesses,
> And find I am alone felicitate
> In your dear highness' love.
> CORDELIA
> [*Aside*] Then poor Cordelia!
> And yet not so since, I am sure, my love's
> More richer than my tongue. (68–80)

Again, there's eloquence. Again, Cordelia is uncomfortable with it. We should understand Cordelia's situation well by this point. It's either (a) give Lear the kind of speech he wants—fawning, and elaborate—and feel uncomfortable doing it, or (b) love, and be silent. After Lear awards Regan her share of the kingdom, Cordelia chooses option (b):

> KING LEAR
> Now our joy,
> Although the last, not least.
> […] what can you say to draw
> A third more opulent than your sisters? Speak.
> CORDELIA
> Nothing, my lord.
> KING LEAR
> Nothing!
> CORDELIA
> Nothing.
> KING LEAR

Nothing will come of nothing. Speak again.
CORDELIA
Unhappy that I am, I cannot heave
My heart into my mouth. I love your majesty
According to my bond, nor more nor less. (84–95)

The choices available to Cordelia are pretty clear. Edmund's response to his father—simple, short, polite answers—is one form of polite speaking available to *King Lear*'s world's children. And so when Lear becomes enraged, we understand that he's not angry because Cordelia's behavior is unprecedented. Good manners in *King Lear* don't always look like flowery speeches. Instead, we understand that Lear is angry because Cordelia's behavior, while dutiful, ran contrary to Lear's specific expectations.

Shakespeare brings this point home by building a Kent/Lear web, in which each character responds differently to Cordelia's speech:

KENT
What wilt thou do, old man?
Thinkest thou that duty shall have dread to speak
When power to flattery bows? To plainness honor's bound
When majesty stoops to folly. Reverse thy doom
And, in thy best consideration, check
This hideous rashness. Answer my life my judgment:
Thy youngest daughter does not love thee least,
Nor are those empty-hearted whose low sound
Reverbs no hollowness. (152–60)

Here, Kent reiterates a distinction between the two types of speech that we've already seen. There's plainness (from Cordelia and Edmund) and flattery (from Goneril and Regan). The difference between them is that plainness is the language of duty—of authenticity, in other words. When Cordelia tells Lear that she loves him no more, and no less, than her bond, she speaks with an unpretentious honesty that Lear ought to appreciate.

But Lear's not having it. He exiles Kent:

KING LEAR
Kent, on thy life, no more.
KENT
My life I never held but as a pawn
To wage against thy enemies. Nor fear to lose it,
Thy safety being the motive.
KING LEAR
Out of my sight!
[…]
Five days we do allot thee, for provision
To shield thee from diseases of the world,
And on the sixth to turn thy hated back

Upon our kingdom. If, on the tenth day following,
Thy banished trunk be found in our dominions,
The moment is thy death. Away! by Jupiter,
This shall not be revoked. (161–90)

Lear also disinherits and exiles Cordelia.

This first scene weave tells us a lot about the choices available to Cordelia. Flattery is possible in the world of *King Lear*, but Cordelia's plainness is also a model for good behavior. We've already seen, in the exchange between Gloucester, Kent, and Edmund, that children whose parents put them in awkward situations can be well served by saying very little.

This scene (I.i) concludes with a few other nice pieces of context. First, the king of France (who values Cordelia's unpretentious plainness) decides to marry her. This tells us that people other than Kent value her choice to speak plainly.

Second, Regan and Goneril note that, although Lear has always been temperamental, his mood swings are getting worse:

REGAN
It is the infirmity of his age. Yet he hath ever
but slenderly known himself.
GONERIL
The best and soundest of his time hath been but
rash. Then must we look to receive from his age,
not alone the imperfections of long-engraffed
condition, but therewithal the unruly waywardness
that infirm and choleric years bring with them.
REGAN
Such unconstant starts are we like to have from
him as this of Kent's banishment. (315–23)

This passage tells us that Lear's banishing Kent also reads as patently unreasonable. The takeaway from this scene, in other words, is that Lear is completely out of line. Flattery might win Regan and Goneril pieces of Lear's kingdom, but it doesn't win any moral high ground. In fact, Lear seems to be the only character who values flattery over plain speech.

The next scene, I.ii, tells us something about Edmund. Despite his plain speaking, it turns out that he's upset about his lot as Gloucester's bastard son and plans to steal his legitimate brother, Edgar's, inheritance:

EDMUND
Thou, nature, art my goddess. To thy law
My services are bound. Wherefore should I
Stand in the plague of custom, and permit
The curiosity of nations to deprive me,
For that I am some twelve or fourteen moon-shines
Lag of a brother? Why bastard? Wherefore base?

When my dimensions are as well compact,
My mind as generous, and my shape as true,
As honest madam's issue?
[...] Well then,
Legitimate Edgar, I must have your land.
Our father's love is to the bastard Edmund
As to the legitimate. Fine word—legitimate!
Well, my legitimate, if this letter speed
And my invention thrive, Edmund the base
Shall top the legitimate. I grow! I prosper!
Now, gods, stand up for bastards! (1–23)

Immediately after this, Edmund uses a complicated plot, involving a forged letter, to convince Gloucester that Edgar (Edmund's brother) intends to murder him (Gloucester) in order to come into his inheritance early.

The parallels between Edmund and Cordelia, Regan, and Goneril's situation ought to be clear. Each one of these characters has the opportunity to inherit land from their father. Three of the four—that is, Regan, Goneril, and Edmund—decide to do this by attacking their fathers' weaknesses. Among the play's children, only Cordelia (and later, Edmund's legitimate brother, Edgar) choose to protect their aging fathers rather than exploiting them for personal gain. The early scene weave in *King Lear*, which lays out a crucial distinction between flattery and plain speech, gives us an early read of each of these characters; Regan and Goneril could have chosen to give a plain speech response to Lear's prompting. We know that because we've already seen plain speech from Edmund. Cordelia could have chosen to flatter Lear instead of speaking honestly. We know that because we've seen Regan and Goneril flatter Lear and get away with it.

And we know what good behavior in *King Lear* looks like, too. When Gloucester embarrasses Edmund in front of Kent, Edmund's response—plain speech rather than elaborate, long-winded tropes about how much he loves Gloucester—tell us which kinds of behavior read as honest and trustworthy. Plain speech is prized by everybody except Lear; the people around Lear—Kent, Gloucester, and Regan, Cordelia, and Goneril—indulge Lear's taste for flattery for their own political advantage. We learn all of this in the first 1,500 words of the play—the first five minutes—not because of what happens in any individual scene, but because of how each scene relates to the others.

King Lear's scene weave doesn't stop there. Later, after both Gloucester and Lear chase away their good children (Edgar and Cordelia), their good children return to help each of their fathers to a revelation. These revelations occur in scenes that immediately follow one another, so that they can be more easily contrasted. Gloucester, who has been blinded and attempted suicide, learns that he needs to trust that his life still has value:

GLOUCESTER
You ever-gentle gods, take my breath from me.

Let not my worser spirit tempt me again
To die before you please! (IV.vi.238–40)

On being reunited with Cordelia, Lear's revelation is simpler:

LEAR
Pray you now, forget and forgive. I am old and foolish. (IV.vii.97)

Each of these characters, in other words, learns their own kind of humility: Their judgment is fallible. But the juxtaposition of these revelations also highlights some subtle differences between them. Lear sees his past behavior as an offense against other people, while Gloucester sees his past behavior as an offense against metaphysical forces—fate, the gods, or some divine plan. That's a distinction you might miss if Lear and Gloucester's revelations weren't placed right beside each other.

Let's try one more of Shakespeare's scene weaves. This one's from *Hamlet* I.ii. In it, both Laertes and Hamlet appear before King Claudius. The reason? Both of them want to leave Denmark. Before either of them approach Claudius, however, we get a chance to see how things ought to operate in the throne room. Claudius opens with a speech about Old Hamlet's death and Fortinbras's immanent invasion of Denmark, and lays out a plan to convince Fortinbras's uncle, Old Norway, to squelch Fortinbras's invasion. This relies on two ambassadors, Cornelius and Voltimand, who will negotiate some settlement with Norway. It's a long, measured, speech, and so I've cut to the end, where Claudius tells everybody what Cornelius and Voltimand ought to do:

KING CLAUDIUS
Now for ourself, and for this time of meeting,
Thus much the business is: we have here writ
To Norway, uncle of young Fortinbras —
Who, impotent and bed-rid, scarcely hears
Of this his nephew's purpose—to suppress
His further gait herein, in that the levies,
The lists and full proportions, are all made
Out of his subject. And we here dispatch
You, good Cornelius, and you, Voltimand,
For bearers of this greeting to old Norway,
Giving to you no further personal power
To business with the king more than the scope
Of these delated articles allow.
Farewell, and let your haste commend your duty.
CORNELIUS & VOLTIMAND
In that and all things will we show our duty. (26–40)

Just like the opening scene in *King Lear*, this scene lays out a set of expectations. Good behavior in front of Claudius means letting him make his speech, and then indicating that you will do whatever it is he wants you to do.

So now it's time for Laertes and Hamlet to approach King Claudius. Laertes goes first:

> KING CLAUDIUS
> And now, Laertes, what's the news with you?
> You told us of some suit. What is it, Laertes?
> You cannot speak of reason to the Dane
> And lose your voice. What wouldst thou beg, Laertes,
> That shall not be my offer, not thy asking?
> The head is not more native to the heart,
> The hand more instrumental to the mouth,
> Than is the throne of Denmark to thy father.
> What wouldst thou have, Laertes?
> LAERTES
> My dread lord,
> Your leave and favor to return to France
> From whence, though willingly I came to Denmark
> To show my duty in your coronation,
> Yet now, I must confess, that duty done,
> My thoughts and wishes bend again toward France
> And bow them to your gracious leave and pardon.
> KING CLAUDIUS
> Have you your father's leave? What says Polonius?
> LORD POLONIUS
> He hath, my lord, wrung from me my slow leave
> By laborsome petition and, at last,
> Upon his will, I sealed my hard consent.
> I do beseech you, give him leave to go.
> KING CLAUDIUS
> Take thy fair hour, Laertes. Time be thine,
> And thy best graces spend it at thy will! (42–64)

We've looked at this moment before, and seen how it introduces Laertes's flaws: he's self-centered enough to think that permission to return to France depends more on his own behavior than on his father's (Polonius's) permission. But this scene also sets up expectations for how a young person ought to address the king. Laertes leads with an honorific—calling Claudius "dread lord"—and, like Cornelius and Voltimand, Laertes gives Claudius plenty of room to speak. Those behaviors aren't flawless, but they are evidence that Laertes is at least trying to comport himself.

Then comes Hamlet:

> KING CLAUDIUS
> But now, my cousin Hamlet, and my son —
> HAMLET
> A little more than kin and less than kind.
> KING CLAUDIUS
> How is it that the clouds still hang on you? (65–67)

Hamlet interrupts Claudius with a snide remark. Because Laertes, Cornelius, and Voltimand have been polite to Claudius, and that this politeness has passed without comment, we know that it isn't common practice to interrupt the king.

Claudius's method for dealing with Laertes was to involve Laertes's parent, Polonius. Here, Hamlet's parent Gertrude gets involved, but not at Claudius's request.

> HAMLET
> Not so, my lord. I am too much in the sun.
> QUEEN GERTRUDE
> Good Hamlet, cast thy nighted color off
> And let thine eye look like a friend on Denmark.
> Do not for ever with thy vailed lids
> Seek for thy noble father in the dust.
> Thou knowest it is common: All that lives must die,
> Passing through nature to eternity.
> HAMLET
> Ay, madam, it is common.
> QUEEN GERTRUDE
> If it be,
> Why seems it so particular with thee?
> HAMLET
> "Seems," madam! Nay, it is! I know not "seems."
> It is not alone my inky cloak, good mother,
> Nor customary suits of solemn black,
> Nor windy suspiration of forced breath,
> No, nor the fruitful river in the eye,
> Nor the dejected behavior of the visage,
> Together with all forms, moods, shapes of grief,
> That can denote me truly. These indeed "seem,"
> For they are actions that a man might play,
> But I have that within which passeth show,
> These but the trappings and the suits of woe. (68–86)

The juxtaposition between Laertes and Hamlet's scenes makes something clear: Claudius is not in control of the relationship between Hamlet and Gertrude in the same way that he's in control of the relationship between Laertes and Polonius. Those two—like Cornelius and Voltimand—know their cues. But once Hamlet and Gertrude get into it, there's not much room for Claudius. The juxtaposition of the conversations between Claudius's subjects (Cornelius, Voltimand, Laertes) and his family (Gertrude and Hamlet) highlights the differences between them.

This contrast serves a writerly purpose. As we've seen in this chapter, scene weave uses logical implication—similarities and differences—to economically illustrate relationships. Sometimes, scene weaves illustrate how one set of character relationships is different from another. Sometimes, they show us how things have (or haven't) changed. When scene weave is well done, we hardly notice that it's happening at all.

The same is true for another of Shakespeare's storytelling tools, and the subject of our next section: symbols.

5.2 Symbols

Maybe no storytelling tool is as maligned as the symbol. Symbols represent everything many of us learned to hate about our high school literature classes, because an uninspired approach to them—one that doesn't understand what symbols actually do—turns a good story into a boring riddle.

So let's start with what symbols do. Witness Stephen King: "Symbolism," he writes, "exists to adorn and enrich, not to create a sense of artificial profundity" (2002, p. 200).

I'll say it in my own words: symbols aren't in a story to make you think. Instead, symbols help an audience understand relationships between characters.

How they do this is a little complicated—but not so complicated that you need a PhD in literature to understand it. In Shakespearean storytelling, symbols have two basic qualities. The first is that they represent some abstract idea. Maybe, for instance, they represent a way of dealing with problems: confronting the problem directly, or confronting it with deception and treachery.

The second quality of symbols is that they have some relationship to a character. Whether a character likes or dislikes a symbol—whether they pick up a book or throw it away—tells the audience about that character's attitude toward the abstractions, or to the values, that the symbol represents.

Shakespeare's symbols often share a third quality, too: Shakespeare arranges symbols in webs, the same way that he arranges characters. Very often, symbols will be introduced together, so that each symbol helps define and clarify the meanings of the others.

Here's an example: In *Hamlet*, both swords and poison are symbols. Swords represent loyalty, knowledge, and duty. People who use swords deal with conflict openly and directly. Poison, on the other hand, represents deceit, treachery, and manipulation. People who use poison deal with conflict surreptitiously, and by protecting themselves with elaborate plans.

In *Hamlet*, swords and their values are good. Poison, and its values, are evil. How characters react to each of these weapons—or, if you prefer, "methods of confrontation and problem solving"—tells us who they are.

These symbols help an audience understand *Hamlet*'s characters. For instance: Hamlet and Laertes have a lot in common. Both plan to avenge their fathers' murders, and do so using a combination of deception and direct violence. Each of them ultimately kills their father's murderer.

Because of that, it might seem like Hamlet and Laertes live according to similar values and that their ways of thinking and acting are, morally speaking, equally legitimate. Arguing that one of them is more right than the other is like arguing that Coke tastes better than Pepsi. So Shakespeare uses symbols to clarify the issue. Let's see how.

First, Shakespeare uses Hamlet's encounter with the ghost (in I.v) to invest each symbol—that is, poison and swords—with a set of values. Poison comes first, as the ghost tells the story of his murder to Hamlet:

> GHOST
> [...] Now, Hamlet, hear:
> It is given out that, sleeping in my orchard,
> A serpent stung me, so the whole ear of Denmark
> Is by a forged process of my death
> Rankly abused. But know, thou noble youth,
> The serpent that did sting thy father's life
> Now wears his crown. (34–40)

The ghost tells us that he's about to unfold a story of *deception*. Whatever the details of this story are about to be, the values that inform it are pretty clear. As the ghost's speech continues, he fills in the details:

> Ay, that incestuous, that adulterate beast,
> With witchcraft of his wit, with traitorous gifts —
> O wicked wit and gifts, that have the power
> So to seduce—won to his shameful lust
> The will of my most seeming-virtuous queen.
> O Hamlet, what a falling-off was there!
> From me, whose love was of that dignity
> That it went hand in hand even with the vow
> I made to her in marriage, and to decline
> Upon a wretch whose natural gifts were poor
> To those of mine!
> But virtue, as it never will be moved,
> Though lewdness court it in a shape of heaven,
> So lust, though to a radiant angel linked,
> Will sate itself in a celestial bed,
> And prey on garbage. (41–57)

In case you missed it, the ghost tells us that deception leads to corruption—both of values and of people. The ghost uses words like *adulterate, witchcraft, shame,* and *treason*.

This is the first inkling that *Hamlet* exists in a specific kind of moral universe. In some kinds of stories—heists and capers, for instance—deception is good. The heroes are the ones who trick banks and casinos out of their ill-gotten riches. A character in another play of this same period—Ben Jonson's *Bartholomew Fair* (1614) or *The Alchemist* (1610)—might well congratulate Claudius on tricking Old Hamlet out of his crown and his wife.

But that's not what we get here. The ghost spends a few more lines driving his point home:

Sleeping within my orchard —
My custom always of the afternoon —
Upon my secure hour thy uncle stole,
With juice of cursed hebenon in a vial,
And in the porches of my ears did pour
The leperous distilment, whose effect
Holds such an enmity with blood of man
That swift as quicksilver it courses through
The natural gates and alleys of the body,
And with a sudden vigour doth posset
And curd, like eager droppings into milk,
The thin and wholesome blood. So did it mine.
And a most instant tetter barked about,
Most lazar-like, with vile and loathsome crust,
All my smooth body.
[…]
O, horrible! O, horrible! Most horrible!
If thou hast nature in thee, bear it not.
Let not the royal bed of Denmark be
A couch for luxury and damned incest. (59–83)

In no particular order, the ghost associates poison (the "juice of cursed hebenon") with deception and corruption (and adultery, shame, and treason), along with images of curdling milk and crusty lepers, and with taboos like incest. Poison-style deception isn't just bad. It's physically, spiritually, and conceptually repulsive.

Immediately after the ghost relates the story of its murder to Hamlet (and still in I.v), Hamlet swears his friends and fellow ghost-witnesses to secrecy. This is where Shakespeare introduces a countersymbol: the sword.

Here's how he does it. First, Hamlet asks Horatio and Marcellus to take an oath:

> HAMLET
> For your desire to know what is between us [that is, Hamlet and the ghost]
> Overmaster it as you may. And now, good friends,
> As you are friends, scholars, and soldiers,
> Give me one poor request.
> HORATIO
> What is it, my lord? We will.
> HAMLET
> Never make known what you have seen tonight.
> HORATIO & MARCELLUS
> My lord, we will not.
> HAMLET
> Nay, but swear it.
> HORATIO
> In faith,
> My lord, not I.

MARCELLUS
Nor I, my lord, in faith. (139–47)

What values are implicit here? Hamlet asks Horatio and Marcellus to take an oath as they are "friends, scholars, and soldiers." The values that these relationships represent—something like loyalty, knowledge, and duty—will come to oppose the values represented by Claudius's poison: deception, corruption, and treason. While this passage is barren of imagery—there's no curdling milk or leprous scabs—both Marcellus and Horatio use the word "faith" in affirming Hamlet's oath. It's a rare instance of clear-cut decency.

Now that we understand the values at work in Hamlet's oath, Shakespeare associates those values with the sword. He does this through the simple expedient of having Hamlet insist that Horatio and Marcellus swear their oaths on a sword—even though, as Marcellus points out, they've already sworn the oath once:

HAMLET
Upon my sword.
MARCELLUS
We have sworn, my lord, already.
HAMLET
Indeed, upon my sword, indeed.

And, just to give the whole thing a stamp of metaphysical approval, the ghost joins in:

GHOST
Swear. (147–49)

We get it. The oath, and that it gets sworn on the sword, are both important. But, in case we missed the point, Hamlet and the ghost keep badgering Horatio and Marcellus to swear their oaths on the sword:

HAMLET
[...] Come on—you hear this fellow [...]
Consent to swear.
HORATIO
Propose the oath, my lord.
HAMLET
Never to speak of this that you have seen.
Swear by my sword.
GHOST
Swear.
HAMLET
Hic et ubique? Then we'll shift our ground.
Come hither gentlemen,

And lay your hands again upon my sword.
Never to speak of this that you have heard,
Swear by my sword.
GHOST
Swear. (151–61)

You'd think that would be enough, but Shakespeare really, really wants to make sure we understand what the sword represents, and so he has everyone—Hamlet, the ghost, Marcellus, and Horatio—repeat the cycle one more time:

HORATIO
O day and night, but this is wondrous strange!
HAMLET
And therefore as a stranger give it welcome.
There are more things in heaven and earth, Horatio,
Than are dreamt of in your philosophy. (164–67)

This time, though, Shakespeare spells out exactly how we should read what Hamlet decides to do next:

HAMLET
But come
Here, as before: never, so help you mercy,
How strange or odd so ever I bear myself —
As I perchance hereafter shall think meet
To put an antic disposition on —
That you, at such times seeing me, never shall
With arms encumbered thus, or this headshake,
Or by pronouncing of some doubtful phrase,
As, "Well, well, we know" or, "We could, an if we would,"
Or, "If we list to speak" or, "There be, an if they might,"
Or such ambiguous giving out, to note
That you know aught of me. This not to do,
So grace and mercy at your most need help you, swear.
GHOST
Swear.
HAMLET
Rest, rest, perturbed spirit!
They swear (164–81)

In case you missed it: Hamlet, Marcellus, and Horatio (and presumably the ghost) are fighting for a set of values: loyalty, knowledge, and duty. Hamlet is about to start doing things that might appear to run counter to those values—like acting "odd," or feigning an "antic disposition." At this moment, we're given to understand that Hamlet and his confederates agree that this is a legitimate course of action—that is, that Hamlet's actions are in line with the values of loyalty, knowledge, and duty that the sword represents.

What we get out of I.v., in other words, are two sets of values. One set—the Values of Poison—involves deception, treachery, corruption, and treason. In case these things weren't self-evidently bad, they're associated with curdling milk, leprosy, and incest. The other set of values—the Values of the Sword—involve loyalty, knowledge, and duty, and are associated with faith and friendship.

You might be thinking that Shakespeare goes to an awful lot of effort to draw this line. After all: do we really need to be told that dishonesty and murder are bad, and that friendship, loyalty, and duty are good? Does *Hamlet* really need to establish a complex moral iconography in order for the audience to tell the good people from the bad ones?

Yes. *Hamlet* is set in a complex moral universe. Characters who are supposed to be morally in the right do many of the same things as the characters who are supposed to be morally in the wrong. For instance, both Claudius and Hamlet kill the rightfully elected king of Denmark. Maintaining that Claudius's murder was wrong while Hamlet's was right is not intellectually trivial.

Likewise, *Hamlet*'s nominally good characters—like Hamlet—do some genuinely awful things. For instance, Hamlet's plan to avenge his father's death involves him making Ophelia feel responsible for his (feigned) insanity. Also, Hamlet murders Ophelia's father, Polonius. These, in combination, drive Ophelia first into insanity and then to suicide. It's not a good look.

Fortunately, Shakespeare's symbols lend *Hamlet* a sense of moral clarity. One good example of how they do this is in IV.vii, when Claudius and Laertes join forces to plot against Hamlet. In the lead-up to this scene, Laertes has left Denmark for France, only to learn that his father (Polonius) has been murdered. Laertes returns to Denmark and raises a makeshift army, intending to remove Claudius from the throne. But Claudius, ever the sly one, convinces Laertes that Polonius's death is Hamlet's fault. Here's how their plan unfolds:

> KING CLAUDIUS
> Laertes, was your father dear to you?
> Or are you like the painting of a sorrow,
> A face without a heart?
> LAERTES
> Why ask you this?
> KING CLAUDIUS
> Not that I think you did not love your father,
> But that I know love is begun by time
> And that I see, in passages of proof,
> Time qualifies the spark and fire of it.
> […]
> Hamlet comes back. What would you undertake
> To show yourself your father's son in deed
> More than in words?
> LAERTES

To cut his throat in the church.
KING CLAUDIUS
No place, indeed, should murder sanctuarize.
Revenge should have no bounds. But, good Laertes,
Will you do this, keep close within your chamber.
Hamlet returned shall know you are come home.
We'll put on those shall praise your excellence
And set a double varnish on the fame
The Frenchman gave you, bring you in fine together
And wager on your heads. He, being remiss,
Most generous and free from all contriving,
Will not peruse the foils so that, with ease,
Or with a little shuffling, you may choose
A sword unbated, and in a pass of practice
Requite him for your father. (107–39)

Claudius's plot involves a fencing match in which Laertes will have a real sword and Hamlet will have a standard, harmless, fencing foil. The reason for this plot, according to Claudius, is to make Hamlet's death look like an accident.[2]

But Laertes's moral standing is harder to divine. *Hamlet* is full of sons avenging their murdered fathers, and so Laertes's deciding to kill Hamlet hardly seems out of bounds. And while Laertes might engage in a bit of deception to carry out his revenge, Hamlet's been doing more than a little deceiving himself. Furthermore, Hamlet has to this point been whining, violent, and self-indulgent—indifferent to other people's feelings, and outright abusive toward Ophelia.

So are we supposed to read Laertes as a sort of anti-Hamlet—as a character who has just as much right to his revenge as Hamlet has to his own? Is Laertes a better-behaved Hamlet—actually the hero? Or are we supposed to see Laertes's plotting as somehow worse than Hamlet's, and Laertes himself as doing something wrong?

Shakespeare turns his symbols loose to help us figure it out.

LAERTES
I will do it
And, for that purpose, I'll anoint my sword.
I bought an unction of a mountebank
So mortal that, but dip a knife in it,
Where it draws blood no cataplasm so rare,
Collected from all simples that have virtue
Under the moon, can save the thing from death
That is but scratched withal. I'll touch my point
With this contagion, that, if I gall him slightly,

---

[2] In Claudius's words: "And for his death no wind of blame shall breathe, / But even his mother shall uncharge the practice / And call it accident."

It may be death. (139–48)

There we go. Up until this point, Laertes and Claudius shared a common interest: killing Hamlet. But by volunteering to poison Hamlet, instead of fighting him (un)fairly, Laertes has shown us that he and Claudius share common values, too. Had Shakespeare not gone to such pains to tell us what poison means, Laertes's willingness to poison Hamlet might read as straightforward practicality. But since Shakespeare has spilled a lot of ink associating poison with all sorts of political, spiritual, and physical corruption, we immediately read this scene differently: Laertes is corrupt. He might have entered this scene morally in the right, but at this moment he is in the wrong.

Claudius drives this point home with an elaboration on their plot:

> KING CLAUDIUS
> Let's further think of this.
> Weigh what convenience both of time and means
> May fit us to our shape if this should fail,
> And that our drift look through our bad performance,
> It were better not assayed. Therefore this project
> Should have a back, or second, that might hold
> If this should blast in proof. Soft! Let me see.
> We'll make a solemn wager on your cunnings. I have it:
> When in your motion you are hot and dry —
> As make your bouts more violent to that end —
> And that he calls for drink, I'll have prepared him
> A chalice for the nonce whereon but sipping,
> If he by chance escape your venomed stuck,
> Our purpose may hold there. (148–62)

Again, in case we missed it: Shakespeare reminds us that Claudius is a poisoner, and gives us a moment to remember what poison means in the context of *Hamlet*. Never mind that Claudius and Laertes's plot has crossed an invisible line that separates "making Hamlet's death look like an accident" from "making Hamlet's death look as suspicious as possible." This scene is meant to show us that Laertes—who, at the beginning of this play, was a decent if self-centered young man—has become a villain. His plot to avenge his father's death doesn't have the moral legitimacy of Hamlet's plot to avenge his.

That's not because the facts of their two cases differ, or because Old Hamlet is more deserving of vengeance than Polonius, but because of a purely connotative piece of symbol work. Had Laertes challenged Hamlet to a duel, rather than poisoning his foil, we would be more inclined to read him as Hamlet's moral peer. But the weight that Shakespeare puts on poison—the heavy load of values and connotations he piles on to it with the ghost's speech in I.v—makes Laertes's resort to poisoning Hamlet look more like a piece of evil than a piece of expedient heroism.

Shakespeare uses symbols only rarely. There's no Shakespearean play that doesn't use conflict, character webs, scene weave, or moral vision in service of its storytelling. But not every play uses symbols. *Hamlet*, as a complex and sometimes subtle piece of storytelling, uses them constantly. We've already seen the ways that swords and poison represent a mutually defining set of complex competing values, but there are also moments where it uses symbols more economically.

Consider one of the most famous symbols: the skull. In the scene that features it—or really them, since there are several—Hamlet and Horatio cross paths with two gravediggers, and their different responses to skulls help build a simple character web. Each character responds to the skull differently, and this tells us how each character is different from the others. Here's V.i:

> FIRST CLOWN (GRAVEDIGGER)
> *He digs and sings*
> In youth, when I did love, did love,
> Methought it was very sweet,
> To contract, O, the time, for, ah, my behove,
> O, methought, there was nothing meet.
> HAMLET
> Has this fellow no feeling of his business, that he
> sings at grave-making?
> HORATIO
> Custom hath made it in him a property of easiness. (59–63)

There's our first piece of symbol-driven character webbing. It's quick—blink, and you'll miss it—but it gets the job done. We haven't seen the skull yet, but Hamlet and Horatio's exchange frames this scene. It's about death. That might seem obvious, but it's only that way because Shakespeare makes it so. If Hamlet had said something like "wow, that guy can really dig," or "amazing that he can work so hard when it's so hot out," the scene would be about something more like work ethic or perseverance.

> FIRST CLOWN
> [*Sings*]
> But age, with his stealing steps,
> Hath clawed me in his clutch,
> And hath shipped me intil the land,
> As if I had never been such.
> *Throws up a skull*
> HAMLET
> That skull had a tongue in it and could sing, once.
> How the knave jowls it to the ground, as if it were
> Cain's jaw-bone that did the first murder! It
> might be the pate of a politician—which this ass
> now over-reaches—one that would circumvent God,
> might it not?

> HORATIO
> It might, my lord. (66–76)

There's our next piece of character webbing. The gravedigger, who sings as he tosses a skull out of the grave he's digging, is indifferent to death. Hamlet, on the other hand, is sensitive to it—not necessarily in the sense that he feels, but in the sense that the reality of death prompts him to reflect on the state of human beings vis-à-vis their inevitable mortality.

They continue:

> HAMLET
> Or of a courtier, which could say "Good morrow,
> sweet lord! How dost thou, good lord?" This might
> be my Lord Such-a-one that praised my Lord
> Such-a-one's horse when he meant to beg it, might it not?
> HORATIO
> Ay, my lord.
> HAMLET
> Why, even so. And now my Lady Worm's: chapless, and
> knocked about the mazzard with a sexton's spade.
> Here's fine revolution, if we had the trick to
> see it. Did these bones cost no more the breeding
> but to play at loggats with them? Mine ache to think on it. (77–86)

We get the idea. In response to the skull, the gravedigger keeps digging, but Hamlet is prompted to draw conclusions about the meaning of life, and inevitably concludes that, no matter how a person lives, they all come to the same end:

> HAMLET
> Alexander died, Alexander was buried,
> Alexander returneth into dust. The dust is earth. Of
> earth we make loam. And why of that loam, whereto he
> was converted, might they not stop a beer-barrel?
> Imperious Caesar, dead and turned to clay,
> Might stop a hole to keep the wind away.
> O that that earth, which kept the world in awe,
> Should patch a wall to expel the winter flaw! (195–202)

For our purposes, the conclusion that Hamlet comes to is less important than the fact that he comes to a conclusion while other characters do not. Despite everything that's happened to Hamlet—a visit from his father's ghost, his murder of Polonius, and being kidnapped by pirates—he remains thoughtful in ways that complicate the otherwise simple task of avenging his father's death. The gravedigger's indifference to each skull he throws out of the grave, and Horatio's habit of marking Hamlet's thoughts without adding any of his own, remind us that this thoughtful quality of Hamlet's makes him unique among the play's characters.

Symbols, whether deployed in isolation (like the skull) or set up in webs (like swords and poison) are comparatively uncommon in Shakespeare's storytelling. Not every play has them. But many do. You can spot some of them by looking for moments, usually early in a play, where characters attach values to simple concepts or objects by explaining what they mean at length. The ghost in *Hamlet* goes on about poison in the same way that Antonio and Shylock go on about the pound of flesh (and the moral standing of interest-bearing bonds) in *The Merchant of Venice*, or the way that Macbeth goes on about daggers.

You can spot other symbols by looking at the ways that different characters react differently to the same physical object, presence, or phenomenon on stage. The gold chain in *The Comedy of Errors*, and the storms in *The Tempest* and *King Lear*, and the weddings, proposals, and other matchmaking spectacles that end *Much Ado About Nothing*, *As You Like It*, *All's Well That Ends Well*, *Measure for Measure*, and a half-dozen others, tell us about how characters are different from one another, and punctuate the ways they've changed since their stories began in Act I.

There is one final matter. Symbols don't need to be inanimate objects. Characters can be symbols, as can non-objects like England or Rome. In *Hamlet*, both Old Hamlet and Claudius are fully realized characters (meaning that they have their own motivations, goals, and flaws), but also represent different ways of thinking and acting. Old Hamlet is a swords kind of guy, while Claudius is more like poison. Lavinia (in *Titus Andronicus*) also acts as a symbol, as do characters like Nell (in *The Comedy of Errors*). Very often, characters who are also symbols end up implicated in the ethics of a piece of storytelling, or the baseline statement that Shakespeare's plays make about how people ought to behave toward one another. That concept, moral vision, is the subject of our next section.

5.3 Moral Vision

Stories aren't just entertainment. A piece of storytelling follows its characters as they pursue their motivations, and tells us something about how they change—or fail to change—in order to be seen as good sons, mothers, fathers, friends, or lovers. In the process, it tells us something about the hows and whys of human life. We have to change in order to become whoever our world needs us to be.

We've discussed the five steps of Shakespeare's stories at length by now, so we know that each of Shakespeare's characters begins their story with flaws (ways that they hurt themselves and other people), and that most of Shakespeare's characters have revelations. That is, characters learn how they ought to behave toward other people—maybe, for instance, they need to become more authentic, honest, and vulnerable—and so they change.

Very often, a piece of Shakespeare's storytelling involves several characters changing. In *Hamlet*, for instance, at least Hamlet and Laertes complete their revelations in Act V. In the ensemble-style Romantic Comedies, like *Much Ado About Nothing* and *A Midsummer Night's Dream* (each of which bring together several romantic couples), every character who ends up in a relationship needs to become more authentic, honest, and vulnerable in order to get there. No character begins their story flawless.

In a piece of storytelling where several characters change, they usually change in coordinated ways. These changes converge on an abstract position about how people ought to behave toward one another. I like to call this abstract statement a *moral vision*.

Moral visions aren't original to Shakespeare. The immediate ancestors of Shakespeare's plays, the so-called Morality Plays, were built around heavy-handed statements about what it meant to be a good Christian. Everyman, Mankind, and their compatriots unfailingly learned lessons about faith and piety that directly translated into lessons about how real human beings in the real (off-stage) world ought to live.

Shakespeare, however, advanced two changes to the idea of moral vision that later writers have largely adopted.

The first change is that Shakespeare's moral visions are each restricted to the world of their play. Some plays seem to present sound advice for real human beings in the real world. For instance, real people in real relationships are often well-served by being authentic, honest, and vulnerable.

Others, not so much. The moral vision of *Hamlet*, for instance, is something like "it is morally necessary, and perfectly reasonable, to kill bad people." While this idea might be on the right side of some abstract moral line, you'd be on the wrong side of more clearly drawn lines if you started killing bad people yourself.

The second change: Shakespeare's moral visions concern how people ought to behave toward other people. In some kinds of storytelling, like Morality Plays, characters discover that they need to get right with God. In others, characters learn that nature will get them if they monkey around with the Wrong Kinds of Science (like in 1954's *Godzilla*, or countless remakes-in-spirit where pollution, global warming, or forbidden science unleash city-destroying catastrophes). But Shakespeare is all about people. Their morality is entirely defined by how they act toward one another.

Much—but not all—modern storytelling follows Shakespeare's lead. Any amount of playgoing, reading, or movie watching will lead you to moral visions like these:

> *It's a Wonderful Life* (1946): Wealth isn't defined by money; instead, it's defined by service to friends and family.
> *The Sting* (1973): It's OK to do bad things to people if that keeps them from doing worse things to other people.

Ulysses (1922): The non-epic struggles of ordinary people are morally and socially significant. In these struggles, victory looks less like an epic journey and more like a quest for human understanding and connection.
Copenhagen (1998): No matter how smart you are, you can only do right by recognizing that we all live in a world of profound moral uncertainty, and by appreciating the consequences of being wrong.
Citizen Kane (1941): A man who tries to force the world to love him will always be alone. You can't form meaningful relationships with other people unless you let them know who you really are and, in the process, risk their criticism or even their rejection.

These moral visions, and countless others, are deeply Shakespearean. To most of us, they are also probably sensible. Is it OK to do something bad in order to keep somebody from doing something worse? Most of us would probably say yes. Even if we didn't, we could probably grant real-world moral legitimacy to people who do. It's easy to do that when Shakespeare (and other storytellers) present moral visions that don't rub us the wrong way.

But Shakespeare's moral visions are sometimes uncomfortable. In *The Taming of the Shrew*, for instance, Petruchio's treatment of Kate is—by modern, real-world standards—criminally abusive. A critical reader might note that Petruchio starves Kate and indulges in a healthy bit of gaslighting, too. Here's IV.v:

> PETRUCHIO
> Good Lord, how bright and goodly shines the moon!
> KATHARINA
> The moon? The sun. It is not moonlight now.
> PETRUCHIO
> I say it is the moon that shines so bright.
> KATHARINA
> I know it is the sun that shines so bright.
> PETRUCHIO
> Now by my mother's son, and that's myself,
> It shall be moon, or star, or what I list,
> Or ere I journey to your father's house.
> Go on and fetch our horses back again.
> Evermore crossed and crossed. Nothing but crossed!
> HORTENSIO
> Say as he says or we shall never go.
> KATHARINA
> Forward, I pray. Since we have come so far,
> If be it moon, or sun, or what you please.
> An if you please to call it a rush-candle,
> Henceforth I vow it shall be so for me.
> PETRUCHIO
> I say it is the moon.
> KATHARINA

I know it is the moon. (2–17)

And once Kate agrees with him, he changes course and insists that it's the sun:

> PETRUCHIO
> Nay, then you lie. It is the blessed sun.
> KATHARINA
> Then, God be blessed, it is the blessed sun.
> But sun it is not when you say it is not,
> And the moon changes, even as your mind.
> What you will have it named—even that it is.
> And so it shall be so for Katharina. (18–23)

If we saw actual human beings in an actual relationship behave this way, we might call the police. But in *Taming*, Petruchio's behavior goes unpunished. What's more, Kate ends the play seeming not to mind it. Here's V.ii:

> KATHARINA
> Such duty as the subject owes the prince
> Even such a woman oweth to her husband.
> And when she is froward, peevish, sullen, sour,
> And not obedient to his honest will,
> What is she but a foul contending rebel
> And graceless traitor to her loving lord?
> I am ashamed that women are so simple
> To offer war where they should kneel for peace,
> Or seek for rule, supremacy, and sway,
> When they are bound to serve, love, and obey. (167–76)

She goes on like this, and concludes by laying her hand beneath her husband's foot—a gesture she thinks demonstrates her duty as a wife.

Kate and Petruchio's relationship isn't comfortable—or good—in any world that I've ever lived in. But it is a good one in the world of *The Taming of the Shrew*, where the moral vision appears to be something like *love works the way it works. If adults want to get weird, let them.*

Thousands of romance novels, along with billion-dollar franchises like *Fifty Shades of Grey* (2012), John Hughes movies, and small-release films like *Secretary* (2002) or *Lars and the Real Girl* (2007) share similar moral visions. That is, they play with similar degrees of divergence from our ordinary understanding of what makes a polite, functional, or legal romantic relationship.

Beyond those are another thousand stories in which action heroes, small-town girls, and docile princesses land their ideal romantic partners as a reward for demonstrating some other quality that—in the world of the story—is considered a virtue. We all (hopefully) understand that real relationships don't work that way. Love, sex, and relationships aren't rewards you get for being kind, rich, smart, or good-looking. But—in the worlds of those stories—that's exactly what happens.

Many of Shakespeare's moral visions get described at the end of the play, usually in statement by a character who's been lucky enough to survive the Act V massacre. Here's Marcus from *Titus Andronicus* V.iii:

> MARCUS
> You sad-faced men, people and sons of Rome,
> By uproar severed like a flight of fowl
> Scattered by winds and high, tempestuous gusts:
> O, let me teach you how to knit again
> This scattered corn into one mutual sheaf,
> These broken limbs again into one body,
> Lest Rome herself be bane unto herself,
> And she whom mighty kingdoms curtsy to,
> Like a forlorn and desperate castaway,
> Do shameful execution on herself. (68–74)

He might as well have said "a house divided cannot stand." That's a fine close to a play where political infighting ends in a pile of bodies. And, like most moral arguments, this one tells us how the characters in the play compare to one another. Lucius gives us a catalog of the characters whose actions have divided Rome:

> LUCIUS
> [...] be it known to you
> That cursed Chiron and Demetrius
> Were they that murdered our emperor's brother,
> And they it were that ravished our sister.
> For their fell faults our brothers were beheaded,
> Our father's tears despised, and basely cozened
> Of that true hand that fought Rome's quarrel out
> And sent her enemies unto the grave.
> [...]
> I am the turned forth, be it known to you,
> That have preserved her welfare in my blood
> And from her bosom took the enemy's point,
> Sheathing the steel in my adventurous body. (97–113)

There it is: good guys and bad guys, laid neatly out. Albany's closing lines (in *King Lear* V.iii) offer a less detailed moral vision:

> The weight of this sad time we must obey:
> Speak what we feel, not what we ought to say. (383–84)

"Speak what we feel, not what we ought to say" is a moral verdict in a play whose troubles began with Lear exiling his closest adviser and his only good daughter for being honest. That verdict divides the play's characters neatly into the good and honest (Cordelia, Edgar, and Kent) and the evil and dishonest (Regan, Goneril, and Edmund).

Hamlet gets a two-parter in its last scene, V.ii. First there's Horatio, who has vowed to tell Hamlet's story:

> Of that I shall have also cause to speak.
> And from his mouth whose voice will draw on more,
> But let this same be presently performed
> Even while men's minds are wild, lest more mischance
> On plots and errors happen. (375–79)

The story Horatio intends to tell is a kind of morality play about the dangers of "mischance on plots and errors"—that is, the misfortunes that come from too much plotting from trickster characters like Claudius. And, just in case we missed the point that Hamlet himself was torn between being a trickster (like Claudius) and a warrior (like Old Hamlet), and ultimately chose the warrior side, Fortinbras stitches it all up for us:

> Let four captains
> Bear Hamlet like a soldier to the stage,
> For he was likely, had he been put on,
> To have proved most royally. And for his passage,
> The soldiers' music and the rites of war
> Speak loudly for him. (380–85)

Done and done. Horatio and Fortinbras divide the world up into those that work through "plots and errors" and those who work "most royally." Hamlet is a soldier (or at least "like a soldier"), even though he's also a career college student who's spent most of his life—really every minute up until Act V—avoiding anything like armed conflict.

It's also worth noting that Fortinbras has never met Hamlet, and therefore doesn't have any sound basis for his judgments about Hamlet's potential as a king. His speech is a kind of mouthpiece for the revelation that the audience was supposed to have about Prince Hamlet—just in case they've made it to the end of the play without having one.

These closing speeches aren't the entirety of each play's moral vision. Instead, a moral vision is built up from the moment a play begins, from the choices that characters make, and the actions that they take, in pursuit of their desires. By creating character webs—that is, by placing characters in similar situations and having them respond differently—Shakespeare lays out a spectrum of possible choices, and the progress of the play tells an audience which choices a character ought to make.

And so, by the end of *Hamlet*, we're left with little doubt about what Hamlet should have done. The world of *Hamlet* doesn't allow him to sit down and negotiate with Claudius, or appeal to higher authorities about his father's murder. His choices are limited to sanity or insanity, and either becoming a warrior or a trickster. While we might wish that he had other choices, or that his world were not so circumscribed, those are the rules of the story.

Points of Review

In this chapter we've looked at some of the tools that Shakespeare uses to build a piece of storytelling. While a story concerns a single character, and that character's progress from motivation to revelation, a piece of storytelling combines several characters' stories in such a way that moments from each character's story highlight and define moments in the others.

Specifically, we've learned about scene weave, symbols, and moral vision. As a piece of storytelling progresses, it gradually expresses a moral vision, or a baseline statement about how characters ought to behave toward one another. As that moral vision becomes clearer, we can see whether the ways a character is changing are likely to help them become who their world needs them to be. Moral vision is specific to a piece of storytelling. Depending on the moral vision of a play, a character who learns to become a better liar might be becoming a better (more prudent) person, or might be wading into a sink of corruption.

Scene weaves and symbols, on the other hand, are principally used to build character webs. Scene weave places significant moments in characters' stories right next to one another so that an audience can compare them. Very often, it shows us characters behaving differently—or making different choices—in response to a similar prompt. For instance: in *Richard III*, we see two commanders (Richard and Henry) preparing for battle. How they treat the people around them, or cope with pre-battle jitters, tells us how they are different from one another. In other plays— like the ensemble Romantic Comedies—characters have their revelations in quick succession. This helps the audience see that, while each character changes a bit differently, they all change in the same direction. While each character begins their story with different flaws, they overcome those flaws by becoming more authentic, honest, and vulnerable.

Symbols also build character webs, but do it a bit differently. If you've taken a literature class before, you probably learned that symbols are tangible objects that represent intangible ideas. While writers think of symbols in lots of different ways, Shakespeare uses them to help us understand how characters' attitudes and values compare to one another, and always does so according to the same basic formula. First, he tells us what a symbol means—usually by having a character explain its meaning at length, and often associating the symbol with all kinds of emotionally loaded images. In *Hamlet*, the ghost talks about poison by associating it with betrayal and—in case we were confused about whether betrayal was OK—he attaches it to images of spoiled milk and leprosy.

Second, Shakespeare has different characters react to a symbol. This tells us whether the character accepts or rejects the values associated with it. When Laertes agrees to poison Hamlet—rather than duel him more-or-less honorably—we understand that Laertes has crossed a significant moral line. His revenge against Hamlet is morally compromised in ways that Hamlet's revenge against Claudius is not.

In the real world, we might not make a distinction between stabbing someone and poisoning them. But in the world of *Hamlet* that distinction is significant. While Laertes and Hamlet seem to have a great deal in common, in the specific sense that they both feel compelled to avenge their fathers' murders, Shakespeare uses symbols like swords and poison to help us understand how each character responds differently to that same basic situation. Whatever his struggles, Hamlet's mission of revenge helps him become a better person. At the moment that Laertes agrees to poison Hamlet, he has become a worse one. Surreptitious poisoning runs contrary to *Hamlet*'s moral vision in a way that stabbings do not.

So far, we've explored the five steps of Shakespeare's stories, and how each story follows a character through five distinct stages. We've also explored the ways that Shakespeare creates a piece of storytelling by weaving stories together, creating patterns that show off the qualities of each story to their best advantage. In our last chapter, we'll explore the types of stories that modern-day writers frequently adapt from Shakespeare. This type of a story, or the type of a piece of storytelling, is most commonly called its genre.

5.4 Further Reading

Structure

These anthologies and monographs are great for further exploring the concepts in this chapter. As is true elsewhere, many of these books work with our concepts under different names. That's a reality we ought to be used to by now.

Scene Weave

Ball, David. *Backwards and Forwards: A Technical Manual for Reading Plays*. Southern Illinois University Press, 1983.

Backwards and Forwards is a short, readable book that deals comprehensively with dramatic structure. Several of its chapters touch on matters pertaining to scene weave. These are generally in the first section ("Part One: Shape") but also include "Exposition," "Forwards," and "Beginnings/Endings."

Brennan, Anthony. *Shakespeare's Dramatic Structures*. Routledge & Kegan Paul, 1986.

Shakespeare's Dramatic Structures uses a different grammar for discussing the concepts in this book, but its first chapter ("Pattern and Variation in Shakespeare's Dramas") touches many of the concepts in this chapter, including symbols and moral vision. Likewise, the chapters on *The Merchant of Venice* and *Romeo and Juliet* discuss elements of each play that this book calls *scene weave*. *Shakespeare's Dramatic Structures* is part of the excellent *Critical Studies* series from Routledge.

Thomas, James. *Script Analysis for Actors, Directors, and Designers*. Focal Press, 2013.

Script Analysis is a textbook and, like *Backwards and Forwards*, it is comprehensive. It has several chapters that deal with what this book calls "scene weave" (under the headings of "progression" and "structure").

Symbols

Ferber, Michael. *A Dictionary of Literary Symbols*. Cambridge University Press, 2007.

A Dictionary of Literary Symbols is exactly what you would expect: an alphabetical listing of symbols that occur in literature, ranging from works by classical authors (like Herodotus) to biblical ones (like Matthew), through the tradition of English letters—including Shakespeare—and to twentieth-century writers like Nathaniel West and Lillian Hellman. It defines symbols more broadly than this book, and focuses primarily on the values or ideas that are consistently attached to them (instead of, for instance, how symbols help develop characters). Readers of this book may find the *Dictionary* useful in identifying symbols in Shakespeare's plays. Some (like the skulls in *Hamlet*) are obvious. Others (like the apes in *Othello*) are harder to spot.

Moral Vision

Bristol, Michael D. (ed.). *Shakespeare and Moral Agency*. Continuum, 2010.

This anthology offers essays from a variety of critics that fit into three basic categories: *Agency* (or how much choice Shakespeare's characters have), *Social Norms* (or what characters' choices mean in their plays' social contexts), and *Moral Characters* (or how Shakespeare's characters' choices belong to categories defined by moral philosophy). The first two of these categories have something in common with moral vision as this book understands it.

References

Capra, Frank. *It's a Wonderful Life*. Directed by Frank Capra. 1946; Hollywood: Paramount. DVD.

Coppola, Francis Ford. *The Godfather*. Directed by Francis Ford Coppola. 1972; Hollywood: Paramount, 2008. Blu-Ray.

Frayn, Michael. (1998) 2000. *Copenhagen*. New York: Anchor Books.

James, E.L. 2012. *Fifty Shades of Grey*. Vancouver: Vintage Books.

Jonson, Ben. (1614) 2004. "Bartholomew Fair." In *Volpone and Other Plays*, ed. Michael Jamieson, 325–462. New York: Penguin Classics.

Jonson, Ben. (1610) 2004. "The Alchemist." In *Volpone and Other Plays*, ed. Michael Jamieson, 185–320. New York: Penguin Classics.

Joyce, James. (1922) 2010. *Ulysses*. Hertfordshire: Wordsworth Editions.

King, Stephen. 1979. *The Dead Zone*. New York: Viking.

King, Stephen. 2002. *On Writing*. New York: Pocket Books.

Lucas, George. *Star Wars Episode IV: A New Hope*. Directed by George Lucas. 1977; Los Angeles: Twentieth Century Fox, 2013. Blu-Ray.

Oliver, Nancy. *Lars and the Real Girl*. Directed by Craig Gillespie. 2007; Beverly Hills: MGM, 2011. Blu-Ray.

Rand, Ayn. (1957) 1996. *Atlas Shrugged*. New York: Signet.

Stowe, Harriet Beecher. (1852) 2005. *Uncle Tom's Cabin*. Dover: Dover Publications.

Ward, David. *The Sting*. Directed by George Roy Hill. 1973; Universal City: Universal, 2019. Blu-Ray.

Welles, Orson. *Citizen Kane*. Directed by Orson Welles. 1941; Burbank: Warner Brothers, 2007. DVD.

Wilson, Erin Cressida. *Secretary*. Directed by Steven Shainberg. 2002; Santa Monica: Lionsgate, 2010. Blu-Ray.

Wright, Richard. (1940) 1989. *Native Son*. New York: Perennial Classics.

CHAPTER 6

Shakespeare's Genres

6.1 What is Genre?

If you've read this far, you've read everything that this book has to say about Shakespeare's storytelling tools. You've also read something about the types of stories that Shakespeare tells. So far, you've learned that Shakespeare tells a specific type of story, in which a character changes in order to get what they want. No matter a character's age, occupation, or desire, each of their stories follows the same five steps. At the beginning of each character's story, we learn about their motivations, goals, and flaws. At the end, we see how the character has changed in order to get what they want, or—sometimes—why and how they failed to change.

In this chapter, we'll return to the matter of Shakespeare's stories. Although modern writers very often use Shakespeare's tools, they also create pieces of storytelling that fit into Shakespearean genres.

Genre is a broad category for a type of text. It is distinct from *form*, which is a similarly broad category that refers both to what a text looks like and what a reader does with it.

Plays, poems, films, television shows, and novels are forms because they look different, and because readers engage with them using different technologies and as part of different processes. A script used to produce a play, for instance, is not the same form as a script used to produce a film, although the two might otherwise look similar. In poetry, pantoums, sonnets, and sestinas are forms because convention determines things like their meter and rhyme scheme. Pantoums all look the same, whether they're written about a puppy or an apocalypse.

© The Author(s), under exclusive license to Springer Nature
Switzerland AG 2021
N. Eastman, *Shakespeare's Storytelling*,
https://doi.org/10.1007/978-3-030-62993-9_6

Love poems, on the other hand, are a genre. A love poem can be a sonnet, pantoum, sestina, lyric, or take any other form. What distinguishes genres from one another are matters of content and subject. A common genre, like Tragedy, can include several different forms. Tragedies can be plays of several varieties, like closet dramas, five-act plays, and one-acts. Tragedies can also be novels, movies, and long-form dramas (like mini-series or movie trilogies). The only limitation on the genre of Tragedy is that whatever form a Tragedy is produced in must allow a character to have a story, and therefore must be able to convey a sequence of events. A comic book or graphic novel can be a Tragedy, but a single panel comic probably can't.

Does this distinction between form and genre get more complicated? Of course. Just for instance: most sonnets (a form) are also love poems (a genre). This is so often true that if you write a sonnet, people are likely to read it as a love poem whether you intend them to or not. Likewise, there's no reason we can't create a form/genre category like "Film adaptations of Broadway Musicals based on Modernist Children's Poems," but that category only has one item (2019's *Cats*). We're better off without it.

In this chapter, we have two rules for approaching genre. The first is that genres are most valuable when they help us make useful distinctions or useful connections. Good generic categories give us the tools we need to talk about how Shakespeare's plays are different from one another. They also give us tools to talk about how Shakespeare's plays are similar to plays, novels, movies, and other pieces of storytelling produced by later writers (since changes in storytelling conventions, along with matters of history, culture, and technology, mean that a modern film looks very different from a sixteenth-century Shakespeare production).

This means that the genres we'll explore are *forward-looking*. Most people who talk about genre in Shakespeare feel the need to look backward: at Greek and Roman definitions of Comedy and Tragedy, or at the conventions of Early Tudor drama. We're not going to do that. Instead, we'll focus on Shakespearean genres that are still in use today.

The second rule is that, while genres are usually conceived as categories, they are also attributes. Sometimes, it makes sense to call a play a Romantic Comedy, since it seems that way from beginning to end. We won't put too much strain on the category of Romantic Comedies if we say that it includes *Much Ado About Nothing*, *As You Like It*, or *A Midsummer Night's Dream*. These are all Romantic Comedy-shaped pegs that fit neatly into Romantic Comedy-shaped holes.

But other Shakespeare plays that are decidedly not Romantic Comedies— such as *Romeo and Juliet* and *Othello*—spend a lot of time looking like Romantic Comedies. It's useful to consider how and why they do this.

Just for instance: *Othello* has a lot in common with *Much Ado About Nothing*. Both plays focus on a socially mismatched couple: a decorated (but insecure) war veteran and a young, civilian bride (Othello and Desdemona/Claudio and Hero). Their relationships are both crossed by a scheming villain (Iago/Don John) who uses a combination of deception, rumor, and misleading spectacle to convince each veteran that the woman he loves is sleeping with somebody else. The result? Each veteran takes revenge against his partner, believes he has killed her, learns that he has been deceived, and immediately atones. In terms of their motivations, goals, and flaws, as well as the structures of their stories, Othello and Claudio look a lot alike.

But *Othello* is a Tragedy. The word is right there in the title (which is *The Tragedy of Othello, the Moor of Venice*), and Tragedies are conventionally defined by how they end, rather than by anything that happens to characters before the ending. The old observation that Shakespeare's Comedies end with weddings and that the Tragedies end in a pile of bodies is an old observation because it's basically correct.

Whether that definition of Tragedy puts too much weight on the ending is a side issue. The fact that *Othello* isn't a Romantic Comedy shouldn't keep us from noting that *Othello* looks a lot more like *Much Ado About Nothing* than, say, *Julius Caesar*. Just because *Othello*'s ending makes it a Tragedy doesn't mean that it didn't spend four acts looking like a Romantic Comedy.

That's a long way of saying that the usual question about genre—something like "Is *Othello* a Tragedy or a Romantic Comedy?"—starts off by making the wrong assumptions. A play can be a Revenge Tragedy and a Coming of Age story for the same basic reasons that a car can be both very expensive and very fast. With very few exceptions, the qualities that include a play in one genre don't necessarily exclude it from others.

In summary: The two rules we'll follow for talking about genre (that generic categories need to be useful, and that they don't exclude one another) will make our conversation about genre sound very different from some you've heard before.

For instance: Many Shakespeare scholars follow the lead of the First Folio and divide Shakespearean drama into Comedies, Histories, and Tragedies. That's fine, but it's not terrifically useful. For instance: Richard III was, however briefly, a non-fictional king of England. This (probably) is what makes *Richard III* a History in the First Folio.

But Richard's unwillingness to change—and that it leads him to end badly—often got the play labeled a Tragedy (as it was in its first Quarto and the Second Folio). Whatever quibbles led editors to assign (or reassign) the play to one category or another, the whole arrangement stinks of generic categories that are too tight in all the wrong places. The central characters in the Histories—your Prince Hals, Lord Talbots, Richards II and III, and platoon of Henrys—don't have much in common. Save that their stories involve the crown, these characters are different in ways that don't lend themselves to productive comparison.

Following that line of reasoning: Among Shakespeare's Histories, most are clearly Tragic in the specific sense that they end poorly for their principal characters. These include (for instance) *Richard II*, the *Henry VI* plays, and *Richard III*. Others, like *1 Henry IV* and *Henry V*, look comic because they feature comic characters (like *Henry IV*'s Falstaff) or end with the kind of matchmaking that is otherwise the provenance of Shakespeare's Comedies.

But if you're a conventional Shakespearean, it's flat out wrong to call the *Henry IV* plays (or *Henry V*) "Comic Histories" (or "Historical Comedies") and call *Richard III* a "Tragical History." Histories are *Histories*, and there are rules against putting too much spin on the ball. You end up sounding like Polonius, who in II.ii introduces *Hamlet*'s troupe of traveling actors as:

> The best actors in the world, either for tragedy, comedy, history, pastoral, pastoral-comical, historical-pastoral, tragical-historical, tragical-comical-historical-pastoral, scene individable, or poem unlimited [...]
> (374–78)

Thankfully, we'll use altogether different generic categories to talk Shakespeare. This list isn't meant to be an encyclopedia. It's just meant to help you, as a reader of Shakespeare, understand how the kinds of stories that Shakespeare told have been adapted by later writers.

Finally: I've kept each genre's definition brief, and kept examples to a minimum. Arguments about genre are arguments of totality—that is, they involve looking at the entire body of a play, rather than choosing bits to read carefully. Most of the Shakespearean examples I've used here ought to be familiar by now, too, and so there's little point in extensive summary. With all that in mind: Let's begin.

6.2 Character Histories

The most conventional genre we'll mention here—and one that is nearly indistinguishable from Shakespeare's category of Histories—is the *Character History*. A Character History is a piece of storytelling that focuses almost exclusively on a single character—usually a character of historical importance—and embeds the five steps of that character's story in a set of significant historical events. The decisions a character makes, and the actions a character takes, cause battles to be won and lost, countries to be founded or conquered, or ways of thinking and living to either ascend or be forgotten.

The thesis of a Character History is that its focal character has a claim on the present. That is, a Character History presents its focal character's thoughts and actions as an explanation for how, or why, present-day things are the way they are. The implicit thesis is that, if the focal character were a different type of person, what we understand to be history would look significantly different.

Consider *Richard III*. At the beginning of the play, Richard's oldest brother, Edward, is king. Though Edward is dying, he has two children ready to serve as heirs, and England itself has entered a long-sought-after peace after a generation of civil war. At the beginning of the play, everybody but Richard is content for the throne to pass to Edward's children with a minimum of fuss.

Had Richard of Gloucester been content to lead a quiet life as the king's youngest brother, England would have seen a peaceful succession. But Richard is Richard. Because he wants to be seen as important, and thinks that the only way to do this is by being a villain, he starts murdering rival claimants to the throne and turning England's political factions against one another. The end result is that Richard briefly becomes king—until the ensuing civil war (which would not have happened except for Richard's meddling) unseats him. The play ends with a new royal family (the Tudors) in charge. The thesis of *Richard III*, in other words, is that the Tudors rule England partly because Richard of Gloucester was on a misguided quest for validation.

This is not history. A historian would point out that the failure of a government, or the re-incitement of a civil war, generally cannot be laid at the feet of a single politician—no matter how ill-intentioned or inept they happen to be. History is driven by individual choices, but also by tidal economic and political forces, and so we ought not to overestimate the importance of any individual's decisions.

But in a Character History, choices matter. Characters' motivations, goals, and flaws—and the thoughts and actions that express them—are mated to historical events that help define their nature and importance. We learn which elements of a character's behavior matter by seeing the consequences of that behavior play out on a magnified (and allegedly historical) scale.

Very often, the title of a Character History is just the name of its focal character. This is often true in Shakespeare. *Richard III* is a good example. But *Julius Caesar* focuses on Brutus, and *Henry IV* Parts 1 and 2 focus more on Prince Hal (later Henry V) than on his father. More recent Character Histories follow this rule almost invariably. You'll get an occasional film like *Hidden Figures* (2016), but for each of those you'll see a dozen like *Lincoln* (2012), *Ray* (2004), or *Forrest Gump* (1994). Sometimes a movie title pulls a *Schindler's List* (1993), and aims just to one side of the convention.

Just because the title characters—and nominal protagonists—of Character Histories are significant does not mean that they are good. Like all Shakespearean characters, the central character in a Character History begins their story with flaws. They have habits of thinking and acting that hurt themselves and other people. Many of these are line traits: ways of thinking and acting that are virtues in one context, but flaws in another. In *Julius Caesar*, Brutus's cultivated even-handedness and stoicism make him an inspiring politician but an inept conspirator. The same is true of Forrest Gump. In both the 1994 film and Winston Groom's 1986 novel, Forrest's combination of perseverance, tolerance, and naiveté are both a reason for his successes and an obstacle to his understanding (and bonding with) other people.

Shakespeare's Character Histories include the ten conventionally recognized Histories.[1] Modern Character Histories are—more often than not—released during Oscar season.

6.3 Coming of Age Stories

In a *Coming of Age story*, a character becomes a fully fledged adult by observing what their society does and choosing to do things differently. This results in a peculiar form of abstract conflict. In Coming of Age stories, young protagonists are in conflict with other, older, characters because each wants to present the story, philosophy, or worldview that everybody will agree is valid.

In the simplest version of a modern Coming of Age story, a young character is set against their society as a whole. According to this character, everyone in the character's society does things one way, but the protagonist chooses to do them differently. *The Catcher in the Rye* (1951) is one such story (since everyone's a phony except Holden Caulfield), but so is *The Hobbit* (1937). The party line in *The Hobbit* is that hobbits are not adventurers, but Bilbo (with the help of Gandalf and the dwarves) discovers that he is and—more importantly—writes a story that tells the world that this is so.

In Shakespearean Coming of Age stories, characters become fully fledged adults not just by finding their own way, but also by confronting their own flaws for the first time. Their revelations involve not only discovering the specific ways they need to change (in order to stop hurting themselves and other people), but also discovering that changing is necessary. Shakespeare's Coming of Age stories, in other words, focus on characters who are not yet aware of their flaws, but become aware of them as their philosophical contest with society unfolds.

In *Romeo and Juliet*, for instance, both Romeo and Juliet come of age by refusing to let the Montague/Capulet feud rule their lives. That's standard operating procedure for a Coming of Age story, regardless of whether it's Shakespearean.

But Shakespeare adds something else: Romeo, in wooing Juliet, discovers something that many of Shakespeare's lovers do: that Juliet isn't impressed by the usual types of insincere poetry. If he expects to woo Juliet, he needs to take real emotional risks. That is, he needs to be authentic, honest, and vulnerable. However old Romeo is, and however many relationships he's attempted before his failed one with Rosalind (the love interest who directly precedes Juliet), he hasn't yet learned that a partner ought to love him for who he is, rather than for who he pretends to be.

One Shakespearean variation on the Coming of Age story is to invert the usual formula of adolescent self-discovery: instead of a character looking at

---

[1] That is, the two tetralogies (*Henry VI* parts 1–3 plus *Richard III*, and *Richard II*, *Henry IV* parts 1 and 2, and *Henry V*), plus the standalone Histories: *King John* and *Henry VIII*.

their society and deciding to do things differently, a character who's already a nonconformist, and who ought to be a fully fledged adult, decides that they'd have been better off conforming in the first place.

Sometimes, as with Kate in *The Taming of the Shrew*, this variation looks like a typical Coming of Age story in every respect except for the character's initial nonconformity. Prince Hal, in running with his tavern buddies when the rest of the kingdom expects him to act like an ordinary prince, is another example of this type. Both Kate and Hal are young—not children, but not quite fully fledged adults. You can still imagine them in the kind of developmental purgatory we reserve for college students.

At other times, the reverse-Coming-of-Age character revisits their nonconformity later on in their adulthood. Prospero's actual Coming of Age story ends long before Act I of *The Tempest*: where his peers learn and practice politics, Prospero learns and practices magic. As an adult, living on his magical island with his daughter, Miranda, Prospero makes a series of choices that end with him renouncing his magic. After abandoning his real-life responsibilities in order to become a magician, Prospero abandons his magic in order to return to ordinary life.

Beatrice and Benedick (in *Much Ado About Nothing*) have likewise already come of age by choosing not (and never) to marry—although marriage is standard operating procedure in their hometown of Messina. But Don Pedro and Don John's plotting lead both Beatrice and Benedick to confront their flaws, and they renounce their earlier nonconformity by marrying each other. Not only do they marry, but they accept the mainstream value of marriage. "Prince," says Benedick to Don Pedro as the play closes (in V.iv.125–26), "thou art sad. Get thee a wife! Get thee a wife!"

Another feature of Shakespearean Coming of Age stories is that parents often represent the attitudes and values against which characters define themselves. Usually:

1. If a character endorses the attitudes and values of a parent, they struggle to live into those values because they aren't like that parent. For example, Hamlet is not a warrior king like his father, Old Hamlet. No matter how much he thinks he wants to be like his father, Hamlet begins his story unable to deal lethal justice as well, or as easily, as his father did.
2. If a character rejects the attitudes and values of a parent, they struggle because they're very like the parent whose values they reject. For example, Cordelia's stubborn and morally certain criticism of her father (King Lear's) inheritance ceremony produces conflict because Lear is also stubborn and morally certain.

Shakespeare is not the only person to use this system of parental acceptance and rejection to drive conflict in a Coming of Age story. *Death of a Salesman* (1949), *The Godfather* (1972), *Fences* (1986), and the first *Star Wars* trilogy

(Lucas et al. 1977, 1980, 1983) follow this same basic pattern. Luke Skywalker might want to see himself as really different from Darth Vader, but they're the only two people in the galaxy who own light sabers.

More broadly, Coming of Age Stories include some of the most well-known novels of the last two centuries: *Johnny Tremain* (1943), *The Kite Runner* (2003), *The Giver* (1993), *Great Expectations* (1861) and *Twilight* (2005) are all straightforward examples.

6.4   ROMANTIC COMEDIES

We've all seen Romantic Comedies before, whether we wanted to or not. In a Romantic Comedy, a character desires the love of another character. That pursuit of love is attached to their motivation, which is generally to be valued or to be seen as worthy of attention.

Eventually, Romantic Comedy characters learn that receiving love requires that they be (or become) authentic, honest, and vulnerable. That's the moral vision of Romantic Comedies. Generally speaking, all of the romantically eligible characters in a Romantic Comedy begin their stories by lying either to themselves or to other people. "The most important thing in my life is my job," they'll say, or "I have never, ever been interested in marrying anyone—especially Beatrice." But they learn. By the ends of their stories, Romantic Comedy characters will know, and take responsibility for, their desires, and they'll pursue those desires directly—even when that pursuit risks them being hurt.

Shakespeare pitched enough Romantic Comedies to throw the occasional change-up. Sometimes, Shakespeare's Romantic Comedy characters begin their stories wanting to be valued, or to be seen as significant, and they'll begin their stories with some goal other than love in mind. Beatrice and Benedick do this in *Much Ado About Nothing*. Each of them begins their stories thinking that they can be valued by being clever, or by being conspicuously witty. But as their stories progress, they learn that the right way to be valued is by partnering up. The same thing happens in modern Romantic Comedies, where career-focused men and women discover that the right way to be valued involves spending less time at work and more time in relationships with the Right Kind of Person.

Generally speaking, modern Romantic Comedies have two principal characters, the lover (A) and the beloved (B). In their simplest form, A has a weakness that makes B threatening, and the Comedy concludes when a revelation transforms B from being threatening to being accessible. A, for instance, might own an independent bookstore while B is an executive for a big box retailer like Barnes and Noble, and intends to set up shop in some territory that threatens to put A's independent bookstore out of business.[2] Shakespeare

---

[2]This is *You've Got Mail*, a 1998 Romantic Comedy written when chain bookstores were a booming business and it was possible to be optimistic about the internet.

certainly does this. Beatrice and Benedick are a great example. Each one finds the other threatening (i.e. capable of hurting their feelings) until Hero and Claudio's disastrous wedding prompts them to start being vulnerable.

In other Shakespearean Romantic Comedies, the obstacle to A and B's relationship is external. Usually, this involves a father objecting to whoever's courting his daughter. In *A Midsummer Night's Dream*, for instance, Egeus doesn't approve of Lysander (a young man who's interested in Egeus's daughter, Hermia).

As a rule, Shakespearean couples negotiate external obstacles by fleeing their jurisdiction. Hermia and Lysander run away from Athens so that Egeus's objection to their marriage can't be enforced.

When internal, rather than external, obstacles keep characters celibate—for instance, when Beatrice and Benedick object to one another's company, or when Kate objects to every suitor in Padua—Shakespeare introduces new characters as stasis-breakers. Sometimes (as with Beatrice and Benedick in *Much Ado*) these characters act as matchmakers. At others (as with Petruchio in *The Taming of the Shrew*) they represent a different type of romantic partner.

Regardless of whether it appears in a Romantic Comedy, love in Shakespeare's plays is both foolish (prompting characters to do silly things in a misguided attempt to impress someone) and wonderful (profoundly character changing). The comedy in Shakespearean Romantic Comedy is usually driven by characters' outlandish courting behavior. Likewise, characters' revelations may be driven by little other than the discovery that they are loved. This is true even well outside the bounds of ordinary Romantic Comedy stories. Edmund's revelation at the end of *King Lear*, for instance, is driven by his discovery that he was loved by Regan and Goneril.

Elements of Romantic Comedy occur in most of Shakespeare's plays, including the tragedies. *Antony and Cleopatra*, *Othello*, and *Romeo and Juliet*, for instance, all involve characters acting unwisely in the name of romance. *Othello* takes the additional step of positioning itself as a Romantic Comedy very like the Claudio/Hero stories in *Much Ado About Nothing* (in which the obstacle to romance between a distinguished soldier and an innocent young woman is an infidelity rumor spread by a declared villain).

When a Shakespearean Romantic Comedy comprises an entire play (as it does in nearly all the Comedies) it will include a web of several Romantic Comedy stories set up so that the mechanics of each romantic relationship (and its A and B characters) define and clarify the mechanics of the others—effectively building character webs out of each romantic couple. *Much Ado About Nothing* and *The Taming of the Shrew* feature two major Romantic Comedy stories. *A Midsummer Night's Dream* has at least five (Theseus/Hippolyta, Titania/Oberon, Lysander/Hermia, Demetrius/Helena, and Pyramus/Thisbe).

The Shakespearean Romantic Comedy also has several variations. The most common is the Makeover Comedy, in which A transforms B from a threatening to an accessible partner by schooling them in how to behave. Juliet/Romeo (in *Romeo and Juliet*), Petruchio/Kate (in *Taming*), and Rosalind/Orlando (in *As You Like It*) are all examples of this type.

Romantic Comedies remain popular. 2018 saw dozens, with the most noteworthy including *Crazy Rich Asians, Love, Simon, Mamma Mia: Here We go Again*,[3] and Tyler Perry's *Nobody's Fool*.

6.5 Revenge Tragedies

About fifty years ago, the *Saturday Evening Post* published one of the twentieth century's most well-crafted Revenge Tragedies. It began like this:

> People do not give it credence that a fourteen-year-old girl could leave home and go off in the wintertime to avenge her father's blood but it did not seem so strange then, although I will say it did not happen every day. I was just fourteen years of age when a coward going by the name of Tom Chaney shot my father down in Fort Smith, Arkansas, and robbed him of his life and his horse and $150 in cash money plus two California gold pieces that he carried in his trouser band.

The piece of storytelling is Charles Portis's *True Grit* (1968). Portis knew exactly where his story was heading and which type of story it was. In the first two sentences, he lays out every salient element of the modern Revenge Tragedy, and foregrounds the most easily overlooked: Revenge Tragedies are about stories. The structural conflict in Revenge Tragedies concerns which version of a story about a crime becomes official.

This is so important that Portis leads his book with it. His narrator, who we will later learn is Mattie Ross, has already told her story to an audience of disbelievers. Her goal this time—for the generation of the story that she invites us into—is to tell the story convincingly.

As a genre, the Revenge Tragedy dates back to Seneca (approx. 50 CE), and experienced a revival in Renaissance England that coincided with Shakespeare's early career. While many plays involve revenge, the Revenge Tragedy itself focuses on a conflict between the revenger (A) and a criminal (B).

The conflict begins when B commits a crime (usually murder), and B's story about the crime—a cover-up—becomes the official narrative. The A character (who is usually indirectly harmed by B's crime) discovers or develops a counternarrative, and A and B battle over which version the world will believe.

This conflict ends with A's revenge, which demonstrates B's guilt in a public and theatrical way, ensuring that A's story becomes the new, official narrative (and usually that B will be too dead to revise it). In Shakespeare, as in many other Revenge Tragedies, the moment of vengeance and the moment of A's narrative's validation are the same. In others—such as *True Grit*—these moments can be separate. In either case, A's need for validation depends on

---

[3] "Noteworthy" does not always mean "good".

the validation of their narrative, and not on a simple sequence of crime and punishment.

The Revenge Tragedy's concern with crime and punishment may make it sound like a detective story, or a police procedural, and in some respects it is. The earliest Revenge Tragedy, the *Oresteia* (458 BCE), is a kind of fable that ends with the gods themselves introducing a jury system. The moral vision of the *Oresteia* is that truth and falsehood—or which versions of the truth become official—should be adjudicated in an orderly, structured way. Modern detective stories and police procedurals often spend some amount of time in trial, so that the audience can see the right story win.

Unlike detective stories and police procedurals, however, the broader universe of the Revenge Tragedy often involves ghosts (or other supernatural elements), madness (on the part of the revenger), a conspiracy protecting the criminal (usually in creating a fraudulent, official narrative about the crime), and—most important—the revenger's trajectory of increasing eccentricity, instability, and isolation.

This last is driven by the revenger's choice to continue pursuing revenge, even when this pursuit harms innocent people. While Mattie Ross is never haunted by her father's ghost, and never shares Hamlet's moments of delusion, she is very much alone. One piece of Portis's cleverness in *True Grit* is that, by extending the period between the moment of Mattie's revenge and the moment that she tells the official story of it, he can demonstrate just how alone she is, and how unlikely it is that this will ever change.

Among Shakespeare's works, *Hamlet* and *Titus Andronicus* are entirely Revenge Tragedies, and *Hamlet* is often cited as the most artistically successful example of the genre. However, Revenge Tragedy stories appear wholly or partly in other of Shakespeare's plays, including *King Lear*, *Othello*, and *The Merchant of Venice*. Today, "hard-boiled" detective stories (in which a loner, anti-hero detective investigates a crime that occurs in a context of universal corruption) are very often Revenge Tragedies in whole or in part. Examples of these range from *Chinatown* (1974) to *Who Framed Roger Rabbit* (1988).

6.6 Runaway Villains

Runaway Villain stories are built on the spectacle of a clever, manipulative villain harassing their nominally innocent victims. One unusual feature of the Runaway Villain genre is culpability. Characters can "deserve" villainous harassment for being active wrongdoers, for being criminally naive, or—sometimes—for being just plain dull. On the other hand, the villain achieves the text's or audience's endorsement by being clear-minded, capable, or entertaining. The moral visions of Runaway Villain stories are often unusual.

Generally speaking, a Runaway Villain's motivation involves being seen as valuable, formidable, or capable. They think that they can do this by manipulating and hurting other people. Other characters in Runaway Villain stories are less developed and, very often, less fun. They are flawed to the extent that they trust, or allow themselves to be manipulated by, the Runaway Villain character. In the least enjoyable kinds of Runaway Villain stories, they're little more than targets for the Runaway Villain to knock down.

The Runaway Villain genre dates back to the Medieval Morality Comedy, in which hapless Everymen were harassed by demons and other vice characters as a vehicle for slapstick. It was most successfully adapted during Shakespeare's time by rival playwright Christopher Marlowe.

Shakespeare's Runaway Villains are different from Marlowe's in at least one significant way. Marlowe's Runaway Villains pursue increasingly ambitious goals by working increasingly complex plots, which succeed in the face of escalating improbability until one misfires in an unexpected—and usually lethal—way. This is true for many of Shakespeare's Runaway Villains, too, and in Shakespeare's only pure Runaway Villain play, *Richard III*.

However, Shakespeare's Runaway Villains engage in a different form of conflict from Marlowe's. In Marlovian drama, characters who aren't the Runaway Villain are caricatures, or types, and—save for their vices—it is difficult to tell them apart. Marlowe's friars, for instance, are lascivious. His politicians are treacherous. His young women are naive, and his young men headstrong. His Runaway Villains succeed by attacking these characters' stereotypical vices rather than their individual psychological weaknesses.

Shakespeare's Runaway Villains are more intimate. Their plans rely on their ability to manipulate individuals by attacking each of them at their points of weakness, which are almost always related to the ways that these characters pursue validation. Richard would not be able to woo just any woman the way that he woos Anne. Iago's plotting likewise relies on Othello being Othello and Roderigo being Roderigo.

A more detailed example from *Much Ado About Nothing*: When Don John attacks Claudio by slandering Claudio's fiancée, Hero, he's attacking Claudio's path to validation.

The background: Claudio's wartime bravery has made him eligible to marry a woman who would otherwise be above his social station—not just because of her birth, but because of her reputation. If Claudio were a simple social climber, Hero's (his wife's) reputation probably wouldn't matter.

But Claudio sees his marriage to a woman of spotless reputation as a statement about who he is, and about how other people—specifically other men, who are older and more powerful—hold him in their esteem. When he thinks that Hero's cheated on him, he refuses to marry her, and the language of his refusal in IV.i makes his concern over other men's esteem clear:

> CLAUDIO
> Sweet prince, you learn me noble thankfulness.
> There, Leonato, take her back again:
> Give not this rotten orange to your friend.
> (29–31)

Claudio might be upset with Hero, but he's more upset with "sweet prince" Leonato's "noble thankfulness." That is, when Claudio agreed to marry Hero, he thought that his marriage would welcome him to the ranks of the nobility. The marriage was a matter of both social acceptance and personal friendship.

Thanks to Don John's intrigue, however, Claudio thinks that his marriage to Hero is a kind of social slight: Leonato pawning off an embarrassingly loose daughter on Claudio to show the rest of the nobility that Claudio doesn't—and never will—deserve to be a real member of their inner circle.

Shakespeare's development of the Runaway Villain, and especially that Villain's ability to discover the weaknesses peculiar to a single character, leads to some of his greatest dramatic accomplishments. It gives us Claudius and Cleopatra, along with declared villains like Iago and Edmund. It even gives us Hamlet, who struggles with discerning exactly how to target Claudius when he's most vulnerable, but who is also more effective than he means to be at targeting the weaknesses of the people he most cares about, like Ophelia.

Shakespeare's other villains, however, follow Runaway Villain arcs that are otherwise indistinguishable from those of Marlowe's villains: declaring their villainy in a soliloquy at the beginning of the play, and driving the plot forward by using increasingly elaborate forms of intrigue and deception until they are undone at the play's end. Iago (*Othello*), Don John (*Much Ado*), Edmund (*King Lear*), and Iachimo (*Cymbeline*) are all of this type.

There aren't as many modern Runaway Villain films as there are Romantic Comedies. *The Silence of the Lambs* (1991) may represent the greatest level or degree of complexity that pure Runaway Villain stories are capable of. But Runaway Villains, in both their Marlovian and Shakespearean forms, are pretty common. Most Bond villains are good examples of the Marlovian type. Tyrion Lannister (from either *Song of Ice and Fire* or *Game of Thrones*) is, like Richard of Gloucester, an intermediate version—part Marlovian, part Shakespearean, and therefore very interesting.

Shakespearean-style Runaway Villains make for compelling film, too. Katherine Merteuil in *Cruel Intentions* (1999) is one, and so is Regina George in *Mean Girls* (2004). Also in the club: Aaron Stampler in *Primal Fear* (1996), Alonzo Harris in *Training Day* (2001), and Phyllis Dietrichson in *Double Indemnity* (1944). This is all apart from the most famous: Hannibal Lecter in *The Silence of the Lambs* (1991).

6.7 One-Trick Ponies

If the Coming of Age story is about transitioning from childhood to adulthood, the One-Trick Pony story is about transitioning from adulthood to old age or—more generally—from one stage or station of adulthood to another.

In the One-Trick Pony story, a character whose identity is defined by a single skill, talent, or aptitude loses the ability to exercise it, and exhibits some combination of optimism, dedication, and characteristically bad judgment by trying anyway.

The most common modern form of the One-Trick Pony story involves an athlete aging out of competition and attempting a comeback—sometimes because they do not know who they are, or how to live, outside the context of their sport. Rod Serling's *Requiem for a Heavyweight* (1956) may be the earliest storytelling of this type. *The Wrestler* (2008) may be the best. A lucky few of these stories, like *The Rookie* (2002), trend toward optimism. But one thing they have in common is a focal character who struggles with the passage of time.

This is a common flaw for a One-Trick Pony: they do not understand, or are unwilling to accept, that the world changes, and that their own happiness requires that they change in response. They're the mother you hear crying in an H&M dressing room, or the thirty-year-old townie you keep seeing at college parties. They're doing something that they used to enjoy, or used to be good at, long past the point when it makes sense.

King Lear is Shakespeare's most straightforward One-Trick Pony story. Lear was himself a warrior king who has aged past the point when he could lead an army. The traits that might have made him an inspiring commander—decisiveness, readiness to violence, and pride—don't serve him well once he's aged past his sword-bearing years. A sense of injured merit might be inspiring in a warrior king, but in an old man it looks a lot like petulance.

Othello is also a One-Trick Pony story, even though Othello is still well-suited to military life. In his story, Othello discovers that his inclination to understand and control his surroundings—a trait that makes him a successful military leader—does not serve him well when he is married to a young, attractive socialite. As a commander, Othello has the luxury of thinking of most problems as conflicts that can be won. That might be a good way to run an army, but it's a bad way to run a marriage.

We can say the same of *Julius Caesar* and Brutus's peculiar, stoic form of integrity, which serves him well as a senator but makes him an inept revolutionary. Brutus is dedicated to principle, and to what modern politicians and executives insufferably call "optics" (which is a way of talking about the way a decision looks to outside observers). Because of that, once he becomes a revolutionary, the choices he makes are invariably wrong. Instead of shutting down rival political factions, or—more prudently—assassinating them, he gives them a free hand to rouse the rabble and incite a counter-revolution. What looks like the right thing is, in Brutus's world, different from what actually works.

In all these cases, the defining characteristic of the One-Trick Pony protagonist is the line trait: a character attribute that is an asset in some contexts (like military life or politics) but a flaw in others (like romance or conspiracy). Modern versions of One-Trick Pony stories work with line traits extensively, to the point where these traits can almost completely define central characters.

For example: in *Death of a Salesman* (1949) Willy Loman's unfounded belief in his own excellence gives him the courage to face rejection from any number of clients. It also prevents him from recognizing, taking responsibility for, and learning from, his shortcomings as a husband and father.

Likewise: in *Fences* (1986) Troy's persistence in pursuing what he thinks is best, coupled with his rigid worldview and outsized sense of entitlement, has helped him become the first Black truck driver in his company. It also leads him to alienate his son, Cory, when they disagree over whether Cory can become a successful athlete.

6.8 Contest Stories

In a Contest story, a character plays a game in which the prize for winning is a real-life reward. This isn't gambling, where people bet money as part of the game itself. Instead, the Contest story relies on a forced and novel incongruity between the game and the prize.

Contest stories have a long history. One of Stephen King's earliest novels—written under the pseudonym of Richard Bachman—is *The Long Walk* (1979). In it, the winner of a mentally and physically grueling forced-march contest called "The Walk" receives anything he wants for the rest of his life. Because this is a dystopia, the winner is the only survivor. The rest of the competitors (all of them teenage boys) get shot like broke-leg horses if they stop walking.

This might sound suspiciously like *The Hunger Games* (2008), which is also a Contest story, as is Stephen King's aka Richard Bachman's *The Running Man* (1982), as are a thousand other dystopian novels intended for young people who have just learned that the highly artificial achievements that attend success in rule-governed environments are not a pathway to real-world happiness or success.

Shakespeare (thankfully) never wrote an entire play of this type, although he wrote several plotlines in which a character wins a bride by winning a game—usually, specifically, by answering a riddle. The most famous of these is the "casket game" in *The Merchant of Venice* (where Bassanio wins the right to marry Portia by choosing the right casket from a row of three).[4] But the strangest game-riddle gets posed to Pericles (in *Pericles, Prince of Tyre* I.i) by Antiochus, the father of the princess that Pericles wants to marry:

---

[4]The caskets are made of gold, silver, and lead, and each of the three comes with a different inscription, too.

Bassanio doesn't choose the right casket by being clever or perceptive. Instead, Portia helps him cheat by bringing in a musician who provides some Jeopardy-style background music as Bassanio makes his choice:
"Tell me where is fancy bred," the song goes:

> *Or in the heart, or in the head?*
> *How begot, how nourished?*
> *Reply, reply.*
> (III.ii.63–66)

Bassanio, being Bassanio, spends three dozen lines (72–107) figuring out that "bred," "head," and "nourished" (here pronounced "nour-ish-ED") don't rhyme with "gold" or "silver."

PERICLES [*reading the riddle*]
I am no viper, yet I feed
On mother's flesh which did me breed.
I sought a husband, in which labor
I found that kindness in a father.
He's father, son, and husband mild;
I mother, wife, and yet his child.
How they may be, and yet in two,
As you will live, resolve it you.
(64–71)

The answer to the riddle is that Antiochus is sleeping with his own daughter. If this seems weird, Antiochus doubles down on that weirdness by (a) being genuinely surprised that Pericles guesses the answer, and (b) vowing to murder Pericles to keep the secret quiet:

ANTIOCHUS
Heaven, that I had thy head! He has found
the meaning! [...]
He must not live to trumpet forth my infamy,
Nor tell the world Antiochus doth sin
In such a loathed manner,
And therefore instantly this prince must die:
For by his fall my honor must keep high.
(145–51)

This isn't *The Hunger Games*. It's also not Shakespeare's best play. Neither is *Love's Labour's Lost*, which priminently features a Contest story in which several friends see who can go the longest without the company of women.

With the exception of *The Merchant of Venice*, Shakespeare's plays seem fundamentally opposed to the idea that you can find the right (or even a good) partner by being good at rule-driven enterprises like dancing, wrestling, or poetry. Where Contest stories occur in Shakespeare's comedies, they are usually set in opposition to romantic values that include authenticity, honesty, and vulnerability.

Points of Review

Speaking broadly, Shakespeare has influenced modern writers in three ways. First, he invented a type of story—the Shakespearean story—in which a character changes in order to get what they want. Second, Shakespeare also invented several tools that help tell this type of story effectively. These range from character motivations to character webs to symbols and moral vision.

Third, Shakespeare developed several different categories, or genres, of stories that are still in our common storytelling vocabulary. When we watch a Romantic Comedy like *Crazy Rich Asians*, a Runaway Villain story like *The Silence of the Lambs*, or a One-Trick Pony story like *Fences*, we're not just seeing Shakespearean characters and storytelling tools. We're seeing a subtype of the five-step Shakespearean story that features its own specific set of conventions.

One last reminder: Traditional approaches to Shakespeare and genre emphasize either Shakespeare's classical influences, or the ways that Shakespeare's own audience would have categorized his plays. These approaches can be informative, but should not exclude an approach that emphasizes Shakespeare's influence on the modern craft of storytelling.

6.9 Further Reading

Shakespeare's Genres

These anthologies and monographs explore issues related to the genres we've look at in this chapter. Some of them do this as genre studies—for instance, looking at the ways that the conventions of Romantic Comedy have been adapted to other genres, or by exploring the history of the Coming of Age story. Others touch on complex issues that might inform how we understand the genres in this chapter. For instance, Maurice Charney (who has two books on this list) has written both about Shakespeare's villains and about the ways that age and aging are presented in Shakespeare's plays. These can help us understand our Runaway Villains and One-Trick Ponies.

There are dozens of sensible ways to categorize Shakespeare's plays, and to make connections between them and the pieces of storytelling that have come afterward. For an overview of the generic traditions (and expectations) that were in place during Shakespeare's day, see Lawrence Danson's *Shakespeare's Dramatic Genres* (Oxford University Press 2000) and Barbara Lewalski's *Renaissance Genres: Essays on Theory, History, and Interpretation* (Harvard University Press 1986).

Character Histories

Saccio, Peter. *Shakespeare's English Kings*. Oxford University Press, 2000.

Now in its second edition, *Shakespeare's English Kings* explores the sources of Shakespeare's history plays (mostly Medieval and Tudor chronicles) and contrasts this with the content of Shakespeare's plays as well as with history as understood by modern-day researchers. It also includes handy material like genealogical charts and appendices of royal family names and titles.

Coming of Age stories

Graham, Sarah (ed.). *A History of the Bildungsroman*. Cambridge University Press, 2019.

The *Bildungsroman* is a specific form of the Coming of Age story that focuses on a character's process of maturation during their childhood's formative years, and includes most of what modern readers think of when they think of Coming of Age stories. *History* focuses on the traditions of the Bildungsroman that originated in continental Europe, as well as Britain, and how these traditions influence the specific types of Bildungsromane we see today—including those for women, children, and lesbian, gay, and trans persons, as well as the Bildungsroman in forms like graphic narrative.

One-Trick Ponies

Charney, Maurice. *Wrinkled Deep in Time: Aging in Shakespeare*. Columbia University Press, 2009.

While this book isn't a genre study, it is an excellent piece of historical and literary research on the attitudes toward age and aging in Shakespeare, and on how those attitudes are different from our own. It also explores conventions about age and aging in texts that influenced Shakespeare, such as Roman Comedies.

Revenge Tragedy

Kerrigan, John. *Revenge Tragedy: From Aeschylus to Armageddon*. Oxford University Press, 1998.

Revenge Tragedy surveys the genre of Revenge Tragedy, and representations of revenge dating back to Homer, using concepts from anthropology, social theory, and moral philosophy.

Romantic Comedy

Deyleto, Celestino. *The Secret Life of Romantic Comedy*. Manchester University Press, 2009.

Where other genre studies take a hidebound approach to Romantic Comedy, *Secret Life* defines the genre flexibly in order to show how the conventions of Romantic Comedy show up in films that aren't ordinarily considered to be part of the genre.

Frye, Northrop. *A Natural Perspective*. Columbia University Press, 1995.

Northrop Frye is one of the most well-respected Shakespeare critics of the late-twentieth century, and in *Natural Perspective* he explores the conventions that define some of Shakespeare's most challenging late comedies: *The Tempest*, *Cymbeline*, *Pericles, Prince of Tyre*, and *The Winter's Tale*. While these are all properly Romantic Comedies, they are also complicated enough to warrant serious critical guidance.

Runaway Villain Stories

Charney, Maurice. *Shakespeare's Villains*. Fairleigh Dickenson University Press, 2011.

Shakespeare's Villains closely considers the way that Shakespeare's villains are developed in terms of language, imagery, and nonverbal stage effects. It includes chapters on Iago, Tarquin, Aaron, Richard of Gloucester, Shylock,

Claudius, Polonius, Macbeth, Edmund, Goneril, Regan, Angelo, Tybalt, Don John, Iachimo, Lucio, Julius Caesar, Leontes, and Duke Frederick—in short, nearly every Shakespearean villain you're likely to encounter.

REFERENCES

Aeschylus. (458 BCE) 1984. *The Oresteia*. Trans. Robert Fagles. New York: Penguin Classics.
Albertalli, Becky. *Love, Simon*. Directed by Greg Berlanti. 2018; Hollywood: Twentieth Century Fox, 2018. Blu-Ray.
Ayer, David. *Training Day*. Directed by Anton Fuqua. 2001; Burbank: Warner Home Video, 2008. Blu-Ray.
Chandler, Raymond, and Billy Wilder. *Double Indemnity*. Directed by Billy Wilder. 1944; Universal City: Universal Pictures, 2018. Blu-Ray.
Collins, Suzanne. (2008) 2010. *The Hunger Games*. New York: Scholastic.
Coppola, Francis Ford. *The Godfather*. Directed by Francis Ford Coppola. 1972; Hollywood: Paramount, 2008. Blu-Ray.
Danson, Lawrence. 2000. *Shakespeare's Dramatic Genres*. Oxford: Oxford UP.
Dickens, Charles. (1861) 2002. *Great Expectations*. New York: Penguin Classics.
Ephron, Nora. *You've Got Mail*. Directed by Nora Ephron. 1998; Burbank: Warner Brothers, 1999. DVD.
Fey, Tina. *Mean Girls*. Directed by Mark Waters. 2004; Hollywood: Paramount, 2019. Blu-Ray.
Forbes, Esther Hoskins. (1943) 2011. *Johnny Tremain*. New York: HMH Books for Young Readers.
Groom, Winston. (1986) 2012. *Forrest Gump*. Vancouver: Vintage.
Hackford, Taylor. *Ray*. Directed by Taylor Hackford. 2004; Universal City: Universal, 2011. Blu-Ray.
Hosseini, Khaled. (2003) 2013. *The Kite Runner*. New York: Riverhead Books.
King, Stephen. (1979) 2016. *The Long Walk*. New York: Gallery Books.
King, Stephen. (1982) 2016. *The Running Man*. New York: Pocket Books.
Kumble, Roger. *Cruel Intentions*. Directed by Roger Kumble. 1999; Culver City: Sony Pictures Home Entertainment, 2016. Blu-Ray.
Kushner, Tony. *Lincoln*. Directed by Steven Spielberg. 2012; Burbank: Walt Disney Studios, 2013. Blu-Ray.
Lewalski, Barbara. 1986. *Renaissance Genres: Essays on Theory, History, and Interpretation*. Cambridge: Harvard UP.
Lim, Adele, and Peter Chiarelli. *Crazy Rich Asians*. Directed by John M. Chu. 2018; Burbank: Warner Brothers, 2018. Blu-Ray.
Lowry, Lois. 1993. *The Giver*. New York: HMH Books for Young Readers.
Lucas, George, and Lawrence Kasdan. *Star Wars Episode VI: Return of the Jedi*. Directed by Richard Marquand. 1983; Los Angeles: Twentieth Century Fox, 2013. Blu-Ray.
Lucas, George, Leigh Brackett, and Lawrence Kasden. *Star Wars Episode V: The Empire Strikes Back*. Directed by Irvin Kershner. 1980; Los Angeles: Twentieth Century Fox, 2013. Blu-Ray.
Lucas, George. *Star Wars Episode IV: A New Hope*. Directed by George Lucas. 1977; Los Angeles: Twentieth Century Fox, 2013. Blu-Ray.

Meyer, Stephanie. 2005. *Twilight*. New York: Little, Brown Books for Young Readers.

Miller, Arthur. (1949) 1976. *Death of a Salesman*. New York: Penguin Books.

Parker, Ol. *Mamma Mia: Here We go Again*. Directed by Ol Parker. 2018; Universal City: Universal, 2018. Blu-Ray.

Perry, Tyler. *Nobody's Fool*. Directed by Tyler Perry. 2018; Hollywood: Paramount Pictures, 2019. Blu-Ray.

Portis, Charles. (1968) 2010. *True Grit*. New York: Harry N. Abrams.

Price, Jeffrey, and Peter Seaman. *Who Framed Roger Rabbit?* Directed by Robert Zemeckis. 1988; Burbank: Touchstone Pictures, 2013. Blu-Ray.

Rich, Mike. *The Rookie*. Directed by John Lee Hancock. 2002; Burbank: Walt Disney Pictures, 2008. DVD.

Roth, Eric. *Forrest Gump*. Directed by Robert Zemeckis. 1994; Burbank: Warner Brothers, 2013. Blu-Ray.

Salinger, J.D. (1951) 2001. *The Catcher in the Rye*. London: Back Bay Books.

Schroeder, Allison. *Hidden Figures*. Directed by Theodore Melfi. 2016; Los Angeles: Twentieth Century Fox, 2017. Blu-Ray.

Serling, Rod. *Requiem for a Heavyweight*. Directed by Ralph Nelson. 1956; Culver City: Sony Pictures Home Entertainment, 1998. VHS.

Siegel, Robert. *The Wrestler*. Directed by Darren Aronofsky. 2008; Los Angeles: Fox Searchlight, 2009. Blu-Ray.

Tally, Ted. *The Silence of the Lambs*. Directed by Jonathan Demme. 1991; Beverly Hills: MGM Studios, 2007. DVD.

Tolkien, J.R.R. (1937) 2012. *The Hobbit*. New York: Houghton Mifflin Harcourt.

Towne, Robert. *Chinatown*. Directed by Roman Polanski. 1974; Burbank: Warner Brothers, 2012. Blu-Ray.

Wilson, August. 1986. *Fences*. New York: Plume.

Zaillian, Steve. *Schindler's List*. Directed by Steven Spielberg. 1993; Universal City: Universal, 2018. Blu-Ray.

CHAPTER 7

Applications and Exercises

7.1 Application: Introduction and Starter Questions

So far, you've learned about Shakespeare's stories, the five steps they follow, and how the characters in each story progress from motivations, goals, and flaws to revelation. You've also learned about several tools that Shakespeare uses to combine characters' stories into a piece of storytelling, and learned about the types (or genres) of storytelling that Shakespeare produced.

In this chapter, you'll apply this book's concepts both to Shakespeare's plays and to pieces of storytelling from modern-day writers. This section isn't a bank of questions and answers like you'd find in the back of a physics textbook. There, it's easy to tell the difference between right and wrong answers quickly. Here, the proper distinction is between answers that demonstrate understanding of a concept and answers that don't. This is more involved. We can both understand a concept like motivation perfectly well, but disagree about what motivates a character like Richard of Gloucester.

So for this section, I've written three application exercises. The first two exercises ask straightforward questions about characters' motivations, goals, and flaws, using examples from *King Lear*, *Hamlet*, and *Star Wars: Episode IV*. I've included discussions of the answers, too. That way it's easier to separate interpretive differences from more substantial misunderstandings.

The third application section is a little different. There, I'll ask you to rewrite a non-Shakespearean story in order to make it Shakespearean. In the discussion of that section, I'll outline what some versions of your new, Shakespearean story might do. I'd be surprised, and maybe a little suspicious, if your story and mine ended up looking very much alike.

But if you have a yen for simple questions, I'll give you some. These assume that you have access to at least the first five minutes of a couple Disney/Pixar films: *Wreck-It Ralph* (2012) and *Inside Out* (2015). Kids' movies. How hard can it be?

Wreck-It Ralph

In order to answer the following questions, you'll need to watch the first four minutes of *Wreck-It Ralph*. Like Richard of Gloucester (in *Richard III*), Ralph has an opening monologue. If there's one thing you should know about an opening monologue, it's that any Shakespearean character who has one will use it to tell you about their motivations, goals, and flaws.

Have you watched the monologue yet? Good. Here are a few simple questions to check your understanding.

Which of these is Ralph's motivation? Choose one:

a. Ralph wants to enjoy another 30 years as a working video game character.
b. Ralph wants his own video game, away from Felix and the Nicelanders.
c. Ralph wants to be seen as a good guy.
d. We don't see Ralph's motivation in this opening monologue.
e. Ralph wants to be seen as authentic, honest, and vulnerable.

The answer is (c). Motivation is about how a character wants to be seen, and Ralph ends his monologue telling us that he wants to be seen as a good guy. It's possible that a character could tell us that they want to be seen one way when they really want to be seen in another, but *Wreck-It Ralph* is a kids' movie. That said, even complicated stories won't misdirect their audiences about essential issues like characters' motivations. When a character tells you what they want, believe them.

Let's try another question, still based on Ralph's opening monologue:
Which of these are Ralph's flaws, and why? Choose one or more:

a. Ralph lacks empathy: Even though Ralph acknowledges the existence of other people, he doesn't understand that other people's physical and emotional struggles might be similar to his own.
b. Ralph is evil: He opens his monologue by saying "My name is Ralph, and I'm a bad guy."
c. Ralph is impulsive and temperamental: He says, "I've got a bit of a temper on me," which sounds like he's minimizing the consequences of a real problem.

The answer is (a) and (c) together. (b) isn't a meaningful answer because it's not specific enough. Flaws are ways of thinking and acting that hurt other people. Just being evil isn't sufficient. If you want to hurt people, you have to get up and do something.

On (a): Ralph comes across as authentic, honest, and vulnerable in this opening monologue. He might not have a sophisticated understanding of his own feelings, but he's also not obviously self-deluding. He tells the truth about himself, even when this means that his listeners—whoever they are—might reject him for it.

At the same time, Ralph sees himself as almost uniquely unlucky. If you watch more than the first two minutes of *Wreck-It Ralph*, you'll learn that Ralph's world is full of Bad Guys whose struggles are very like his. They do a necessary job that nobody appreciates. They also offer good advice that Ralph doesn't take.

On (c): A character who admits to a flaw will never be totally wrong. A character who points out someone else's flaws is never totally wrong, either. If a character says, "I make sure things get done," you can bet that someone else will say, "he's obsessive and controlling." They're saying the same thing in different words.

Let's try one more question:

Which of these is likely to be one of Ralph's goals? Choose one:

a. Ralph wants to live in a nicer place (that is, not in the dump).
b. Ralph wants to kill Fix-it Felix and take his place as the game's hero.
c. Ralph wants a medal. Ralph wants to be seen as a "good guy," and having a medal would confirm, or validate, that he is one.

The answer is (c). It's the longest answer (which is always a giveaway). But it's also the only answer that makes a connection between a goal and a motivation—that is, it's the only answer that tells us how attaining a thing, whatever it is, will help Ralph be seen in the way that he wants to be seen. It's possible that Ralph wants to live in a nicer place, but that's just something he wants. If it doesn't pertain to his motivation, it's not a goal.

Let's try another children's movie.

Inside Out

To answer these questions, you'll need to watch the first couple minutes of *Inside Out*. Like *Wreck-It Ralph*, *Inside Out* begins with a monologue that describes one character, Joy's, motivations, goals, and flaws in an abbreviated way. Unlike *Wreck-It Ralph*, *Inside Out* pounds straight on to establishing conflicts and character webs.

Have you watched the first three minutes yet? Good.

How would you describe the Shakespearean conflict between Joy (the yellow character) and Sadness (the blue character)? Choose one:

a. Joy and Sadness obviously dislike each other—they shove each other to get to the giant button that controls Riley (the baby's) emotions.
b. Joy wants the baby, Riley, to be happy. Sadness wants Riley to be, well, sad.

c. This is a trick question. Joy and Sadness aren't in conflict at all. Instead, they're working together to control the way that the baby, Riley, feels.
d. Both Joy and Sadness want to control how the baby (Riley) feels and behaves.

The answer is (d). Both (a) and (b) might be true, but Shakespearean conflict only happens when characters want the same thing. This can sometimes look like characters cooperating, but when characters agree to do the same thing you can bet that they'll disagree about how it ought to be done. The conflicts between the Nurse and Friar Lawrence in *Romeo and Juliet* often take this form.

Next question:

Which of Joy's and Sadness's actions help establish their character web? You may choose more than one:

a. The different ways that Joy and Sadness react to their environments. Both of them spontaneously appear in Riley's (the baby's) mind. Joy reacts to this with curiosity and wonder, while Sadness focuses only on pushing the button.
b. The different ways that Joy and Sadness try to control the button. Both of them want to control it, but use different strategies: Joy shoves (politely) while Sadness just stays put.
c. The character design. Because Joy is tall and Sadness is short, we're supposed to understand that they are different types of characters.
d. The music. The sad tuba music that plays when Sadness introduces herself shows us that she is a different type of character than Joy.

The answers? (a) and (b), but it's tricky. Both of these are examples of the most basic kind of character webbing, where characters react differently to the same thing. Character design, music, and other cues can help us tell characters apart, but they're not character webbing in the Shakespearean sense. That involves only the things that characters say and do, rather than (for instance) their costumes, their stature, or their theme music.

Here's one more question:

True or False: Because Joy and Sadness both try to keep each other from pushing the button, they are opponents.

This is another tricky one. It's false, but—if the sequence had played out longer, or at a different point in *Inside Out*—it could have easily been true.

Opponents attack other characters' weaknesses, generally over the course of an entire piece of storytelling. At this early stage, one character might attack another's weaknesses in order to keep her from pressing the button. Sadness, for instance, might know that Joy is non-confrontational, and attack that weakness by staying put, knowing that Joy doesn't have the mettle to shove her out of the way. But we haven't seen enough of *Inside Out* to know whether this will be a sustained attack.

If questions like these are your idea of fun, you can continue on to the next two Application sections, where we'll work with *King Lear*, *Hamlet*, and *Star Wars* (1977).

7.2   APPLICATION: *KING LEAR*

We'll begin our practice with *King Lear*. If you've read (or are reading) *King Lear*, and you understand motivations, goals, flaws, and revelations, you should be able to apply those concepts by answering two questions:

1. What are Gloucester's motivations, goals, and flaws?
2. What is Edmund's revelation?

If you haven't read *King Lear*, I've provided quotes and summaries that should allow you to answer these questions anyway. I've also provided answers and explanations, so you can see how each of my answers is accountable to what each of these characters says and does.

What are Gloucester's motivations, goals, and flaws?

Before you answer this question, here's what you need to know: In the first scene of *King Lear* (I.i), we meet three characters: Kent (an advisor to the king), Gloucester (a nobleman), and Gloucester's illegitimate son, Edmund. We learn about Edmund this way:

> GLOUCESTER
> [...] I have, sir, a son by order of law, some year elder than this, who yet is no dearer in my account. Though this knave came something saucily into the world before he was sent for, yet was his mother fair. There was good sport at his making, and the whoreson must be acknowledged. Do you know this noble gentleman, Edmund?
> EDMUND
> No, my lord. (20–27)

Gloucester makes a few points in this introduction, and they get progressively stranger:

1. My son Edmund, who you see here, is illegitimate, and has an older and legitimate brother.
2. I don't think that Edmund's older, legitimate brother is any more valuable than Edmund.
3. That said, I didn't really love that Edmund was born.
4. By the rules of having enjoyed sex with Edmund's hot mom, I've got to acknowledge that Edmund is my son.
5. By the way, Edmund, do you know this guy I'm talking to?

Based on this introduction alone, what do you suppose are Gloucester's motivations, goals, and flaws?
The Answer

> **Motivations**: Gloucester wants to be seen as responsible. He does what he must, where "must" specifically means bending to whatever legal or moral principles say that he should acknowledge Edmund as his son.
> **Goals**: Gloucester wants to convince Kent—and perhaps Edmund—that he is a responsible person by explaining how and why he has met his obligations to Edmund.
> **Flaws**: Gloucester thinks that he is being responsible and fair by acknowledging that Edmund is his son, but his conduct toward Edmund is distant and insensitive. He talks about Edmund as a responsibility that deserves to be met, rather than as a child who deserves to be loved.

Discussion

Gloucester doesn't seem to know, or care, much about Edmund. His introduction of Edmund talks about Edmund's brother, and Edmund's mother, and how Gloucester feels about them, but there's nothing about Edmund and how Gloucester feels about him. Edmund is the Amazing Invisible Kid.
What is Edmund's revelation?

Before you answer this question, here's some context: *King Lear* progresses unhappily through another set of equally awkward parenting blunders, while Edmund (who turns out to be a genuine villain in the tradition of Richard of Gloucester) double-crosses his brother and father, and then pits King Lear's daughters Goneril and Regan against each other. They're evil, too. Naturally, they both fall in love with Edmund. In their fight over him, Goneril poisons Regan and then kills herself.

Meantime Edmund lies dying, having lost a duel with his nobler, older, more legitimate brother. His final scene (V.iii) begins:

> ALBANY
> Speak, Edmund. Where's the king? And where's Cordelia? See'st thou this object, Kent?
> *The bodies of GONERIL and REGAN are brought in.*
> KENT
> Alack, why thus?
> EDMUND
> Yet Edmund was beloved.
> The one the other poisoned for my sake,
> And after slew herself.
> ALBANY
> Even so. Cover their faces.
> EDMUND
> I pant for life. Some good I mean to do,
> Despite of mine own nature. (279–87)

Based on this exchange, and on what we already know about Edmund's story, what do you think is Edmund's revelation?
The Answer
I'd start by looking at Edmund's first line after Goneril and Regan's bodies are brought in: "Yet Edmund was beloved." It's a twisted line—love doesn't ordinarily take the form of murder/suicide—but it speaks to Edmund.

With a father like Gloucester, who blushes to acknowledge that Edmund is his son, Edmund's motivation is little more than to be seen or—more specifically—to be seen as significant to someone else. What Edmund realizes at this moment is that he has been significant to ("beloved" by) Regan and Goneril. He doesn't need to seek attention by being unrelentingly evil.
Conclusion
Those two questions, and their answers, describe how Edmund moves from one way of thinking to another, or from flaw to revelation. It's only one of several stories in *King Lear*: there's the story of Edmund's father, Gloucester, and Edmund's brother, Edgar. There's the story of Kent, and of Goneril and Regan (and their husbands, Albany and Cornwall), and their youngest sister, Cordelia. And there's the story of King Lear himself—the story that is central to the play.

But it is not the entire play. The arrangement of stories in *King Lear* is especially artful; the characters highlight one another's most important qualities, and the way that each character's story is told places important events in positions that contrast one another. The play, all in all, is like a well-composed painting that uses perspective, color, and light to present every element as a consistent, artistic whole.

In the next chapter, we'll see how one writer has used Shakespeare's system of motivations, goals, flaws, and revelations to produce a modern-day version of an essentially Shakespearean story.

7.3   Application: *Hamlet* and *Star Wars: Episode IV*

If your work with *King Lear* has convinced you that you understand motivations, goals, flaws, and revelations, you're ready to see how other writers have used these tools of Shakespeare's in modern-day storytelling. In a moment, I'm going to ask you to read *Hamlet* and watch *Star Wars* (1977). Here's why:

At the center of *Hamlet* is a story in which a young person (Hamlet) becomes an adult by choosing loyalties between two different parental figures (Old Hamlet and Claudius) who represent different ways of thinking and acting.

That definition of Hamlet's story is expansive enough to include books like *Coraline* (2002), *Fun Home* (2006), and *Matilda* (1988), along with movies like *Batman Begins* (2005), *Iron Man* (2008), *Get Rich or Die Tryin'* (2005) and dozens—if not hundreds—of others. Read (or watch) any of them carefully, and you'll find several characters whose stories echo the stories in *Hamlet*.

Star Wars is no exception, and it makes an excellent reference text for *Hamlet*. Comparing the characters in *Hamlet* to their counterparts in *Star Wars*, using what we know about motivations, goals, flaws, and revelations, can give you insights about both sets of characters that you might be unlikely to have if you looked at either set of characters in isolation.

So if you've never read *Hamlet*, now's the time. If you've never seen *Star Wars*, it's that time, too. Reading *Hamlet* can take as long as four hours, and watching *Star Wars* takes about two. This should be six hours well spent.

At the end of them, if you understand motivations, goals, flaws, and revelations, and have carefully read (and watched) *Hamlet* and *Star Wars*, you should be able to answer these three questions:

1. What do Hamlet and Luke's motivations, goals, flaws, and revelations have in common? (Just to clarify, let's start with the goals that Hamlet and Luke have at the beginnings of their stories. After that, their worlds are too different to allow brief and meaningful comparison.)
2. What is Han Solo's revelation, and when in his story does it occur?
3. Princess Leia and Ophelia are different from one another in several important respects. But their flaws are similar. How?

In the section below, I've provided an overview of some basic similarities between *Hamlet* and *Star Wars*. I've also answered these questions, and explained how each answer is accountable to the texts.

Now that you've read *Hamlet*, seen *Star Wars*, and answered the questions...

Here's what should be obvious: *Hamlet* and *Star Wars* are built from fundamentally similar stories and use fundamentally similar storytelling techniques. You may have noticed that:

- Both *Hamlet* and *Star Wars* are Coming of Age stories set against a backdrop of military conflict, in which a young man (Hamlet/Luke) must discover his strengths as a warrior in order to preserve the values inherent in his father's legacy.
- In both stories, Hamlet and Luke discover these strengths by avenging their father's betrayal and murder, which was committed by an anti-father figure (Claudius/Darth Vader) who represents a competing set of values.
- This revenge is aided by an arrogant and self-centered foil (Laertes/Han Solo) who complicates the young man's romance with a young woman (Ophelia/Leia), and who ultimately abandons his self-centered behavior in service of both the young man's revenge and the interests of the nation (Denmark/the Rebel Alliance).

There's more, but that should be enough to convince you that we are working with a set of deeply similar stories. So let's start with a comprehensive question—the big one.

What do Hamlet's and Luke's motivations, goals, flaws, and revelations have in common?
The Answer

> **Motivations**: Both Hamlet and Luke begin their stories wanting to be seen as loyal sons to their dead fathers.
> **Goals**: Both Hamlet and Luke believe they can accomplish this using a twofold strategy of (a) demonstrating contempt for their adoptive father's lifestyle, worldview, and values, and (b) escaping their family (by going to college).[1]
> **Flaws**: Neither Hamlet nor Luke know how to approach conflicts using their father's values (that is, by being straightforward, capable warriors who fight for The Right Way of Doing Things). Instead, they approach conflicts using a combination of complaint, whining, and deception.
> **Revelations**: Both Hamlet and Luke discover their strengths as warriors by learning to trust that a system larger than themselves (divine providence/the Force) will lend them the strength to discover, confront, and thwart the plans laid by their anti-father figures, Claudius and Darth Vader.

Discussion

I haven't shown my work in that first answer—there's probably a book in that all by itself. You might disagree with my answer, too, and that's fine. I'm willing to bet you've seen elements of both Hamlet's and Luke's stories that you've never seen before, and that's the point of exercises like that first question. That, and helping you check that you really understand concepts like motivations, goals, flaws, and revelations.

If you do understand them, and you're confident in your answer to the first question, you're ready for the next two questions. These are more specific, and I've shown how I got to my answers as quickly and neatly as possible.

We have discussed Laertes's motivations, flaws, and revelation already, and in this section we've also identified Han Solo as the Laertes figure in Star Wars.
What is Han Solo's revelation and where in his story does it occur?
The Answer

Han Solo's flaws closely mirror Laertes's: he's self-centered. Other characters in *Star Wars* make this observation constantly. Let's look at the dialogue in the scene that begins Han's revelation:

---

[1] In Hamlet's case, Wittenberg. In Luke's, it's the Academy.

LUKE
So... you got your reward and you're just leaving then?
HAN
That's right, yeah! I got some old debts I've got to pay off with this stuff. Even if I didn't, you don't think I'd be fool enough to stick around here, do you? Why don't you come with us? You're pretty good in a fight. I could use you.
LUKE
Getting angry
Come on! Why don't you take a look around? You know what's about to happen, what they're up against. They could use a good pilot like you. You're turning your back on them.
HAN
What good's a reward if you ain't around to use it? Besides, attacking that battle station ain't my idea of courage. It's more like suicide.
LUKE
All right. Well, take care of yourself, Han. I guess that's what you're best at, isn't it?
Luke goes off and Han hesitates, then calls to him.
HAN
Hey, Luke... may the Force be with you!
Luke turns and sees Han wink at him. Luke lifts his hand in a small wave and then goes off. Han turns to Chewie who growls at his captain.
HAN
What're you lookin' at? I know what I'm doing.

Here, we see both Luke and Chewie opposing Han's decision to abandon the battle against the Empire and its Death Star. Han still leaves, but there are hints that his attitude is changing: he and Luke are able to part on friendly terms thanks to Han's "may the Force be with you." This is the first moment in *Star Wars* that Han shows much consideration of anybody else's feelings.

We know that Han's revelation is complete, however, when he returns to aid Luke in his assault on the Death Star. His revelation is extremely similar to Laertes's, in the sense that both characters abandon their self-centered behavior and choose to return to, and protect the interests of, their community.

Discussion

Both Laertes and Han are starkly drawn characters with well-defined flaws and sudden—even abrupt—revelations. I don't know that either warrants much further commentary, save that the exact moment that Laertes's revelation begins is hard to pinpoint. It could begin the moment that Laertes returns from France, if you think his weightiest flaw is that he's indifferent to the fate of his country. For what it's worth, I think that Laertes's revelation begins very late: when he starts to lose the fencing match with Hamlet and realizes that for all of Hamlet's eccentricities, there is something in him that is worthy of respect.

Let's try our next question.

Princess Leia is the Ophelia figure in *Star Wars*, although she and Ophelia are different from one another in several important respects. But their flaws are similar. How?
The Answer

Both Ophelia and Leia begin their stories with the same flaw: they underestimate the intelligence, perceptiveness, and competence of the people they're in conflict with.

This flaw of Ophelia's and Leia's gets illustrated in the same oddly specific way: both characters begin their stories trying to lie their way out of a problem, protesting their innocence long after a more perceptive character would have abandoned that strategy for another.

Let's start with Ophelia. In her first scene (I.iii) she and her father (Polonius) are bidding farewell to Laertes, who's leaving for France. Before he leaves, Laertes warns Ophelia not to put too much faith in her relationship with Hamlet. It's a long speech, but the key lines go something like this:

> LAERTES
> Then weigh what loss your honor may sustain
> If with too credent ear you list his songs,
> Or lose your heart, or your chaste treasure open
> To his unmastered importunity. (29–32)

Don't sleep with Hamlet, in other words. Ophelia responds this way:

> OPHELIA
> I shall the effect of this good lesson keep
> As watchman to my heart. But, good my brother,
> Do not, as some ungracious pastors do,
> Show me the steep and thorny way to heaven
> Whiles, like a puffed and reckless libertine,
> Himself the primrose path of dalliance treads,
> And recks not his own rede.
> LAERTES
> O, fear me not.
> I stay too long: but here my father comes.
> *Enter POLONIUS.* (49–52)

This exchange exists for a few reasons. For our purposes, the most important reason is to tell us that Laertes knows that Hamlet and Ophelia are in a relationship, and that Ophelia wants that relationship to continue—that's why she shoots back at Laertes with the "puffed and reckless libertine" bit instead of saying something like "I'm done with Hamlet. His drama is already past its expiration date."

The second reason is to show us that Ophelia isn't naive. She knows what Laertes is getting up to in France—it's exactly the same kind of business he's warning her against with Hamlet, which is why she calls him out for being a hypocrite.

So then we get her conversation with Polonius:

> LORD POLONIUS
> What is it, Ophelia, he hath said to you?
> OPHELIA
> So please you, something touching the Lord Hamlet. (88–89)

Ophelia is already in trouble. I think that Polonius already knows what Laertes has been talking to Ophelia about, and he's probing her. (This is exactly the same strategy he suggests that Reynaldo use to spy on Laertes in II.i.) A cunning father might even have put Laertes up to warning Ophelia away from Hamlet instead of doing the job himself.

But even if you don't buy that, any teenager in the habit of lying to their parents could tell you that Ophelia's response, "something touching the Lord Hamlet," is too evasive to end a line of fatherly questioning. Polonius jumps on it:

> LORD POLONIUS
> Marry, well bethought.
> It is told me he hath very oft of late
> Given private time to you, and you yourself
> Have of your audience been most free and bounteous. (90–93)

Let's ignore what Polonius is implying about Ophelia's "free and bounteous" gifts (sex), and focus on the state of Ophelia's cover. It's blown. The game is over. Laertes knows where Ophelia and Hamlet's relationship is heading, and Polonius has just revealed that he does, too. But Ophelia retrenches:

> OPHELIA
> He hath, my lord, of late made many tenders
> Of his affection to me.
> LORD POLONIUS
> Affection! pooh! you speak like a green girl,
> Unsifted in such perilous circumstance. (99–103)

"Green" here means "naive," and so we can see the drift of Ophelia's plan: she's playing innocent. *Sex? What's that?* Again, she gives herself away by being so vague that her answers look evasive. Polonius doesn't buy it.

> LORD POLONIUS
> Do you believe his tenders, as you call them?
> OPHELIA
> I do not know, my lord, what I should think. (103–104)

This is the second time in a half-dozen lines that Ophelia tries to play naive—and, again, does it badly. Polonius shows his contempt for this with a bit of condescension:

> LORD POLONIUS
> Marry, I'll teach you. Think yourself a baby,
> That you have taken these tenders for true pay
> Which are not sterling. Tender yourself more dearly
> Or [...] you'll tender me a fool. (105–109)

To her credit, Ophelia gives up playing dumb and tries a new line: Hamlet is noble and honest:

> OPHELIA
> My lord, he hath importuned me with love
> In honorable fashion.
> LORD POLONIUS
> Ay, fashion you may call it. Go to, go to.
> OPHELIA
> And hath given countenance to his speech, my lord,
> With almost all the holy vows of heaven.
> LORD POLONIUS
> Ay, springes to catch woodcocks. I do know,
> When the blood burns, how prodigal the soul
> Lends the tongue vows. These blazes, daughter [...]
> You must not take for fire. (110–120)

Polonius isn't having any of it, and their conversation concludes:

> LORD POLONIUS
> I would not, in plain terms, from this time forth,
> Have you so slander any moment's leisure
> As to give words or talk with the Lord Hamlet.
> Look to it, I charge you. Come your ways.
> OPHELIA
> I shall obey, my lord. (132–36)

Another character in the same position might have done better. Had Ophelia said, "I was just warning Laertes to stay away from French hookers," she might have put this whole exchange to bed in line one.

Failing that, Ophelia's conversation with her father might have gone better if she'd abandoned her pretext of total innocence and demonstrated her ability to handle a delicate situation more carefully. "Yes," she might have said, "I've been seeing Hamlet. He's like a dog trying to get into the refrigerator. I'm not going to let him, but it's fun to watch him work at it."

Leia works the same way. *Star Wars* opens with Darth Vader and his Stormtroopers forcibly boarding Leia's ship. Leia, meantime, is loading a secret message on to R2D2. There's a firefight, and when the Stormtroopers reach Leia she pulls a gun and starts shooting. Then she's captured.

That's our establishing moment—the *Star Wars* version of Ophelia's conversation with Laertes. We know that Leia is up to something when she loads a message onto R2D2, and we also know that she's the kind of person who'd rather shoot a Stormtrooper than surrender to one. That frames Leia's first conversation with Darth Vader, where she complains about her ship being boarded:

> LEIA
> Lord Vader, I should have known. Only you could be so bold. The Imperial Senate will not sit for this, when they hear you've attacked a diplomatic—
> VADER
> Don't play games with me, Your Highness. You weren't on any mercy mission this time. You passed directly through a restricted system. Several transmissions were beamed to this ship by Rebel spies. I want to know what happened to the plans they sent you.
> LEIA
> I don't know what you're talking about. I'm a member of the Imperial Senate on a diplomatic mission to Alderaan—
> VADER
> You're a part of the Rebel Alliance and a traitor. Take her away!

Darth Vader might be evil, but he's right. Leia *is* part of the Rebel Alliance, and *has* been in contact with Rebel agents who have sent her the plans to the Death Star. Darth Vader's intentions are more severe than Polonius's, but there's still no point in Leia insisting on her cover story. The chances of success are zero. Vader wouldn't have boarded the ship, searching for the plans, if he didn't already know that they were there.

Again, this situation might have turned out better if Leia had abandoned her pretext of total innocence and told a different lie instead: "You're too late, Vader! Our double agent has the plans and is already inside the Death Star!"

Discussion

Though Ophelia and Leia begin their stories with similar flaws, they end their stories differently. Leia overcomes her flaw of holding other people in low esteem only with her last line—in this case, to Han:

> LEIA
> *Laughing*
> Hey, I knew there was more to you than money.

That line is the first moment that Leia openly declares her confidence in someone else's positive qualities.

That's not much to go on, but *Star Wars* ends with a scene in which there's no spoken dialogue: a throne-room ceremony. There, Leia awards medals of honor to both Luke and Han in front of hundreds of assembled Rebel soldiers (and C3PO, R2D2, and Chewbacca). The last scene of the movie, in other words, drives home the point that Luke has become brave enough to be honored, Han has become selfless enough to be honored, and Leia has learned that other people are competent enough to deserve being honored. It's really quite clever that way.

Ophelia never gets a scene like this, and whether she has a revelation at all depends on lots of good questions about her character that don't have certain answers.

Let's begin with her suicide. It's reasonable to read it as driven by guilt. Her father is dead, murdered by her insane boyfriend as the consequence both of her own plans and of a plot in which she allowed herself to be used as an instrument. From Ophelia's perspective, that could very well make everything her fault.

But it's also reasonable to read Ophelia's suicide as driven by anger—specifically, anger over being ignored, or treated as an instrument in other people's plans, or as an obstacle to their happiness. If that's how you read Ophelia, she has absolutely had a revelation: she's learned that other people are capable, but also that they're indifferent to her well-being.

There are probably a dozen other ways to read Ophelia's death, and as many more to read moments that precede it. I think that readers work against the text when they read Ophelia as naive. We have her opening scene with Laertes, and her mid-play (III.ii) banter with Hamlet, to vouch for her cleverness and sophistication. But outside of that misreading, nearly anything goes.

7.4 Application: From Story to Shakespeare

So far, you've braved the terrors of a half-dozen multiple choice and short-answer questions about motivations, goals, flaws, conflict, character webs, and opposition. Now, we're going to do a comprehensive exercise that ties together these and other concepts by writing our own Shakespearean story.

Don't panic. I'm not asking you to write the next Great American Novel. Instead, I'm going to ask you to take a simple story and turn it into something Shakespearean.

So let's start the simplest possible story, in which we learn what a character does in order to get what they want. Here it is:

> Once upon a time there was a young man named Alex who wanted a Tropical Island card from *Magic, the Gathering*.[2] He mowed lawns until he earned enough money to buy it. Then he bought it.

---

[2]To quote CompleteSet.com: "Valued between $2,600 and $3,000, Tropical Island isn't actually part of the legendary Power 9 but it is widely regarded as one of the most valuable *Magic: The Gathering* Cards putting it into most Top 10 lists and edging up to the #9 spot for ours. Containing serene, island art by Jesper Myrfors this pretty little card is incredibly useful for generating mana just when you need it most; especially if you are playing a green and blue mixed deck."

Over the next five subsections, you'll revise this story so that it follows each of Shakespeare's five steps. For each step, we'll also revise it so that it uses some of Shakespeare's storytelling tools. Some of those—like motivations, goals, and flaws, we've already worked with in the last two sections. Others, like symbols, are concepts that we'll be working with for the first time. By the end of this section, we'll have revised this simple story about Alex into a Shakespearean journey of self-discovery and change.

One warning: This section may feel heavy on review. It's our last chance to get things right. If you feel like we're re-covering familiar territory, it's because we are. You're not having an episode of *déjà vu* and (probably) not having a stroke.

Ready? Let's begin.

7.4.1 Step One: Motivations, Goals, and Flaws

Let's begin with *Step One: Motivations, Goals, and Flaws*. For reference, here's our simple story:

> Once upon a time there was a young man named Alex who wanted a Tropical Island card from *Magic, the Gathering*. He mowed lawns until he earned enough money to buy it. Then he bought it.

Prompt

Revise this story so that Alex has a well-defined motivation, at least one clearly defined goal, and both a psychological and a moral flaw.

In this exercise, it's OK to add characters, background, and whatever else to this story. By itself, it doesn't tell you everything you need to know in order to introduce Shakespeare's storytelling concepts.

Discussion

This story already tells us something about Alex's goals. He wants a Tropical Island card. At some point, he'll plan to get it by mowing lawns. Then he'll get it.

But we're missing Alex's motivation. To review: Motivations are general, ongoing needs. While, in the world of stories, those needs can be anything from a glass of water to freedom from oppression, Shakespeare's characters need validation. In every Shakespeare play, and for every Shakespearean character, it's possible to discuss this need for validation in terms of how a character wants to be seen. Sometimes, a character wants to be seen as valuable, or worthwhile. Sometimes, they want to be seen as a responsible parent, a loyal son, or a protective patriarch.

So: in this story, the Tropical Island card is Alex's goal. It's a specific, concrete, tangible thing. It's *what* he wants; his motivation is the *why*.

So why does Alex want the Tropical Island card? Maybe he thinks that having a Tropical Island card will make him the envy of his *Magic*-playing friends, so that they'll love him, accept him, or see him as worthy of respect.

We're all (hopefully) adult enough to understand that you don't get acceptance, love, or validation by buying expensive things and showing them off to your friends. All the lawn mowing and card buying in the world won't get Alex what he really wants. We know that, but he doesn't.

That's the third ingredient of Step One: flaws. Alex has a misperception about the world, or an element of his personality, that hurts him. That's a psychological flaw. It's usually evident in the way that a character connects their motivation (to be seen as worthy of love and acceptance) to their first goal (buying the Tropical Island card).

If Alex is like most Shakespearean characters, his misperceptions will also lead him to hurt other people. If they do, they constitute a moral flaw. If we want Alex to have a moral flaw, his story will need at least one other character. And so we'll introduce one: Alex's mother, Mom.

With her in the mix, a Shakespearean version of Alex's story might open like this:

> MOM
> I can't believe you're still up in your room.
> ALEX
> Everybody hates me.
> MOM
> They don't even know you. Go to that comic shop you like so much and make some friends.

That banter between Alex and Mom will take us to *Step Two: Conflict*.

7.4.2 Step Two: Conflict and Opponents

If you've already created motivations, goals, and flaws for Alex, the next step is to introduce at least one conflict.

Prompt

Rewrite Alex's story so that it includes at least one overt conflict, a structural conflict, and an opponent.

Discussion

We left Alex in conversation with his mother. That conversation went something like this:

> MOM
> I can't believe you're still up in your room.
> ALEX
> Everybody hates me.
> MOM
> They don't even know you. Go to that comic shop you like so much and make some friends.

Conflict happens when two characters both want the same thing. It sometimes doesn't look that way at first. In Alex's conflict with Mom, it looks like

Alex wants to stay in his room and Mom wants him to make friends. His choice to stay in his room keeps him from being happy, and disappoints his mother. It's a symptom of both a psychological and a moral flaw.

But the conflict between Alex and Mom isn't only about what Alex ought to do. It's over whose version of reality, or which set of shared beliefs, will govern both characters' expectations. Alex wants Mom to believe that everybody hates him. Mom wants Alex to believe that nobody really knows him. Like many Shakespearean conflicts, this one is about the truth, and about which version of it becomes what all of the play's characters accept as their reality.

An aside: Mom has motivations, goals, and flaws as well. She needs validation—specifically, she wants to be seen as a good mother. For her, that means believing that she has a psychologically and emotionally healthy (and therefore socially active) son. Her goal, at least as far as this first conversation goes, is getting Alex out of his room and talking to other kids down at the comic shop.

Her flaw? Nagging Alex probably won't change his behavior. Even if it does, it probably won't change it for reasons that actually meet her emotional needs. Mom wants Alex at the comic shop so that he can meet (or make) friends, not because she orders him to go. She wants him out of his room because he's socially active and wants to be out of his room—not because she's increased the emotional costs of staying in bed. In other words, Mom is hurting herself (and Alex) by making it harder for each of them to get the kind of validation that they actually need.

Now for opponents. Another *Magic* player at the comic shop could want the Tropical Island card for themselves. Let's call that player Bob. In the outline of our simple story, this conflict over the Tropical Island card is a structural conflict. It's going to drive this piece of storytelling until the end.

The only other ingredient for opposition is that Bob needs to attack Alex's weaknesses. We can detail how in the next section, but—just for now—let's assume that he'll attack Alex by exploiting Alex's need to be seen as worthy of love and respect.

That said, Bob's reason for being in this story can't be just to oppose Alex. He needs to have his own motivations, goals, and flaws. How will getting the Tropical Island card validate Bob? Let's suppose that, in order to feel valued, Bob needs to beat Alex at whatever Alex is trying to do. If Alex wants something, Bob needs to get it first.

Bob's flaw—like Alex's and Mom's—involves a kind of disconnect between his motivation and his first goal. In trying to one-up Alex, Bob's hurting himself even if he doesn't know it. Trying to get something just because your friend wants it isn't a good look. Bob might think that people will see him as somehow better than Alex if he keeps one-upping him, but if Bob gets the Tropical Island card by hurting Alex, other people will most likely see him as envious, spiteful, and insecure.

Either way: if Bob expects to get the Tropical Island card before Alex does, he'll need a way to do it. This takes us to *Step Three: Plans*.

7.4.3   Step Three: Plans

Let's refresh our original story:

> Once upon a time, Alex wanted a Tropical Island card from *Magic, the Gathering*. He mowed lawns until he earned enough money to buy it. Then he bought it.

The second sentence in that story—the one about mowing lawns—is the germ of *Step Three: Plans*. Now that we have an opponent, we can introduce the kinds of sustained intrigues and madcap plotting that make Shakespeare's villains so much fun.

Prompt

Rewrite Alex's story so that Alex and his opponent each have a plan to buy the Tropical Island card.

Discussion

Alex and Bob could each plan to buy the Tropical Island card independently. In that case, their conflict would basically be a race. Maybe they set up rival lawnmowing businesses. That could be fun for an audience, but it's not Shakespearean. A piece of storytelling about characters who all play by the rules isn't very interesting.

So maybe Alex mows lawns to get his cards, but Bob browbeats his grandfather until the old man hands over his last pension check. Then, once Alex and Bob both have their money in hand, there's a foot race to the comic shop. That can make for a fun story—a Contest story, like *Better off Dead* (1985), *The Karate Kid* (1984), and a lot of movies about sports—but it still feels a little too fair. It's lacking in opposition.

As an opponent, Bob will attack Alex by exploiting Alex's flaws. Once Bob learns that Alex is mowing lawns to buy the Tropical Island card, they might have a conversation like this.

> BOB
> It's no fun playing if you're not there. Everybody says so.
> ALEX
> I still need another thousand. I'm mowing every day straight through to Halloween. If I can't get it by then I've got to wait 'til Spring.
> BOB
> Just play.
> ALEX
> I've got to mow.
> BOB
> We miss you, bro.

Bob's plan of attack here is pretty straightforward: use Alex's need for validation and acceptance to keep Alex playing *Magic*—and away from mowing lawns—until Bob's grandfather coughs up his year-end pension check. Then the Tropical Island card (and the sweet, sweet gamer prestige that comes with it) will be all his.

But plans usually don't work that simply. In a piece of Shakespearean storytelling, you can expect Alex and Bob's plans to fail, get revised, and fail again. Maybe Bob's grandfather dies, or starts to think that Bob should spend his Christmas check on something more worthwhile, like college tuition.

And maybe Alex's race against the end of mowing season hits an unexpected snag when Bob pulls the spark plug out of Alex's lawnmower, or the weather runs unseasonably dry, or—get this—Alex figures out something about himself. That takes us to *Step Four: Battles and Revelations*.

7.4.4   Step Four: Battles and Revelations

We've just introduced an opponent to Alex in the form of rival gamer Bob, and outlined the plan Bob will use to buy the Tropical Island card for himself: keep Alex from mowing lawns until Bob's grandfather signs over his year-end pension check. If that's the direction Bob is heading, he and Alex will eventually have it out. That takes us to *Step Four: Battles and Revelations*.
Prompt
Rewrite Alex's story so that he and his opponent have a battle, and so that Alex has a revelation. Just for fun, include at least one symbol.
Discussion

The battle portion of this question is easy enough to understand: eventually, Bob and Alex fight it out. Maybe that fight is just a culmination of their intrigue—Bob slips into the comic shop one night, buys the Tropical Island card, and vanishes like D.B. Cooper. But their fight could be an honest-to-God battle, too. Maybe Alex finds out the deception Bob's been planning and they katana-duel to the death.

Those things can happen in Shakespearean stories, but not without a revelation. Alex's plan, and its continued failings and reversals, will eventually lead him to recognize his flaws and change his behavior. That is, Alex will find a better way to be seen as worthy of love and respect, but his desire to be seen that way won't change.

Often—and very often in the comedies—the impetus for a character's revelation is good old-fashioned love. So: Imagine that Alex and Bob are both in the depths of their planning. Alex (according to his plan) mows lawn after lawn in order to make one thousand dollars by Halloween. Bob (according to his plan) tries to talk Alex into more *Magic* playing and less mowing.

And then, while mowing on one unseasonably hot September afternoon, Alex sees somebody. Since most Shakespearean characters are heterosexual, I'll call her Cassie. She is achingly beautiful (at least to Alex) and he forgets all about the Tropical Island card. At that moment, we're poised for a revelation.

To recap: At the beginning of his story, Alex needed validation—to be seen as worthy of love and respect. That never changes.

Alex thought that he could be seen as worthy of love and respect by buying a Tropical Island card, and by using it to become the envy of his *Magic*-playing friends. We've already indicated that this thinking is one of Alex's flaws. At the moment he sees Cassie and falls head-over-heels in hormone, he realizes he can meet those needs another way: romantic love.

But what comes of that process is very often complicated. Shakespeare offers us at least two possibilities:

One is that Alex learns about a new way to meet his needs, but what he learns doesn't actually address his flaw (which is his misperception that having something other people envy is the key to making friends and being happy). In that case, Alex sees Cassie as a better version of the Tropical Island card, and develops a plan to win her in order to impress his friends.

In that situation, Alex doesn't actually discover anything about himself—in fact, instead of improving, he actually gets worse. The revelation that he ought to have instead comes to us, the audience. For us, it's painfully obvious how Alex ought to change, and we'll probably groan because Alex's flaw, which at first interfered only with his and Mom's happiness, now threatens Cassie's, too. A few characters from Shakespeare's comedies, like Jaques (from *As You Like It*) and Malvolio (from *Twelfth Night*), go that route. They're constantly doubling down on their flaws.

A second possibility is that Alex learns something about himself. "Wait a minute," he might think, "I shouldn't be looking for ways to be loved because of what I have. I should instead seek love from people whose love helps me become a better version of myself. That's the only honest path to validation."

In that story, Alex correctly perceives his flaws, and pursues his new goal (according to a new plan) instead of pursuing his old goal (according to the old one). That doesn't mean that one desire simply and immediately replaces another. Instead, characters often struggle to live according to the values, or to address the flaws, that their revelation says they ought to.

This is a classic fork—the kind we see when Hamlet chooses between two different father figures who represent different sets of values. In this case, both Cassie and the Tropical Island card are symbols. They represent different philosophies about what Alex ought to value and how he ought to act.

In a more detailed version of this story, Alex might be forced to choose between mowing lawns to buy his Tropical Island card or spending time with Cassie. His decision about which to do tells us which set of values he's adopted.

Revelations are an important storytelling tool. They clarify and deepen character, which keeps the story interesting. In a well-crafted story, like many of Shakespeare's plays, they also produce new conflicts by changing the goals (and plans) of several characters, rather than only the one who had the revelation. This produces new, and (hopefully) more interesting conflicts.

Consider the conflict between Alex and his mother, Mom. Both these characters need love and validation, although they try to meet those needs in different ways.

Alex pursues love and validation indirectly at first (by buying the card that gets his friends to envy, and therefore validate, him), and then directly (through Cassie).

Mom, however, pursues validation by demonstrating her competence as a parent which—to her—means keeping her son from being hurt. In their first conflict, this made her goal one thing: for Alex to get out of his room and make friends. But once Alex has his revelation and his goal changes, Mom's goal is likely to change, too.

The same is true of the conflict between Alex and Bob. Bob pursues validation by doing better than Alex. In their first conflict, this made Bob's goal one thing: to buy the Tropical Island card. But when Alex's goal changes, Bob's goal also has to change.

So: Imagine that Alex has told everyone he's getting ready to ask Cassie out on a date. He's got a pocket full of lawnmowing money, so he's going fancy: dinner at the Cheesecake Factory. Here's how the conflict between Alex, Bob, and Mom might play out:

> MOM
> I just don't see why you have to.
> ALEX
> It's got to be special.
> BOB
> Just be careful.
> MOM
> What do you mean?
> BOB
> I don't want to say anything.
> MOM
> You don't have to, Bobby. That girl just wants a ten-dollar piece of cheesecake.
> BOB
> Her ex just got a new Camry.
> ALEX
> What?
> BOB
> She hangs out with him all the time. I didn't want to tell you, but—
> MOM
> Hush, Bobby. You need to think about this, Alex. You need to think about a girl who rides in foreign cars. You need to think about all that before you go buy her a ten-dollar piece of cheesecake.

Alex's goal has changed, so Bob's and Mom's goals have, too. Mom makes her suspicions about Cassie clear—after all, that's what her version of a good mother might do to keep her only son from getting hurt.

Bob, meantime, gets busy planting seeds of doubt. By making up an ex-boyfriend who can afford a new car, he's playing on one of Alex's early flaws: thinking that people will love and respect you based on what you own (like a Tropical Island card), rather than on how you behave. "Of course Cassie would choose that guy over me," Alex might think, "he's got better stuff than I could ever buy."

That's just one step in Bob's plan. Once Alex gives up on Cassie—maybe for a Sara Lee cheesecake and Ford Festiva kind of girl—Bob can swoop in with his grandfather's pension check and treat Cassie to the whole Cheesecake Factory dessert menu. Even the fresh strawberries.

Bob's plan will either work or it won't, just as Alex will end up choosing either Cassie or the card. Either way, we'll end at *Step Five: New Equilibrium*.

7.4.5 Step Five: New Equilibrium

Here's the simple version of our story, one last time:

> Once upon a time, Alex wanted a Tropical Island card from *Magic, the Gathering*. He mowed lawns until he earned enough money to buy it. Then he bought it.

So far, we've introduced three new characters: Alex's mom (who wants to be seen as a responsible parent), fellow-gamer Bob (who thinks he can be valued by one-upping Alex), and Cassie (who, right now, is a symbol instead of a fully realized character). She represents the value that one finds real validation through romantic love, rather than material attainments like Tropical Island cards.

When we left our last step, *Battles and Revelations*, Bob decided to pursue Cassie for himself. Meantime, Alex's mother, Mom, demonstrated her protectiveness by warning Alex away from getting into a romantic relationship with Cassie. If he did that, he might get hurt.

Eventually the battle ends. Alex either chooses the card over Cassie, or Cassie over the card, and gets what he wants or is forced to stop trying.

So let's write *Step Five: New Equilibrium*.

Prompt

Rewrite Alex's story so that Alex either gets what he wants or is forced to stop trying.

Discussion

Eventually, thankfully, Alex's story has to end. Let's pretend that our story ends the way that our simple story did: with Alex buying the Tropical Island card.

We've already established that both the card and Cassie are symbols. They represent two different ways of thinking. Alex, at the beginning of his story, believed that the way to be seen as worthy of love and respect was to have something that his friends didn't. As a symbol, the Tropical Island card represents that way of thinking. The more Alex thinks about it, pursues it, or treasures it, the more we understand that Alex wants to be envied.

Cassie represents another set of values. Earlier in our story, as part of his revelation, Alex realized that it was possible to be seen as worthy of love and respect by actually being loved by somebody else (in this case, Cassie). As a symbol, she represents that way of thinking. The more Alex thinks about her, romantically pursues her, or values her, the more we understand that Alex wants to love and be loved in return.

If we follow this story to its original end, Alex has to buy the Tropical Island card. That could be kind of depressing because it might mean that, at the end of his story, Alex hasn't learned anything. He's choosing to act according to the same flaws he had at the beginning of his story, and choosing his friends' envy over Cassie's love.

Your story doesn't have to end that way, though. Maybe your story ends with Alex and Cassie flying to a destination wedding, still with their pockets full of lawnmowing money, with Bob shaking his fists at Alex and Cassie's plane as it flies overhead.

Or maybe your story ends with Alex sitting in the back room of the comic shop, playing his Tropical Island card for the first time, but in a way that isn't depressing at all. Whether any of these endings are good or bad, happy or unhappy, depends on your piece of storytelling's moral vision: its baseline statement about how people ought to behave toward one another.

Suppose we had a subplot where Alex's mom was dating the comic shop owner, Dave. Suppose it turned out that Dave was a real louse. Suppose it also turned out that Cassie was the cheesecake-and-Camry-chasing hussy that Mom always feared she was. The moral vision for our piece of storytelling might be that romantic love is better off avoided. We'd all be happier relating to other people in rule-governed environments like *Magic, the Gathering* tournaments.

Or suppose we had a subplot where Dave turned out to be a great guy, and he and Alex's mom have a happy downstairs relationship while, upstairs, Alex stays in his room, mostly alone, with his collection of *Magic* cards sliding into ever-more-untidy heaps. If Alex were unhappy, the moral vision of this story is that romantic love is the One True Path to Happiness. If they were all happy, the moral vision might be different: there are many paths to happiness, and some of them are quirky.

Whatever the case, the story will have settled into a new state of stability—a balance of opposing forces. Alex might end his story married or dead, happy or unhappy, but only after the question about whether he has overcome his flaws has been settled certainly or—in some rare cases—left tantalizingly ambiguous. This is the New Equilibrium.

References

Bechdel, Alison. (2006) 2007. *Fun Home*. New York: Mariner Books.
Dahl, Roald. (1988) 2007. *Matilda*. New York: Puffin Books.
Fergus, Mark, and Hawk Otsby. *Iron Man*. Directed by Jon Favreau. 2008; Burbank: Walt Disney Studios, 2013. Blu-Ray.
Gaiman, Neil. (2002) 2012. *Coraline*. New York: Harper Collins.

Goyer, David S. *Batman Begins*. Directed by Christopher Nolan. 2005; Burbank: Warner Brothers, 2008. Blu-Ray.

Holland, Steve. *Better Off Dead*. Directed by Steve Holland. 1985; Hollywood: Paramount Pictures, 2011. Blu-Ray.

Kamen, Robert Mark. *The Karate Kid*. Directed by John C. Avildsen. 1984; Culver City: Sony Pictures Home Entertainment, 2015. DVD.

Lee, Jennifer, and Phil Johnston. *Wreck-It Ralph*. Directed by Rich Moore. 2012; Burbank: Walt Disney Studios, 2013. Blu-Ray.

LeFauve, Meg, and Josh Cooley. *Inside Out*. Directed by Pete Doctor. 2015; Burbank: Walt Disney Studios, 2015. Blu-Ray.

Lucas, George. *Star Wars Episode IV: A New Hope*. Directed by George Lucas. 1977; Los Angeles: Twentieth Century Fox, 2013. Blu-Ray.

Moore, Chuck. 2016. "The 10 Rarest *Magic: The Gathering* Cards." Complete Set. https://www.completeset.com/the-10-rarest-magic-the-gathering-cards. Accessed July 9, 2020.

Winter, Terence. *Get Rich or Die Tryin*. Directed by Jim Sheridan. 2005; Hollywood: Paramount Pictures, 2006. DVD.

CHAPTER 8

Conclusion

You've done it. You're at the end. Assuming you've read this book from the beginning, you've learned the five steps of Shakespeare's stories—from *Motivations, Goals, and Flaws* to *New Equilibrium*—and learned about the tools with which Shakespeare weaves his stories together. These tools—from character webs to scene weave to symbols—contrast, define, and highlight the most important elements of each character's story. The effect? Even if a character like Lord Capulet or Laertes has only a handful of scenes, we understand more about them than we see on stage. Each character, however briefly presented, undergoes a profound process of self-discovery and change. A lifetime's journey, outlined in a few hundred words.

The great accomplishment of Shakespeare's storytelling tools is that they represent this journey so clearly and economically. They do this by focusing almost entirely on the questions central to our own lives: what does life mean? How do we discover and create that meaning? Shakespeare's answer is different for every character. Some characters, like Hamlet, are out for justice. Others, like Beatrice, are out for love. But they all want to be valued. In order to be valued, they must recognize how their own ways of thinking and acting hurt other people, and learn to think and act differently.

This type of story—the Shakespearean story—is still frequently told today in novels, films, TV shows, short stories, and even comic books. And writers who tell other kinds of stories still universally use Shakespeare's tools. Probably, somewhere, you can find a piece of storytelling that doesn't have a character web, or doesn't use scene weave. But it's like finding a seven-wheeled car. It probably doesn't work well. Whoever built it just wanted to be unconventional.

You understand all that, now that you've finished this book. There's just one more thing.

In this book, we've looked at novels, movies, TV shows, comics, and other pieces of storytelling that use Shakespearean tools. Until now, we've thought about the relationships between these modern-day pieces of storytelling and Shakespeare's own plays as a convenient way to define our concepts. If you've seen *Star Wars* (1977), you probably understand how the light saber (or the Millennium Falcon) is a symbol, even if you didn't think (or care) about calling it one. Once you understand that, it's easy to understand how symbols like swords and poison work in *Hamlet*. But that's not the end of the story.

When a modern-day writer creates a piece of Shakespearean storytelling, they're actually using a set of well-understood conventions to draw our attention to specific elements of character (like motivations and flaws) and specific elements of storytelling (like moral vision).

Sometimes—as in *House of Cards* (2013)—they'll invite us into a Runaway Villain story by giving their pet villain (Frank Underwood) an opening monologue that looks very like Richard of Gloucester's. When we see that kind of monologue, we know we're going to see Frank ascend to the heights of power using Richard's trademark mixture of deception and underhanded violence.

But there's something else going on: If you recognize that Frank Underwood begins his story with a *Richard III*-style monologue, you might compare Frank Underwood and Richard of Gloucester to one another. If you did, you'd see differences between them that highlight and define elements of their characters. For instance: Frank Underwood trusts his wife, Claire. Richard, on the other hand, is incapable of trusting anyone.

This is a character web but, unlike the character webs we've looked at in earlier chapters, this one involves characters from different texts. Frank Underwood's opening monologue in *House of Cards*, in other words, defines Frank's character by inviting us to compare him to Richard of Gloucester.

This isn't unique to *House of Cards*. In *The Warrior's Apprentice* (1986), Lois McMaster Bujold, whose books about space mercenary Miles Vorkosigan have won her a handful of Hugo awards, has Miles quote Richard's seduction of Anne (*Richard III* I.ii) while trying to woo his would-be girlfriend, Elena. Why? Miles suffers from a degenerative bone disease, and has consequently learned to solve problems using a combination of manipulation, improvisation, and strategic thinking. So far as that goes, Miles is just Richard of Gloucester in space.

But when Bujold invites us to compare the Miles/Elena relationship with the Richard/Anne relationship, she highlights a difference: Miles actually loves Elena. This intertextual character web is one of several tools that Bujold uses to makes Miles's habits of deception and plotting look heroic, rather than villainous.

George R.R. Martin, whose *Game of Thrones* (1996) became the HBO series of the same name, does the same thing with Tyrion Lannister. Tyrion is very like Richard of Gloucester aka Miles Vorkosigian—not "shaped for sportive tricks" or a gifted soldier. But he's a quick wit, a clever thinker, and an excellent strategist. Martin, however, introduces a second character modeled on Shakespeare's Richard of Gloucester: Stannis Baratheon. This gets us a three-point character web, in which Stannis's and Tyrion's similarities to Richard of Gloucester highlight the differences between them. Tyron, it turns out, has inherited Richard's cleverness and charisma and so—like Richard—we generally see Tyron's crimes as entertainment. Stannis, on the other hand, contends for the throne in a grim, joyless way that makes his other sins seem less forgivable.

This practice of inviting intertextual comparison is embedded in our art, regardless of whether that art is Shakespearean. When an Australian rock band names itself *Rolling Blackout*, you can bet that they're inviting you to compare them to the granddaddy of all Australian rock bands, *AC/DC*. When *Run the Jewels* invites Zack De La Rocha[1] to perform on a track like "JU$T," you can bet that they're inviting you to compare their act's political and social dimension to *Rage Against the Machine*'s. When, in *Frankenstein* (1818), the monster spends a dozen pages talking about his experience of reading *Paradise Lost* (1667), or in *The Stand* (1978), Stuart Redman spends more time reminiscing about *Watership Down* (1972) than about his dead wife, you can bet that the writers behind these characters (Mary Shelley and Stephen King) are inviting us to compare their pieces of storytelling to someone else's.

These invitations help us understand the diversity of human experience. Often, writers will approach the same genres, forms, and subjects as other artists, so that they can show you how they see these things differently. For instance: Sara Teasdale and Claude McKay both wrote sonnets about New York City—"Broadway" and "The Tropics of New York," respectively—and even though these are both fourteen-line poems about early-twentieth-century New York, you will never, ever confuse them with one another. That they have a common form and a common subject only sharpens the differences between them. "You know how other people see New York," each sonnet says. "Here's how I see it differently."

If you don't care for poetry, consider Steven Spielberg's *Poltergeist* (1982) and Toni Morrison's *Beloved* (1987). Both are Haunted House stories in which some collective social sin causes the family in the Haunted House to lose a daughter. Furthermore, both stories oscillate between moments of abject terror and absurdist humor. In terms of genre and convention, in other words, *Poltergeist* and *Beloved* are very much alike. But evil—or collective social sin—in *Poltergeist* takes the form of estate developers who'll sacrifice anything for a dollar. In *Beloved*, that evil is the insoluble legacy of chattel slavery. These different perspectives on social evil create two pieces of storytelling that, despite their similarities, feel totally distinct.

In other words: Artists don't create a text. They create *relationships between texts*. When artists invite us into the conventions that shape their work, they

---

[1] Former frontman of *Rage Against the Machine*.

also invite us to consider where else those conventions have been used, and how they intend to use those conventions differently. Once upon a time, a seemingly endless parade of blues-influenced rock bands—including Them, AC/DC, Aerosmith, and the Amboy Dukes—covered Big Joe Williams's "Baby, Please Don't Go." If you performed some version of that song today, you'd invite comparison to every other recording of it. But as a musician of a later era, you'd also be writing one piece of a longer story. "Here's how people used to play Big Joe Williams," you'd be saying. "And here's how he's played now."

The same thing is true of Shakespeare's storytelling tools. Shakespeare may have invented character webs in the same way that Edison invented the light bulb, but the story of character webs—like the story of the electric light—is one of continuous adaptation and refinement. Shakespeare's character web in *A Midsummer Night's Dream* might be delightful, but the story of the character web includes other storytellers—Charles Dickens, Toni Morrison, Stephen King, and August Wilson, for instance—who all used the same tool in their own ways.

So here is one thing that you can take away from this book: When you watch a movie, read a novel, or see a play, you can do it with a new kind of attention. You'll see Shakespeare's legacy everywhere. It's alive in the kinds of stories we read and watch, in the tools that writers use to tell them, and in the conventions that have grown out of those tools' constant use.

But here's another: Storytelling has its own story. Shakespeare began that story, or at least the piece of it that involves the invention and refinement of a dozen tools. But Shakespeare is not the entire story. As long as the journey of our lives is a journey of self-discovery, we carry Shakespeare with us. But we also carry other storytellers who have refined, and who continue to refine, the tools Shakespeare invented. They are not lesser storytellers because they happen to have come after Shakespeare. A generation from now, the way we tell stories may owe as much to Hugo winners like N.K Jemisin and Lois Bujold, or to academic darlings like Toni Morrison and Maxine Hong Kingston, or to blockbuster—and bestseller—producers like James Cameron and Stephen King, as it does to Shakespeare.

Storytelling is an ocean. No one way of thinking, no single history, and no set of methods can make sense of it completely. I wrote this book to chart one path from Shakespeare to the present day, by way of a few easy-to-illustrate storytelling tools. That's enough to take you out of the bay, to the near mouth of the vast and ever-changing sea. Where you go next, and how far, is up to you.

References

Adams, Richard. (1972) 1975. *Watership Down*. London: Avon Books.
Bujold, Lois McMaster. (1986) 1991. *The Warrior's Apprentice*. Riverside: Baen Books.

Fincher, David (dir.). *House of Cards*. Season 1, Episode 1, "Chapter One." Aired February 1, 2013, on Netflix.
King, Stephen. (1978) 1990. *The Stand: The Complete and Uncut Edition*. New York: Doubleday.
Martin, George R.R. 1996. *A Game of Thrones*. New York: Bantam Books.
McKay, Claude. "The Tropics of New York." In *Poems of New York*, ed. Elizabeth Schmidt, 76. New York: Everyman's Library, 2002.
Milton, John. (1667) 2003. *Paradise Lost*. New York: Penguin Classics.
Morrison, Toni. (1987) 2004. *Beloved*. Vancouver: Vintage.
Shelley, Mary. (1818) 1994. *Frankenstein*. Dover: Dover Publications.
Spielberg, Steven. *Poltergeist*. Directed by Tobe Hooper. 1982; Burbank: Warner Brothers, 2010, Blu-Ray.
Teasdale, Sara. "Broadway." In *Poems of New York*, ed. Elizabeth Schmidt, 76. New York: Everyman's Library, 2002.

Index

B
battles, 16, 17, 22, 23, 51, 56, 82, 93, 99–102, 104, 131, 138, 144, 164, 174, 177

C
Character History, 138, 139
character web, 5, 17, 19, 52, 54–56, 72–74, 76–80, 85–87, 89–93, 95, 101, 106, 123, 130, 131, 143, 151, 157, 169, 181–184
Comedy of Errors, The, 1, 5, 6, 23, 25, 57, 125
Coming of Age story, 14, 137, 140, 141, 148, 151, 152
conflict
  covert, 60, 61, 63, 91
  multi-point, 75, 89
  overt, 59, 60, 63, 91, 171
  structural, 63, 64, 91, 144, 171, 172
Contest story, 149, 150, 173

D
desire, 4, 12, 18, 22, 23, 43, 45, 46, 63–65, 69, 70, 80, 100, 117, 130, 135, 142, 174, 175

F
five steps of Shakespeare's stories, 125, 132, 181
flaws, 13, 16–18, 22–24, 34–44, 46, 47, 51, 52, 56, 64, 65, 72, 78, 79, 90, 113, 124, 125, 131, 135, 137, 139–141, 148, 149, 155, 157, 159–165, 168–176, 178, 182
moral, 34, 35
psychological, 34, 35, 170–172

G
genre, 7, 132, 135–138, 144–146, 151, 152, 155, 183
goal, 16, 18, 22–24, 27–32, 34, 36, 37, 39, 40, 43, 46, 47, 51, 52, 56, 58, 61, 63, 72, 125, 135, 137, 139, 142, 144, 146, 155–157, 159–163, 169–172, 175, 176, 181

INDEX

H
Hamlet, 1–3, 12, 15–18, 23, 26, 30, 31, 39, 41, 42, 52, 54, 56, 58, 60, 63, 67, 72, 86, 87, 89, 91, 92, 95–98, 112, 115, 116, 120–123, 125, 126, 130–133, 138, 145, 155, 159, 161, 162, 165, 182
Hamlet, v, vii
Henry IV, 46, 137, 139, 140
Henry V, 46, 137–140
Henry VI, 102, 105, 106, 137, 140

K
King Lear, 15–17, 46, 48, 57, 64, 76, 80, 96, 106, 109–112, 125, 129, 141, 143, 145, 147, 148, 155, 159–161
King Lear, vii

L
line trait, 139, 149

M
Merchant of Venice, The, 1, 23, 32, 36, 67, 125, 133, 145, 149, 150
Midsummer Night's Dream, A, 16, 56, 64, 80, 84–86, 91, 143
moral vision, 5, 14, 17, 19, 35, 47, 76, 79, 90, 95, 97, 98, 123, 125–133, 142, 145, 151, 178, 182
motivation, 4, 5, 16–18, 22–27, 30, 32, 34–37, 39, 40, 43, 46–48, 51, 52, 56, 65, 71, 72, 90, 125, 131, 135, 137, 139, 142, 145, 151, 155–157, 159–163, 169–172, 181, 182
Much Ado About Nothing, 24, 43, 56, 64, 97, 125, 126, 136, 137, 141–143, 146

N
new equilibrium, 17, 18, 22, 51, 178, 181

O
One-Trick Pony, 148, 149, 151
opponent, 16, 17, 22, 51, 55, 64, 65, 67, 72, 91, 158, 171–174
opposition.. *See* opponent
Othello, 1, 16–18, 36, 51, 56, 64, 67, 91, 133, 136, 137, 143, 145–148

P
plans, 14, 16, 22, 23, 25, 27–31, 41, 45, 51, 52, 56, 58, 60–63, 65, 67, 68, 72, 77, 93, 103, 110, 112, 115, 120, 146, 163, 166, 168–170, 173–175, 177

R
revelation, 17, 22–24, 39, 41–43, 45–47, 51, 52, 64, 79, 96, 97, 111, 112, 125, 126, 130, 131, 140, 142, 143, 155, 159, 161–164, 169, 174–177
revenge tragedy, 63, 137, 144, 145, 152
Romantic Comedy, 43, 80, 136, 137, 142, 143, 151, 152
Romeo and Juliet, 16, 60, 63, 64, 86, 133, 136, 140, 143, 144, 158
Runaway Villain, 145–147, 151, 182

S
scene weave, 5, 17, 79, 89, 90, 95, 96, 98–100, 103, 105, 106, 110–112, 114, 115, 123, 131, 133, 181
Shakespearean story, 12, 14, 151, 155, 161, 169, 181
storytelling, v–viii, 2–5, 12, 13, 15, 16, 18, 19, 22, 24, 47, 52, 56, 57, 72, 73, 75, 76, 78–80, 90, 92, 95–98, 106, 115, 123, 125, 126, 131, 132, 135, 136, 138, 144, 148, 151, 155, 158, 161, 162, 169, 170, 172, 174, 175, 178, 181–184
symbol, vii, 4, 5, 17, 78, 79, 89, 90, 95, 96, 98, 115–117, 120–123, 125, 131–133, 151, 169, 174, 175, 177, 178, 181, 182

T

Taming of the Shrew, The, 1, 24, 30, 127, 128, 141, 143
Titus Andronicus, 21, 36, 54, 55, 64, 98, 125, 129, 145, 147

U

unwritten, 21, 75